Level 2

BENCHMARK SERIES

Microsoft®

Excel

365
2019 Edition

Jan Davidson
Lambton College
Sarnia, Ontario

PARADIGM
EDUCATION SOLUTIONS

St. Paul

Vice President, Content and Digital Solutions: Christine Hurney
Director of Content Development: Carley Fruzzetti
Developmental Editor: Jennifer Joline Anderson
Director of Production: Timothy W. Larson
Production Editor/Project Manager: Jen Weaverling
Senior Design and Production Specialist: Jack Ross
Cover and Interior Design: Valerie King
Copy Editor: Communicáto, Ltd.
Testers: Janet Blum, Traci Post
Indexer: Terry Casey
Vice President, Director of Digital Products: Chuck Bratton
Digital Projects Manager: Tom Modl
Digital Solutions Manager: Gerry Yumul
Senior Director of Digital Products and Onboarding: Christopher Johnson
Supervisor of Digital Products and Onboarding: Ryan Isdahl
Vice President, Marketing: Lara Weber McLellan
Marketing and Communications Manager: Selena Hicks

Care has been taken to verify the accuracy of information presented in this book. However, the authors, editors, and publisher cannot accept responsibility for web, email, newsgroup, or chat room subject matter or content, or for consequences from the application of the information in this book, and make no warranty, expressed or implied, with respect to its content.

Trademarks: Microsoft is a trademark or registered trademark of Microsoft Corporation in the United States and/or other countries. Some of the product names and company names included in this book have been used for identification purposes only and may be trademarks or registered trade names of their respective manufacturers and sellers. The authors, editors, and publisher disclaim any affiliation, association, or connection with, or sponsorship or endorsement by, such owners.

Paradigm Education Solutions is independent from Microsoft Corporation and not affiliated with Microsoft in any manner.

Cover Photo Credit: © lowball-jack/GettyImages
Interior Photo Credits: Follow the Index.

We have made every effort to trace the ownership of all copyrighted material and to secure permission from copyright holders. In the event of any question arising as to the use of any material, we will be pleased to make the necessary corrections in future printings.

ISBN 978-0-76388-726-1 (print)
ISBN 978-0-76388-709-4 (digital)

© 2020 by Paradigm Publishing, LLC
875 Montreal Way
St. Paul, MN 55102
Email: CustomerService@ParadigmEducation.com
Website: ParadigmEducation.com

Printed in the United States of America

28 27 26 25 24 23 22 21 20 19   1 2 3 4 5 6 7 8 9 10 11 12

Brief Contents

Contents

Achieving Proficiency in Excel

The Benchmark Series, *Microsoft® Excel® 365*, 2019 Edition, is designed for students who want to learn how to use Microsoft's powerful spreadsheet program to manipulate numerical data in resolving financial and other problems requiring data management and analysis. After successfully completing a course in Excel using this courseware, students can expect to be proficient in using Microsoft Excel to do the following:

- Create and edit spreadsheets and worksheets of varying complexity.
- Format cells, columns, and rows as well as entire workbooks in a uniform, attractive style.
- Analyze numerical data and project outcomes to make informed decisions.
- Plan, research, create, revise, and publish worksheets and workbooks to meet specific needs.
- Given a workplace scenario requiring a numbers-based solution, assess the information requirements and then prepare the materials that achieve the goal efficiently and effectively.

Well-designed pedagogy is important, but students learn technology skills through practice and problem solving. Technology provides opportunities for interactive learning as well as excellent ways to quickly and accurately assess student performance. To this end, this course is supported with Cirrus, Paradigm's cloud-based training and assessment learning management system. Details about Cirrus as well as its integrated student courseware and instructor resources can be found on page xii.

Proven Instructional Design

The Benchmark Series has long served as a standard of excellence in software instruction. Elements of the series function individually and collectively to create an inviting, comprehensive learning environment that leads to full proficiency in computer applications. The following visual tour highlights the structure and features that comprise the highly popular Benchmark model.

Microsoft®

Excel Level 2

Unit 1

Advanced Formatting, Formulas, and Data Management

Chapter 1   Advanced Formatting Techniques

Chapter 2   Advanced Functions and Formulas

Chapter 3   Working with Tables and Data Features

Chapter 4   Summarizing and Consolidating Data

Unit Openers display the unit's four chapter titles. Each level of the course contains two units with four chapters each.

Chapter Openers Present Learning Objectives

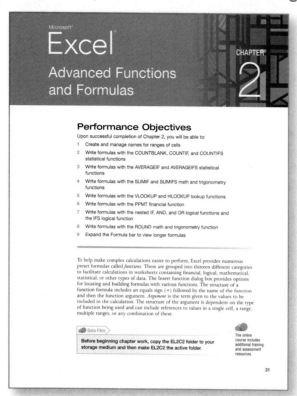

Chapter Openers present the performance objectives and an overview of the skills taught.

Data Files are provided for each chapter.

Activities Build Skill Mastery within Realistic Context

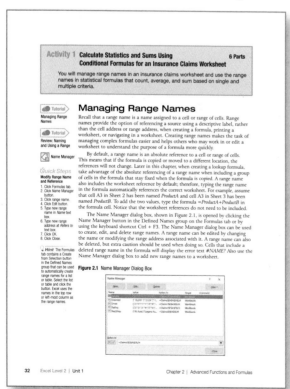

Multipart Activities provide a framework for instruction and practice on software features. An activity overview identifies tasks to accomplish and key features to use in completing the work.

Tutorials provide interactive, guided training and measured practice.

Quick Steps in the margins allow fast reference and review of the steps needed to accomplish tasks.

Hints offer useful tips on how to use features efficiently and effectively.

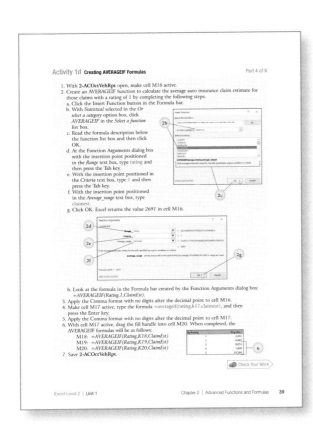

Step-by-Step Instructions guide students to the desired outcome for each activity part. Screen captures illustrate what the screen should look like at key points.

Magenta Text identifies material to type.

Check Your Work model answer images are available in the online course, and students can use those images to confirm they have completed the activity correctly.

Between activity parts, the text presents instruction on the features and skills necessary to accomplish the next section of the activity.

Typically, a file remains open throughout all parts of the activity. Students save their work incrementally. At the end of the activity, students save, print, and then close the file.

Chapter Review Tools Reinforce Learning

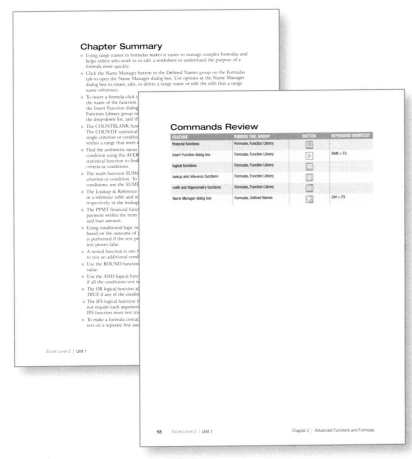

A **Chapter Summary** reviews the purpose and execution of key features.

A **Commands Review** summarizes visually the major features and alternative methods of access.

The Cirrus Solution
Elevating student success and instructor efficiency

Powered by Paradigm, Cirrus is the next-generation learning solution for developing skills in Microsoft Office. Cirrus seamlessly delivers complete course content in a cloud-based learning environment that puts students on the fast track to success. Students can access their content from any device anywhere, through a live internet connection; plus, Cirrus is platform independent, ensuring that students get the same learning experience whether they are using PCs, Macs, or Chromebook computers.

Cirrus provides Benchmark Series content in a series of scheduled assignments that report to a grade book to track student progress and achievement. Assignments are grouped in modules, providing many options for customizing instruction.

Dynamic Training

The online Benchmark Series courses include interactive resources to support learning.

Watch and Learn Lessons include a video demonstrating how to perform the chapter activity, a reading to provide background and context, and a short quiz to check understanding of concepts and skills.

Guide and Practice Tutorials provide interactive, guided training and measured practice.

Hands On Activities enable students to complete chapter activities, compare their solutions against a Check Your Work model answer image, and submit their work for instructor review.

Chapter Review and Assessment

Review and assessment activities for each chapter are available for completion in Cirrus.

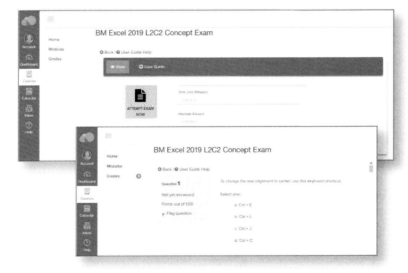

Concepts Check completion exercises assess comprehension and recall of application features and functions as well as key terminology.

Skills Assessment Hands On Activity exercises evaluate the ability to apply chapter skills and concepts in solving realistic problems. Each is completed live in Excel and is uploaded through Cirrus for instructor evaluation.

Visual Benchmark assessments test problem-solving skills and mastery of application features.

A **Case Study** requires analyzing a workplace scenario and then planning and executing a multipart project. Students search the web and/or use the program's Help feature to locate additional information required to complete the Case Study.

Exercises and **Projects** provide opportunities to develop and demonstrate skills learned in each chapter. Each is completed live in the Office application and is automatically scored by Cirrus. Detailed feedback and how-to videos help students evaluate and improve their performance.

Skills Check Exams evaluate students' ability to complete specific tasks. Skills Check Exams are completed live in the Office application and are scored automatically. Detailed feedback and instructor-controlled how-to videos help student evaluate and improve their performance.

Multiple-choice **Concepts Exams** assess understanding of key commands and concepts presented in each chapter.

Unit Review and Assessment

Review and assessment activities for each unit of each Benchmark course are also available for completion in Cirrus.

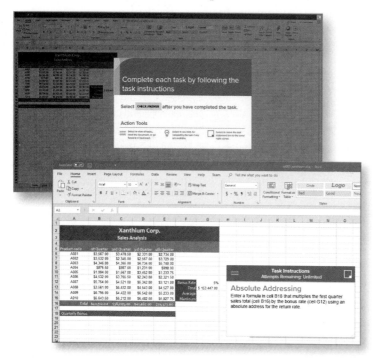

Assessing Proficiency exercises check mastery of software application functions and features.

Writing Activities challenge students to use written communication skills while demonstrating their understanding of important software features and functions.

Internet Research assignments reinforce the importance of research and information processing skills along with proficiency in the Office environment.

A **Job Study** activity at the end of Unit 2 presents a capstone assessment requiring critical thinking and problem solving.

Unit-Level Projects allow students to practice skills learned in the unit. Each is completed live in the Office application and automatically scored by Cirrus. Detailed feedback and how-to videos help students evaluate and improve their performance.

Student eBook

The Student eBook, accessed through the Cirrus online course, can be downloaded to any device (desktop, laptop, tablet, or smartphone) to make Benchmark Series content available anywhere students wish to study.

Instructor eResources

Cirrus tracks students' step-by-step interactions as they move through each activity, giving instructors visibility into their progress and missteps. With Exam Watch, instructors can observe students in a virtual, live, skills-based exam and join remotely as needed—a helpful option for struggling students who need one-to-one coaching, or for distance learners. In addition to these Cirrus-specific tools, the Instructor eResources for the Benchmark Series include the following support:

- Planning resources, such as lesson plans, teaching hints, and sample course syllabi
- Delivery resources, such as discussion questions and online images and templates
- Assessment resources, including live and annotated PDF model answers for chapter work and review and assessment activities, rubrics for evaluating student work, and chapter-based exam banks in RTF format

About the Author

Jan Davidson started her teaching career in 1997 as a corporate trainer and postsecondary instructor and holds a Social Science degree, a writing certificate, and an In-Service Teacher Training certificate. Since 2001, she has been a faculty member of the School of Business and International Education at Lambton College in Sarnia, Ontario. In this role, she has developed curriculum and taught a variety of office technology, software applications, and office administration courses to domestic and international students in a variety of postsecondary programs. As a consultant and content provider for Paradigm Education Solutions since 2006, Jan has contributed to textbook and online content for various titles. She has been author and co-author of Paradigm's Benchmark Series *Microsoft® Excel®*, Level 2, and *Microsoft® Access®*, Level 2 since 2013 and has contributed to the Cirrus online courseware for the series. Jan is also co-author of *Advanced Excel® 2016*.

Microsoft®

Excel Level 2

Unit 1

Advanced Formatting, Formulas, and Data Management

Microsoft®

Excel®

Advanced Formatting Techniques

CHAPTER

1

Performance Objectives

Upon successful completion of Chapter 1, you will be able to:

1 Apply conditional formatting by entering parameters for a rule

2 Create and apply new rules for conditional formatting

3 Edit and delete conditional formatting rules

4 Apply conditional formatting using icon sets, data bars, and color scales

5 Apply conditional formatting using a formula

6 Apply conditional formatting using Quick Analysis

7 Apply fraction and scientific formatting

8 Apply special number formatting

9 Create custom number formats

10 Filter a worksheet using a custom AutoFilter

11 Filter and sort data using conditional formatting or cell attributes

12 Remove a filter from a worksheet

13 Apply an advanced filter

Excel provides many options for formatting worksheets. Buttons are available in the Font, Alignment, and Number groups on the Home tab, as well as on the Mini toolbar. Excel also offers advanced formatting techniques to help users explore and analyze data. One of the most useful is *conditional formatting*. Conditional formatting allows important information to be highlighted using a different format such as a background color or font style. This formatting can help users quickly identify trends and spot critical issues that need to be investigated or monitored.

 Data Files

Before beginning chapter work, copy the EL2C1 folder to your storage medium and then make EL2C1 the active folder.

The online course includes additional training and assessment resources.

Working with a payroll worksheet, you will change the appearance of cells based on criteria related to pay rate and gross pay.

Applying
Conditional
Formatting Using
Top/Bottom Rules

Applying Conditional Formatting

Conditional formatting makes it easier to spot important information in a worksheet and analyze the data for patterns and trends. Cells within a specified range that meet a specific condition can be highlighted using a different format such as a background color or font style. For instance, values that are high or low can be formatted in red font or with a yellow background to make them stand out.

Formatting can be applied based on a specific value or a value that falls within a range or it can be applied by using a comparison operator, such as equal to (=), greater than (>), or less than (<). Conditional formats can also be based on dates, text entries, or duplicated values. Consider using conditional formatting to analyze a question, such as *Which store locations earned sales above their targets?* Using a different color to identify those stores that exceeded their target sales makes it easy to quickly identify the top performers.

Excel provides predefined conditional formatting rules that can be accessed from the Conditional Formatting button drop-down list, as shown in Figure 1.1. Unique conditional formatting rules can also be created. Using options in the *Top/ Bottom Rules* drop-down list, cells can be highlighted based on a top 10 or bottom 10 value or percent or by above average or below average values.

Conditional
Formatting

Quick Steps

Apply Conditional Formatting Using Predefined Rule
1. Select range.
2. Click Conditional Formatting button.
3. Point to rule category.
4. Click rule.
5. If necessary, enter parameter value.
6. If necessary, change format options.
7. Click OK.

Figure 1.1 Conditional Formatting Button Drop-Down List

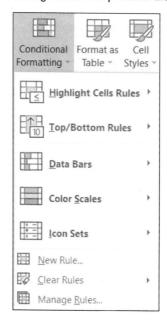

1. Open **VRPay-Oct23**.
2. Save the workbook with the name **1-VRPay-Oct23**.
3. Using conditional formatting, apply green fill with dark green text formatting to the pay rate values to identify employees whose pay rate is less than $11.50 by completing the following steps:
   a. Select the range L6:L23.
   b. Click the Conditional Formatting button in the Styles group on the Home tab.
   c. Point to *Highlight Cells Rules* and then click *Less Than* at the drop-down list.

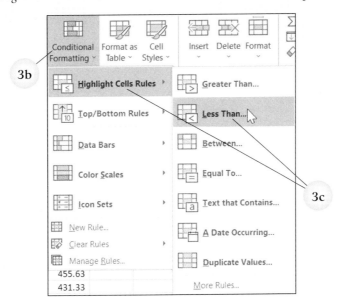

   d. At the Less Than dialog box with the text automatically selected in the *Format cells that are LESS THAN* text box, type 11.50.
   e. Click the *with* option box arrow and then click *Green Fill with Dark Green Text*.

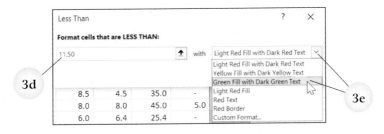

   f. Click OK.
   g. Click in any cell to deselect the range.
   h. Review the cells that have been conditionally formatted.
4. Save **1-VRPay-Oct23**.

1. With **1-VRPay-Oct23** open, apply light red fill with dark red text conditional formatting to the gross pay values to identify employees who earned above average wages for the week by completing the following steps:
   a. Select the range M6:M23.
   b. Click the Conditional Formatting button in the Styles group on the Home tab.
   c. Point to *Top/Bottom Rules* and then click *Above Average* at the drop-down list.
   d. At the Above Average dialog box with *Light Red Fill with Dark Red Text* selected in the *Format cells that are ABOVE AVERAGE* option box, click OK.

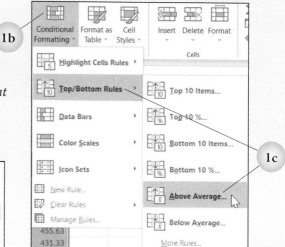

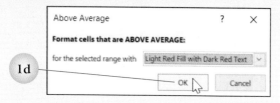

   e. Click in any cell to deselect the range.
   f. Review the cells that have been conditionally formatted.
2. Print the worksheet.
3. Save and then close **1-VRPay-Oct23**.

> Check Your Work

Activity 2 Apply Conditional Formatting to Insurance Policy Data   6 Parts

You will format cells in an insurance claims worksheet by creating, editing, clearing, and deleting conditional formatting rules and by visually identifying trends within the data.

Applying Conditional Formatting Using a New Rule

💡 **Hint** Create a rule to format cells based on cell values, specific text, dates, blanks, or error values.

Applying Conditional Formatting Using a New Rule

Cells are conditionally formatted based on rules. A rule defines the criterion by which cells are selected for formatting and includes the formatting attributes that are applied to cells that meet the criterion. The rules that were applied in Activity 1a and Activity 1b applied conditional formatting using predefined options. At the New Formatting Rule dialog box, shown in Figure 1.2, a custom conditional formatting rule can be created that defines all the parts of the criterion and the formatting. The *Edit the Rule Description* section of the dialog box varies depending on the active option in the *Select a Rule Type* list box.

Create and Apply New Formatting Rule
1. Select range.
2. Click Conditional Formatting button.
3. Click *New Rule*.
4. Click rule type.
5. Add criteria as required.
6. Click Format button.
7. Select formatting attributes.
8. Click OK to close Format Cells dialog box.
9. Click OK to close New Formatting Rule dialog box.

Figure 1.2 New Formatting Rule Dialog Box

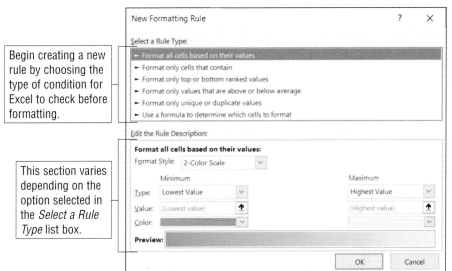

Begin creating a new rule by choosing the type of condition for Excel to check before formatting.

This section varies depending on the option selected in the *Select a Rule Type* list box.

Activity 2a Applying Conditional Formatting Using a New Rule

1. Open **ACInsce**.
2. Save the workbook with the name **1-ACInsce**.
3. The owner of AllClaims Insurance Brokers is considering changing the discount plan for customers with no claims or with only one claim. The owner would like to see the names of customers who meet either of the two claim criteria formatted in color to provide a reference for how many customers this discount would affect. Create the first formatting rule, which changes the appearance of cells in the *Claims* column that contain *0* by completing the following steps:
   a. Select the range H4:H20.
   b. Click the Conditional Formatting button in the Styles group on the Home tab.
   c. Click *New Rule* at the drop-down list.
   d. At the New Formatting Rule dialog box, click *Format only cells that contain* in the *Select a Rule Type* list box.
   e. Click the second option box arrow (which displays *between*) in the *Format only cells with* section and then click *equal to* at the drop-down list.

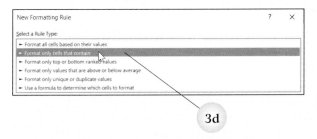

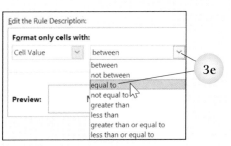

f. Click in the blank text box next to *equal to* and then type 0.
g. Click the Format button.

h. At the Format Cells dialog box with the Font tab selected, apply the Dark Red color (first option in the *Standard Colors* section), apply bold formatting, and then click OK.
i. Click OK at the New Formatting Rule dialog box.
4. Create a second formatting rule, which changes the appearance of cells in the *Claims* column that contain *1*, by completing the following steps:
   a. With the range H4:H20 still selected, click the Conditional Formatting button and then click *New Rule*.
   b. At the New Formatting Rule dialog box, click *Format only cells that contain* in the *Select a Rule Type* list box.
   c. Click the second option box arrow in the *Format only cells with* section (which displays *between*) and then click *equal to* at the drop-down list.
   d. Click in the blank text box next to *equal to* and then type 1.
   e. Click the Format button.
   f. At the Format Cells dialog box with the Font tab selected, apply the Blue color (eighth option in the *Standard Colors* section), apply bold formatting, and then click OK.
   g. Click OK at the New Formatting Rule dialog box.

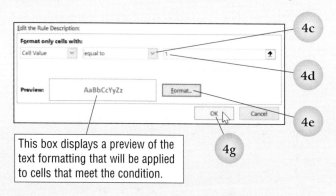

This box displays a preview of the text formatting that will be applied to cells that meet the condition.

Rating	Claims
1	0
1	0
2	1
2	1
5	3
4	2
2	1
5	2
5	2
8	4
5	3
6	3
1	0
3	2
5	3
2	1
1	0

Bold dark red formatting has been applied to cells containing *0*, and bold blue formatting has been applied to cells containing *1*.

5. Click in any cell to deselect the range and review the conditionally formatted cells in the *Claims* column.
6. Save **1-ACInsce**.

Editing and Deleting a Conditional Formatting Rule

Editing and Deleting a Conditional Formatting Rule

To edit or delete a formatting rule, select the range, click the Conditional Formatting button in the Styles group on the Home tab, and then click the *Manage Rule* option to open the Conditional Formatting Rules Manager dialog box. By default, *Show formatting rules for* is set to *Current Selection* when the

Quick Steps

Edit Formatting Rule
1. Select range.
2. Click Conditional Formatting button.
3. Click *Manage Rules.*
4. Click rule.
5. Click Edit Rule button.
6. Make changes.
7. Click OK two times.

Quick Steps

Remove Conditional Formatting
1. Select range.
2. Click Quick Analysis button.
3. Click Clear Format button.

Conditional Formatting Rules Manager dialog box is opened. If a range was not selected and no rules display, click the option box arrow and then select *This Worksheet* to show all the formatting rules in the current sheet. To edit the comparison rule criteria and/or formatting options, click to select the rule to change and then click the Edit Rule button. At the Edit Formatting Rule dialog box, make the required changes and then click OK two times. To remove a rule, click to select the rule to delete, click the Delete Rule button, and then click OK.

Another way to remove conditional formatting is to select the range, click the Conditional Formatting button, point to *Clear Rules* at the drop-down list, and then click either *Clear Rules from Selected Cells* or *Clear Rules from Entire Sheet.* Conditional formatting can also be removed using the Quick Analysis button. Once the range has been selected, click the Quick Analysis button, which appears at the bottom right corner of the selected data, and then click the Clear Format button in the drop-down gallery. The Quick Analysis gallery can also be accessed using the keyboard shortcut Ctrl + Q. Formatting applied to the cells by the deleted rule(s) will be removed.

Activity 2b **Creating, Editing, and Deleting a Conditional Formatting Rule**   Part 2 of 6

1. With **1-ACInsce** open, create a new formatting rule to add a fill color to the cells in the *No. of Autos* column for those auto insurance policy holders who have more than two cars by completing the following steps:

   a. Select the range C4:C20.
   b. Click the Conditional Formatting button and then click *New Rule* at the drop-down list.
   c. Click *Format only cells that contain* in the *Select a Rule Type* list box.
   d. In the *Edit the Rule Description* section, change the parameters for the rule to format only cells with values greater than 2. (If necessary, refer to Activity 2a, Steps 3e–3f, for assistance.)
   e. Click the Format button and then click the Fill tab at the Format Cells dialog box.
   f. Click the *Orange* color (third column, bottom row in the *Background Color* palette) and then click OK.
   g. Click OK to close the New Formatting Rule dialog box.

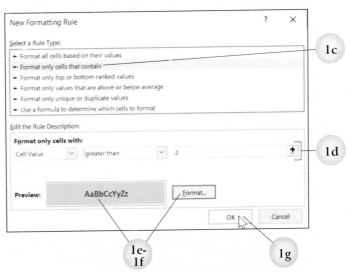

   h. Click in any cell to deselect the range.

2. After the formatted cells have been reviewed, it is decided that cells should be formatted for all policy holders with two or more cars. Edit the formatting rule to include the value *2* by completing the following steps:

a. Select the range C4:C20.

b. Click the Conditional Formatting button and then click *Manage Rules* at the drop-down list.

c. Click *Cell Value > 2* in the Conditional Formatting Rules Manager dialog box to select the rule and then click the Edit Rule button.

Customer ID	Policy ID	No. of Autos
C-025	6512485	2
C-055	6123584	1
C-072	6583157	2
C-085	6124893	3
C-094	3481274	1
C-114	4956875	2
C-124	3354867	1
C-131	6598642	3
C-148	4668457	3
C-155	8512475	4
C-168	6984563	2
C-171	4856972	1
C-184	5124876	1
C-190	6845962	1
C-199	8457326	1
C-201	4968532	2
C-212	2698715	2

Formatting has been applied to cell values greater than 2.

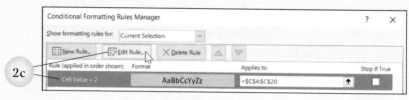

2c

d. Click the second option box arrow (which displays *greater than*) and then click *greater than or equal to* at the drop-down list.

e. Click OK.

f. Click OK to close the Conditional Formatting Rules Manager dialog box.

g. Click in any cell to deselect the range.

3. Save and print the worksheet.

4. To prepare for experimenting with another method of formatting the data, save the revised worksheet with a new name and then delete the formatting rule in the original worksheet by completing the following steps:

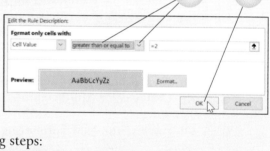

2d   2e

a. Save the workbook with the name **1-ACInsce-Autos2+**. Saving the workbook with a new name ensures that a copy of the workbook with the conditional formatting applied in this activity is kept.

b. Close **1-ACInsce-Autos2+**.

c. Open **1-ACInsce**.

d. Click the Conditional Formatting button and then click *Manage Rules* at the drop-down list.

e. Click the *Show formatting rules for* option box arrow and then click *This Worksheet*.

f. Click *Cell Value >= 2* to select the rule and then click the Delete Rule button.

g. Click OK to close the Conditional Formatting Rules Manager dialog box. Notice that the formatting has been removed from the cells in the *No. of Autos* column.

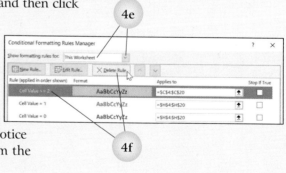

4e

4f

5. Save **1-ACInsce**.

Check Your Work

Applying Conditional Formatting Using an Icon Set

Format a range of values using an icon set to organize data into three to five categories. When this type of conditional formatting is applied, Excel places an icon in a cell to visually portray the value of the cell relative to the values of the other cells within the selected range. Using an icon set, similar data are categorized to easily identify high points, low points, and other trends. Icons are assigned to cells based on default threshold values for the selected range. For example, if the *3 Arrows (Colored)* icon set option is selected, icons are assigned as follows:

- Green up arrows for values greater than or equal to 67%
- Red down arrows for values less than 33%
- Yellow sideways arrows for values between 33% and 67%

The available icon sets, shown in Figure 1.3, are organized into four sections: *Directional*, *Shapes*, *Indicators*, and *Ratings*. Choose the icon set that best represents the number of categories within the range and symbol type, such as directional colored arrows, traffic light shapes, flag indicators, star ratings, and so on. Modify the default threshold values or create unique icon sets by opening the Manage Rules dialog box and editing an existing rule or creating a new rule.

 Green Up Arrow

 Red Down Arrow

 Yellow Sideways Arrow

Quick Steps

Apply Conditional Formatting Using Icon Set
1. Select range.
2. Click Conditional Formatting button.
3. Point to *Icon Sets*.
4. Click icon set.
5. Deselect range.

Figure 1.3 Conditional Formatting Icon Sets Gallery

1. With **1-ACInsce** open, select the range C4:C20.
2. Use an icon set to organize the number of automobiles into categories by completing the following steps:
   a. Click the Conditional Formatting button.
   b. Point to *Icon Sets* and then click *Red To Black* (first column, third row in the *Shapes* section) at the drop-down gallery.
   c. Click in any cell to deselect the range. Notice that Excel assigns an icon to each cell and that these icons correlate with the values of the cells. For example, all cells containing the value *1* have the same icon, all cells containing the value *2* have the same icon, and so on.

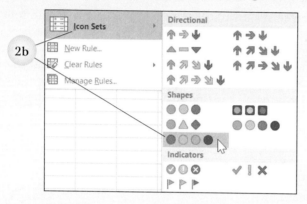
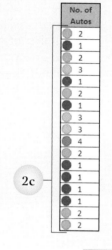

3. Save **1-ACInsce**.

Check Your Work

Applying Conditional Formatting Using Data Bars and Color Scales

Excel also provides the ability to conditionally format cells using data bars, two-color scales, and three-color scales, to provide visual guides for identifying distributions or variations within a range.

Use data bars to easily identify the highest and lowest values within a range. A data bar appears in the background of a cell and the length of the bar depends on the value within the cell. A cell with a higher value within the range displays a longer bar than a cell with a lower value. Excel offers six colors for data bars and each color is available in a gradient or solid fill.

Hint Be careful not to use too many icon sets, color scales, and/or data bars. Readers can quickly lose focus when too many items compete for their attention.

Color scales format a range using a two-color or three-color palette. Excel provides 12 color scale gradients, half of which are two-color combinations and half of which are three-color combinations. The gradation of color applied to a cell illustrates its value relative to the rest of the range. Color scales are useful for reviewing the distribution of data. In a two-color scale, the shade applied to a cell represents either a higher or lower value within the range. In a three-color scale, the shade applied to a cell represents a higher, middle, or lower value within the range.

1. With **1-ACInsce** open, select the range I4:I20.
2. Apply gradient blue data bar formatting to the premium values to easily identify the higher and lower premiums by completing the following steps:
   a. Click the Conditional Formatting button.
   b. Point to *Data Bars* and then click *Blue Data Bar* (first option in the *Gradient Fill* section) at the drop-down gallery.
   c. Click in any cell to deselect the range. Notice that the lengths of the colored bars in the cells reflect various premium amounts, with longer bars representing higher premiums.

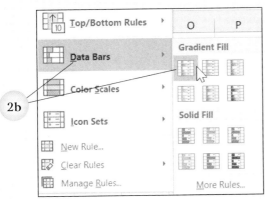
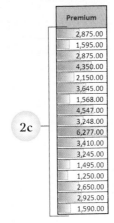

3. Save **1-ACInsce**.

 Check Your Work

 Tutorial

Applying Conditional Formatting Using a Formula

Applying Conditional Formatting Using a Formula

Use conditional formatting and a formula to format a cell based on the value in another cell or using some logical test. At the New Formatting Rule dialog box, choose *Use a formula to determine which cells to format* in the *Select a Rule Type* list box. Enter a formula, such as an IF statement, to determine whether a cell will be formatted.

For example, in Activity 2e, the premium values in column I of the insurance worksheet are formatted based on the rating values for the policies stored in column G. In this activity, the IF statement allows a premium to be conditionally formatted if the rating value for the policy is greater than 3. The IF function's logical test returns only a true or false result. The value in the rating cell is either greater than 3 (true) or not greater than 3 (false). Excel conditionally formats only those cells in the *Premium* column for which the conditional test returns a true result.

The formula that is entered into the New Formatting Rule dialog box in Activity 2e is *=IF(G4:G20>3,TRUE,FALSE)*. Excel treats any formula entered for conditional formatting as an array formula, which means one rule needs to be added for the range G4:G20. In the first cell in the selected range (cell I4), Excel will perform the following test: *Is the value in G4 greater than 3?* In the first row, this test returns a false result, so Excel will not conditionally format the value in cell I4. Excel will apply bold formatting and the standard red font color to those cells in column I for which the test returns a true result based on the corresponding cell in column G.

1. With **1-ACInsce** open, select the range I4:I20.
2. The owner of AllClaims Insurance Brokers would like the premiums for those clients with ratings higher than 3 to stand out in the worksheet. Conditionally format the premiums in column I using a formula that checks the ratings in column G by completing the following steps:
   a. Click the Conditional Formatting button and then click *New Rule* at the drop-down list.
   b. At the New Formatting Rule dialog box, click *Use a formula to determine which cells to format* in the *Select a Rule Type* list box.
   c. Click in the *Format values where this formula is true* text box in the *Edit the Rule Description* section of the New Formatting Rule dialog box and then type =if(g4:g20>3,true,false).
   d. Click the Format button.
   e. At the Format Cells dialog box, click the Font tab and apply the Red font color (second option in the *Standard Colors* section), apply bold formatting, and then click OK.
   f. Click OK to close the New Formatting Rule dialog box and apply the rule to the selected cells.

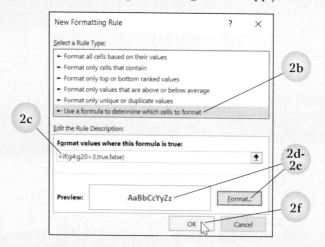

   g. Click in any cell to deselect the range. Notice that the cells in column I with bold formatting and the standard red font color are those for which the corresponding rating values in column G are greater than 3. For the most part, the higher ratings correspond to higher premiums, which are identified by the longer blue data bars.
3. Save **1-ACInsce**.

Rating	Claims	Premium
1	0	2,875.00
1	0	1,595.00
2	1	2,875.00
2	1	4,350.00
5	3	2,150.00
4	2	3,645.00
2	1	1,568.00
5	2	4,547.00
5	2	3,248.00
8	4	6,277.00
5	3	3,410.00
6	3	3,245.00
1	0	1,495.00
3	2	1,250.00
5	3	2,650.00
2	1	2,925.00
1	0	1,590.00

Check Your Work

Applying Conditional Formatting Using Quick Analysis

Use the Quick Analysis button to quickly apply preset conditional formatting. After the data is selected, the Quick Analysis button appears near the fill handle at the bottom right corner of the selection and the options shown in Figure 1.4 become available. Use these options to apply conditional formatting, create charts, add totals, create tables, and add Sparklines. With predefined conditional formatting rules, Excel can quickly analyze and format the data. If more options are required than those provided by the Quick Analysis button, access the rules from the Conditional Formatting button drop-down list.

Figure 1.4 Quick Analysis Button Options

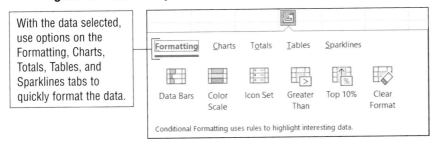

Activity 2f Apply Conditional Formatting Using the Quick Analysis Button

Part 6 of 6

1. With **1-ACInsce** open, apply conditional formatting to apply a light red fill with dark red text for the number of drivers over three by completing the following steps:
   a. Select the range F4:F20.
   b. Click the Quick Analysis button at the bottom right of the selected range.
   c. Click the Greater Than button on the Formatting tab.

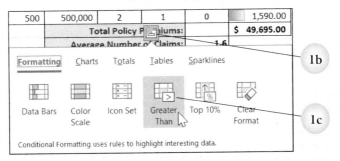

   d. At the Greater Than dialog box with the text already selected in the *Format cells that are GREATER THAN* text box, type 3.
   e. With *Light Red Fill with Dark Red Text* selected, click OK.
   f. Click in any cell to deselect the range. Review the cells that have been conditionally formatted. Notice that cells with values over 3 are formatted with a light red fill and dark red text.
2. Save, print, and then close **1-ACInsce**.

 Check Your Work

Activity 3 Use Fraction and Scientific Formatting Options for a Lesson Plan Worksheet **1 Part**

Using two lesson plan worksheets, you will format cells in a solution column to display the answers for a math tutor.

Tutorial

Applying Fraction and Scientific Formatting

Tutorial

Review: Applying Number Formatting

Quick Steps

Apply Fraction Formatting
1. Select range.
2. Click Number group dialog box launcher.
3. Click *Fraction* in *Category* list box.
4. Click option in *Type* list box.
5. Click OK.
6. Deselect range.

Apply Scientific Formatting
1. Select range.
2. Click *Number Format* option box arrow.
3. Click *Scientific*.
4. Deselect range.

Applying Fraction Formatting and Scientific Formatting

Most worksheet values are formatted using the Accounting Number Format, Percent Style, or the Comma Style button in the Number group on the Home tab. However, some worksheets contain values that require other number formats. When clicked, the *Number Format* option box arrow in the Number group on the Home tab displays a drop-down list with additional format options, including date, time, fraction, scientific, and text options.

Click the Number group dialog box launcher at the bottom right of the Number group on the Home tab to open the Format Cells dialog box with the Number tab active, as shown in Figure 1.5. This dialog box may also be opened by clicking *More Number Formats* at the *Number Format* drop-down list or by using the keyboard shortcut Ctrl + 1. At this dialog box, specify additional parameters for the number format categories. For example, with the *Fraction* category selected, choose the type of fraction to be displayed.

Scientific formatting converts a number to exponential notation. Part of the number is replaced with $E+n$, where E means "exponent" and n represents the power. For example, the number *1,500,000.00* formatted in scientific number format displays as *1.50E+06*. In this example, *+06* means "Add six zeros to the right of the number left of E and then move the decimal point six places to the right." Scientists, mathematicians, engineers, and statisticians often use exponential notation to write very large numbers and very small numbers in a more manageable way.

Figure 1.5 Format Cells Dialog Box with the Number Tab Selected and the *Fraction* Category Active

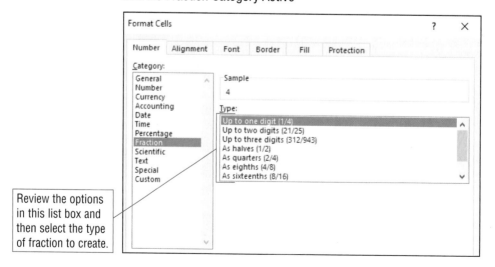

Review the options in this list box and then select the type of fraction to create.

1. Open **JTutor.**
2. Save the workbook with the name **1-JTutor.**
3. Make Fractions the active worksheet by clicking the Fractions sheet tab.
4. Apply fraction formatting to the values in column D to create the solution column for the math tutor by completing the following steps:
   a. Select the range D11:D19.
   b. Click the Number group dialog box launcher on the Home tab.
   c. At the Format Cells dialog box with the Number tab selected, click *Fraction* in the *Category* list box.
   d. Click *Up to two digits (21/25)* in the *Type* list box.

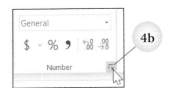

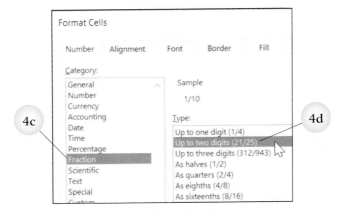

   e. Click OK.
   f. Click in any cell to deselect the range.
5. Click the Exponents sheet tab.
6. Apply scientific formatting to the values in column D to create the solution column for the math tutor by completing the following steps:
   a. Select the range D11:D25.
   b. Click the *Number Format* option box arrow (which displays *Custom*) in the Number group on the Home tab and then click *Scientific* at the drop-down list.
   c. Click in any cell to deselect the range.
7. Print the workbook.
8. Save and then close **1-JTutor.**

Examples	Converted to Scientific Notation
1,000,000,000	1.00E+09
100,000,000	1.00E+08
10,000,000	1.00E+07
1,000,000	1.00E+06
100,000	1.00E+05
10,000	1.00E+04
1,000	1.00E+03
100	1.00E+02
10	1.00E+01
1	1.00E+00
0.1	1.00E-01
0.01	1.00E-02
0.001	1.00E-03
0.0001	1.00E-04
0.00001	1.00E-05

6a-6c

Apply Advanced Formatting Options to a Products Worksheet   **2 Parts**

You will update a products worksheet by formatting telephone numbers and creating a custom number format to add descriptive characters before and after values.

Applying Special Number Formatting

Excel provides special number formats that are specific to countries and languages at the Format Cells dialog box with the Number tab active. As shown in Figure 1.6, when *Special* is selected in the *Category* list box and *English (United States)* is selected in the *Locale (location)* option box, the *Type* list box includes *Zip Code, Zip Code + 4, Phone Number,* and *Social Security Number*. When the *English (Canadian)* option is selected in the *Locale (location)* option box, the *Type* list box includes *Phone Number* and *Social Insurance Number*.

Applying special number formatting can save time and keystrokes, as well as help to ensure consistent formatting. For example, if special social security number formatting is applied to a range, social security numbers can be typed into the range without hyphens because Excel will add them. Typing *000223456* will enter *000-22-3456* in the cell with social security number formatting applied.

Figure 1.6 Format Cells Dialog Box with the Number Tab Selected and the *Special* Category Active

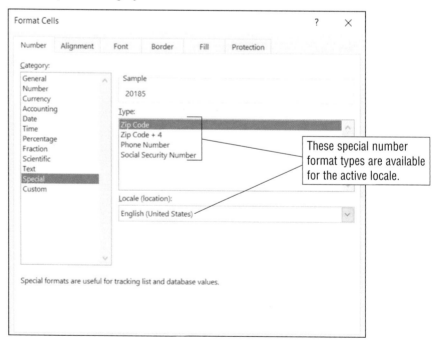

1. Open **Precision**.
2. Save the workbook with the name **1-Precision**.
3. Format the range that will contain telephone numbers to include brackets around each area code and a hyphen between the first three and last four digits of each number by completing the following steps:
   a. Select the range C15:C20.
   b. Click the Number group dialog box launcher.
   c. At the Format Cells dialog box with the Number tab selected, click *Special* in the *Category* list box.
   d. Click *Phone Number* in the *Type* list box and make sure the *Locale (location)* option box is set to *English (United States)*.
   e. Click OK.
   f. Click in cell C15 to deselect the range and make the first cell to contain a telephone number the active cell.

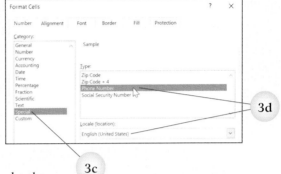

4. Type the telephone numbers for the sales representatives as follows:

   C15: 8005553429
   C16: 8005553439
   C17: 8005553449
   C18: 8005553459
   C19: 8005553469
   C20: 8005553479

14	Regional Sales Representatives		
15	North	Jordan Lavoie	(800) 555-3429
16	South	Pat Gallagher	(800) 555-3439
17	East	Alonso Rodriguez	(800) 555-3449
18	West	Karsten Das	(800) 555-3459
19	Canada	Kelli Olsen	(800) 555-3469
20	International	Bianca Santini	(800) 555-3479

5. Save **1-Precision**.

Check Your Work

 Tutorial

Creating a Custom Number Format

 Quick Steps

Create Custom Number Format
1. Select range.
2. Click Number group dialog box launcher.
3. Click *Custom* in *Category* list box.
4. Select *General* in *Type* text box.
5. Press Delete.
6. Type custom format code.
7. Click OK.
8. Deselect range.

💡 **Hint** Custom number formats are stored in the workbook in which they are created.

Creating a Custom Number Format

Use a custom number format for a worksheet to enter values that do not conform to predefined number formats or values to which punctuation, text, or formatting such as color is to be added. For example, in Activity 4b, a custom number format is created to automatically add two product category letters before each model number.

Formatting codes are used in custom formats to specify the types of formatting to apply. Type unique custom number format codes or select from a list of custom formats and modify the codes as necessary. Table 1.1 displays commonly used format codes along with examples of their uses.

Once a custom format has been created, it can be applied elsewhere within the workbook. To do this, select the text to be formatted, open the Format Cells dialog box with the Number tab selected, select the *Custom* category, scroll down to the bottom of the *Type* list box, click to select the custom format code, and then click OK.

Text, numbers, and punctuation added as part of a custom number format are not saved as part of the cell value. In Activity 4b, a custom number format that displays *PD-* in front of each model number is created. The value in cell A5 displays as *PD-1140* but *1140* is the actual value that is stored. This is important to remember when searching for or filtering data.

Table 1.1 Examples of Custom Number Format Codes

Format Code	Description	Custom Number Format Example	Display Result
#	Represents a digit; type one for each number. Excel rounds numbers if necessary to fit the number of digits after the decimal point.	###.###	Typing *145.0068* displays *145.007*.
0	Also represents a digit. Excel rounds numbers to fit the number of digits after the decimal point but also fills in leading zeros.	000.00	Typing *50.45* displays *050.45*.
?	Rounds numbers to fit the number of digits after the decimal point but also aligns numbers vertically on the decimal point by adding spaces.	???.???	Typing *123.5, .8,* and *55.356* one below the other in a column aligns the numbers vertically on the decimal points.
"text"	Adds the characters between the quotation marks to the entry.	"Model No." ##	Typing *58* displays *Model No. 58*.
[color]	Applies the font color specified in square brackets to the cell entry.	[Blue]##.##	Typing *55.346* displays *55.35*.
;	Separates the positive value format from the negative value format.	[Blue];[Red]	Typing *25* displays as *25* and typing *-25* displays as *25*.

Quick Steps

Delete Custom Number Format
1. Click Number group dialog box launcher.
2. Click *Custom* in *Category* list box.
3. Click custom format code.
4. Press Delete.
5. Click OK.

To delete a custom number format, open the workbook in which the custom format code was created, open the Format Cells dialog box with the Number tab selected, click *Custom* in the *Category* list box, scroll down the list of custom formats in the *Type* list box to the bottom of the list, click the custom format code that was added, and then click the Delete button. Deleting the formatting code also removes the custom formatting from any cells to which it was applied.

Activity 4b **Creating a Custom Number Format**   Part 2 of 2

1. With **1-Precision** open, select the range A5:A12.
2. Create a custom number format to insert *PD-* before each model number by completing the following steps:
   a. Click the Number group dialog box launcher.
   b. Click *Custom* in the *Category* list box in the Format Cells dialog box with the Number tab selected.

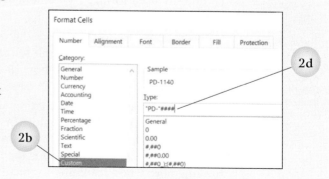

c. Scroll down the list of custom formats in the *Type* list box and notice the various combinations of format codes for numbers, dates, and times.

d. Select *General* in the *Type* text box and then type "PD-"####.

e. Click OK.

f. With the range A5:A12 still selected, click the Center button in the Alignment group on the Home tab.

g. Click in any cell to deselect the range.

3. Create a custom number format to insert *lbs* after the weights in columns D and E by completing the following steps:

a. Select the range D5:E12.

b. Click the Number group dialog box launcher.

c. Click *Custom* in the *Category* list box.

d. Select *General* in the *Type* text box and then type ### "lbs". Make sure to include one space after ###.

e. Click OK.

f. Click in any cell to deselect the range.

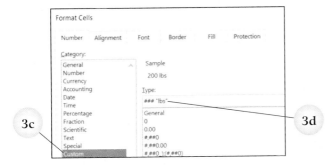

4. Save, print, and then close **1-Precision**.

 Check Your Work

---

Activity 5 **Filter and Sort Insurance and Payroll Data on Values, Icon Sets, and Colors**   **4 Parts**

You will filter an insurance policy worksheet to show policies based on a range of liability limits and by number of claims, filter policies based on the number of automobiles, and filter and sort a payroll worksheet by font and cell colors. You will also remove a filter.

 Tutorial

Filtering a Worksheet Using a Custom AutoFilter

Filtering a Worksheet Using a Custom AutoFilter

The Custom AutoFilter feature is used to display only the rows that meet specific criteria defined using the filter arrow at the top of each column. Rows that do not meet the criteria are temporarily hidden from view. At the top of each column in the selected range or table, click a filter arrow to display a drop-down list of all the unique field values that exist within the column. To filter the values by more than one criterion using a comparison operator, open the Custom AutoFilter dialog box, shown in Figure 1.7. Use the ? and * wildcard characters in a custom filter. For example, filter a list of products by a product number beginning with *P* by using *P** as the criteria.

To display the Custom AutoFilter dialog box, select the range to filter, click the Sort & Filter button in the Editing group on the Home tab, and then click *Filter* at the drop-down list to add filter arrows. Filter arrows can also be added using the keyboard shortcut Ctrl + Shift + L. Click the filter arrow in the column that contains the criteria. Point to *Number Filters* or *Text Filters* and then choose one of the options at the drop-down list. The type of filter and options available depend on the type of data in the column—for example, text or numbers.

Figure 1.7 Custom AutoFilter Dialog Box

Sort & Filter

Use the Custom AutoFilter dialog box to specify two criteria by which to filter using either an *And* or an *Or* statement.

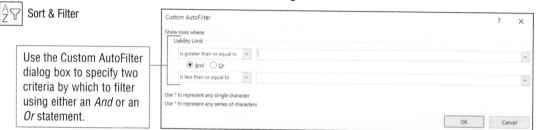

Activity 5a Filtering Policy Information Using a Custom AutoFilter

Part 1 of 4

1. Open **1-ACInsce**.
2. Save the workbook with the name **1-ACInsce-LL**.
3. The owner of AllClaims Insurance Brokers wants to review policies with liability limits from $500,000 to $1,000,000 that have had more than one claim to determine if customers should increase their coverage. Filter the policy information to produce the list of policies that meet the owner's request by completing the following steps:
   a. Select the range A3:I20.
   b. Click the Sort & Filter button in the Editing group on the Home tab.
   c. Click *Filter* at the drop-down list. A filter arrow displays at the top of each column.
   d. Deselect the range.
   e. Click the filter arrow next to *Liability Limit* in cell E3.
   f. Point to *Number Filters* and then click *Between* at the drop-down list.

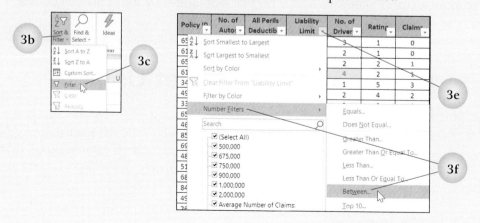

g. At the Custom AutoFilter dialog box with the insertion point positioned in the blank text box next to *is greater than or equal to*, type 500000.

h. Notice that *And* is the option selected between the criteria. This is correct, since the owner wants a list of policies with liability limits greater than or equal to $500,000 *and* less than or equal to $1,000,000.

i. Click in the blank text box next to *is less than or equal to* and type 1000000.

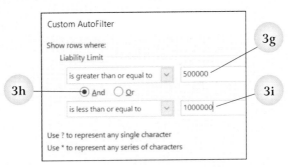

j. Click OK to close the Custom AutoFilter dialog box. The range is filtered to display the rows for customers with liability limits from $500,000 to $1,000,000.

k. Click the filter arrow next to *Claims* in cell H3.

l. Point to *Number Filters* and then click *Greater Than* at the drop-down list.

m. At the Custom AutoFilter dialog box with the insertion point positioned in the blank text box next to *is greater than*, type 1 and then click OK.

4. Print the filtered worksheet.

5. Save **1-ACInsce-LL**.

 Check Your Work

 Tutorial

Filtering Data Using Conditional Formatting or Cell Attributes

💡 **Hint** If an error message about merged cells needing to be the same size appears when sorting, select the range to be sorted and do a custom sort.

Filtering and Sorting Data and Removing a Filter

A worksheet with cells that have been formatted manually or by conditional formatting to change the cell or font color can be filtered by color. In addition, a worksheet conditionally formatted using an icon set can be filtered using an icon. When the data needs to be redisplayed, remove the filter.

Filtering and Sorting Data Using Conditional Formatting or Cell Attributes

To filter by color or icon, select the range, click the Sort & Filter button, click *Filter*, and then deselect the range. Click the filter arrow in the column to filter and then point to *Filter by Color* at the drop-down list. Depending on the formatting that has been applied, the list contains cell colors, font colors, or icon sets. Click the specific color or icon option to filter the column.

Quick Steps
Filter or Sort by Color
or Icon Set
1. Select range.
2. Click Sort & Filter
   button.
3. Click *Filter.*
4. Deselect range.
5. Click filter arrow at
   top of column to be
   filtered.
6. Point to *Filter by
   Color* or *Sort by
   Color.*
7. Click color or icon.

The filter drop-down list also contains a *Sort by Color* option to sort rows within a range or table by a specified cell color, font color, or cell icon. To sort by color, follow steps similar to those used to filter by color. For example, to sort a column by font color, point to *Sort by Color* from the column filter drop-down list and then click the specific font color. Excel sorts the column by placing cells with the specified font color at the top. The list does not sort itself within the different color groupings.

The shortcut menu can also be used to sort or filter data. To do this, right-click a cell that contains the color or icon to filter, point to *Filter,* and then click *Filter by Selected Cell's Color, Filter by Selected Cell's Font Color,* or *Filter by Selected Cell's Icon.*

Removing a Filter

Quick Steps

Remove Filter
1. Click in filtered list.
2. Click Sort & Filter
   button.
3. Click *Clear* at drop-down list.

 Clear

To remove a filter, click in the filtered list, click the Sort & Filter button in the Editing group on the Home tab, and then click *Clear* at the drop-down list. A filter can also be removed by clicking the Clear button in the Sort & Filter group on the Data tab.

Defining a Custom Sort

Define a custom sort in a worksheet when more than one cell or font color is applied to a column. Select the range, click the Sort & Filter button in the Editing group on the Home tab, and then click *Custom Sort* at the drop-down list. At the Sort dialog box, shown in Figure 1.8, define the color by which to sort first and then add a level for each other color in the order in which the sorting is to occur. Select *Values, Cell Color, Font Color,* or *Conditional Formatting Icon* from the *Sort On* drop-down list at the Sort dialog box. Figure 1.8 illustrates a sort definition for a column in which four conditional formatting icons have been used.

Figure 1.8 Sort Dialog Box with a Four-Color Sort Defined

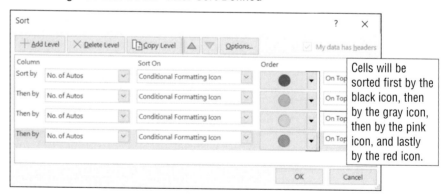

Cells will be sorted first by the black icon, then by the gray icon, then by the pink icon, and lastly by the red icon.

Activity 5b Clearing a Filter and Filtering by an Icon Set   Part 2 of 4

1. With **1-ACInsce-LL** open, save the workbook as **1-ACInsce-1Auto.**
2. Remove the filter by completing the following steps:
   a. Click in the filtered list.
   b. Click the Sort & Filter button.
   c. Click *Clear* at the drop-down list.

3. Filter the worksheet to display the customers with coverage for only one automobile by completing the following steps:
   a. In Activity 2c, the Red to Black icon set was applied to the data in column C. Note that the black circle icon represents the *1* data set. Click the filter arrow next to *No. of Autos* in cell C3.
   b. Point to *Filter by Color* at the drop-down list.
   c. Click the black circle icon in the *Filter by Cell Icon* list.

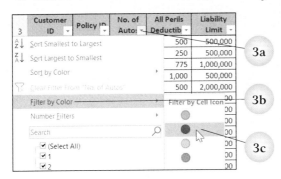

The worksheet has been filtered by the black circle icon representing customers with one auto.

4. Print the filtered worksheet.
5. Save **1-ACInsce-1Auto**.

Check Your Work

Activity 5c Filtering by Font Color

Part 3 of 4

1. With **1-ACInsce-1Auto** open, further filter the list to display the customers that have had zero claims. Recall that zero claims were conditionally formatted by applying a red font color and bold formatting to cells with values equal to 0. Filter the worksheet by the conditional formatting by completing the following steps:
   a. Right-click in cell H5 (or in any other cell in column H with a red font color).
   b. Point to *Filter* and then click *Filter by Selected Cell's Font Color* at the shortcut menu.

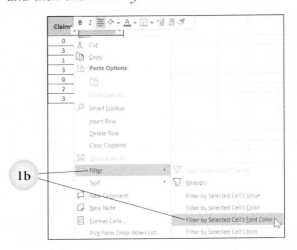

2. Print the filtered worksheet.
3. Save and then close **1-ACInsce-1Auto**.

Check Your Work

1. Open **1-VRPay-Oct23**.
2. Save the workbook with the name **1-VRPay-Oct23-Sorted**.
3. Sort the payroll worksheet by cell color by completing the following steps:

   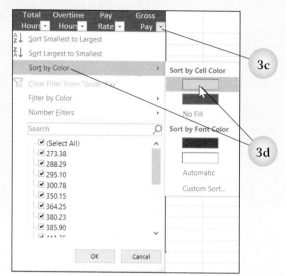

   a. Select the range A5:M23, click the Sort & Filter button, and then click *Filter* at the drop-down list.
   b. Deselect the range.
   c. Click the filter arrow next to *Gross Pay* in cell M5.
   d. Point to *Sort by Color* and then click the pink fill color box in the *Sort by Cell Color* section.
4. Print the sorted worksheet.
5. Save and then close **1-VRPay-Oct23-Sorted**.

> Check Your Work

Activity 6 Apply an Advanced Filter to Create a Client List   2 Parts

You will use an advanced filter to create a list of clients of an insurance company who have a good rating with no claims and filter the same list using And and Or logical operators.

Tutorial

Applying an Advanced Filter

Advanced Filter

Applying an Advanced Filter

Use an advanced filter when a range needs to be filtered on complex criteria. An advanced filter allows the data to be filtered using the And or Or logical operator on more than one field. The list can either be filtered in place or copied to a new location.

To filter a range using an advanced filter, insert five or six rows at the top of the worksheet and then copy the column header row to the new row 1. If your worksheet has a title, insert the rows and the column header row under the title. Enough rows are needed at the top of the worksheet to enter all the required criteria and allow at least one blank row between the criteria range and the data to be filtered. Enter the filter criteria under the appropriate column headers. Click the Data tab and then click the Advanced button in the Sort & Filter group to display the Advanced Filter dialog box. Use options at the dialog box to indicate the filter criteria, as shown in Figure 1.9, and then click OK.

When using the And operator, enter criteria on the same row, and when using the Or operator, enter the criteria in separate rows.

Quick Steps

Apply Advanced Filter in Place
1. Select rows 1 through 5.
2. Right-click and then click *Insert*.
3. Select column header row.
4. Press Ctrl + C.
5. Click in cell A1.
6. Press Ctrl + V.
7. Enter filter criteria under appropriate column headers.
8. Click Data tab.
9. Click Advanced button.
10. Type range to be filtered.
11. Press Tab key.
12. Type range that contains criteria.
13. Click OK.

If you need to filter a range using a criterion that falls between two values in the same field, copy the field name and place it in the first empty cell in the row of the copied column header row. The worksheet in Figure 1.10 has been filtered to show the policies that have at least one claim and a premium between $3,000 and $4,000.

Figure 1.9 Advanced Filter Dialog Box

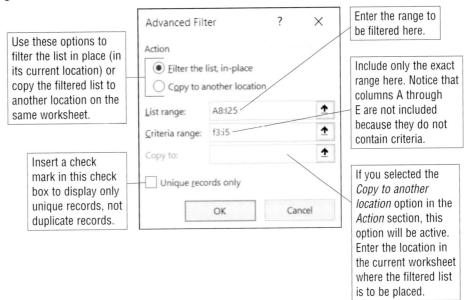

Figure 1.10 Between Filter Applied Using the Advanced Filter Feature

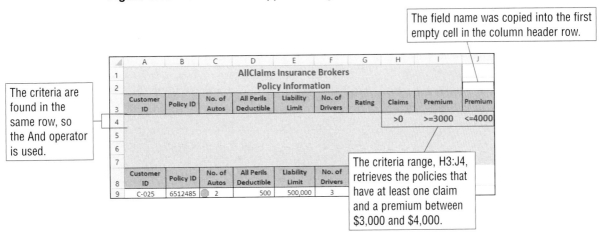

1. Open **1-ACInsce**.
2. Save the workbook with the name **1-ACInsce-AF**.
3. Filter the range and copy the results to a new location for those clients with a rating of 1 who have zero claims by completing the following steps:
   a. Select rows 3 through 7.
   b. Right-click in the selected range and then click the *Insert* option.
   c. Select the range A8:I8, press Ctrl + C, click in cell A3, and then press Ctrl + V. Press the Esc key.
   d. Click in cell G4 and then type 1.
   e. Click in cell H4, type 0 and then click the Enter button on the Formula bar.

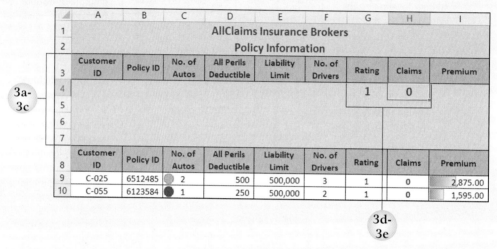

   f. Click the Data tab and then click the Advanced button in the Sort & Filter group.
   g. If a Microsoft Excel message box displays, click OK.
   h. Click the *Copy to another location* radio button.
   i. Select the text in the *List range* text box, type a8:i25 and then press the Tab key.
   j. With the insertion point in the *Criteria range* text box, type g3:h4 and then press the Tab key.
   k. With the insertion point in the *Copy to* text box, type a30.
   l. Click OK.

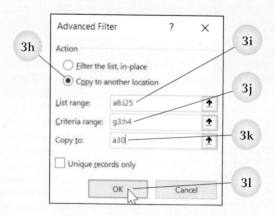

4. Save **1-ACInsce-AF**.

1. With **1-ACInsce-AF** open, filter the range in its current location to show the records
   for policies that have a rating higher than two and more than one claim or that have a
   premium greater than 3,500 by completing the following steps:
   a. Delete the contents of cell G4 and H4.
   b. Click in cell G4 and then type >2.
   c. Click in cell H4 and then type >1.
   d. Click in cell I5 and type >3500, and then press the Enter key.

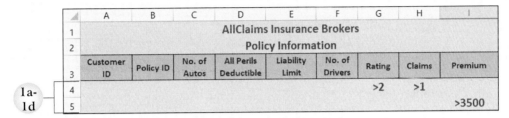

	A	B	C	D	E	F	G	H	I
1				AllClaims Insurance Brokers					
2				Policy Information					
3	Customer ID	Policy ID	No. of Autos	All Perils Deductible	Liability Limit	No. of Drivers	Rating	Claims	Premium
4							>2	>1	
5									>3500

(1a–1d)

   e. Click the Advanced button in the Sort & Filter group.
   f. Verify that the *Filter the list, in-place* radio button contains a bullet.
   g. Verify that the text in the *List range* text box is *$A$8:$1$25* and then press the Tab key.
   h. With the text selected in the *Criteria range* text box, type f3:i5.
   i. Click OK.
2. Save, print, and then close **1-ACInsce-AF**.

Check Your Work

Chapter Summary

- Conditional formatting applies special formatting to cells based on a condition;
  cells that meet the condition have the formatting applied, and cells that do not
  meet the condition remain unformatted.

- Conditional formats can be based on values, dates, text entries, or duplicated values.

- Use the *Top/Bottom Rules* option at the Conditional Formatting button drop-
  down list to conditionally format based on the top 10 or bottom 10 value or
  percent or by above average or below average values.

- Use the *Highlight Cells Rules* option at the Conditional Formatting button drop-
  down list to conditionally format based on a value comparison.

- Conditional formats are based on rules that define criteria by which cells are
  selected for formatting and include the formatting attributes that are applied to cells
  that meet the criteria.

- Create a new conditional formatting rule by selecting *New Rule* at the
  Conditional Formatting button drop-down list.

- Edit or delete a rule at the Conditional Formatting Rules Manager dialog box.

- Apply conditional formatting using data bars, color scales, or icon sets to add
  small bar charts, gradations of color, or icons, respectively, to cells to make it
  easier to identify certain data.

- Apply conditional formatting using a formula to apply formatting to a cell
  based on the value in another cell or using some logical test. Excel treats any
  formula entered for conditional formatting as an array formula, which means
  one rule needs to be added for a selected range.

- An IF statement can be used to conditionally format those cells for which the conditional test returns a true result.
- Use the Quick Analysis button to quickly apply preset conditional formatting.
- Fraction formatting converts decimal values to fractions. To choose the type of fraction to create, open the Format Cells dialog box with the Number tab selected and the *Fraction* category active.
- Scientific formatting displays numbers in exponential notation, in which part of the number is replaced with $E+n$, where E stands for "exponent" and n represents the power.
- Excel provides special number formats that are specific to countries and languages to format entries such as telephone numbers and social security numbers.
- Custom number formats use formatting codes to specify the types of formatting to apply.
- Display the Custom AutoFilter dialog box to filter values by more than one criterion using a comparison operator, such as greater than ($>$) or equal to ($=$).
- A worksheet with cells that have been formatted manually or by conditional formatting can be filtered by color or icon.
- To remove a filter, click anywhere in the filtered list, click the Sort & Filter button in the Editing group on the Home tab, and then click *Clear* at the drop-down list.
- To specify the order of the sorted colors, define a custom sort if the worksheet contains more than one cell color, font color, or cell icon.
- Apply an advanced filter when a range needs to be filter on complex criteria. An advanced filter allows filtering the data using the And or Or logical operator on more than one field. The criteria in an advanced filter are entered directly in the worksheet and establish the criteria range.

Commands Review

FEATURE	RIBBON TAB, GROUP	BUTTON	KEYBOARD SHORTCUT
apply advanced filter	Data, Sort & Filter		
clear all filters	Home, Editing OR Data, Sort & Filter		
conditional formatting	Home, Styles OR Quick Analysis		Ctrl + Q
custom AutoFilter	Home, Editing		Ctrl + Shift + L
custom number format	Home, Number		Ctrl + 1
fraction formatting	Home, Number		Ctrl + 1
scientific formatting	Home, Number		Ctrl + 1
special number formatting	Home, Number		Ctrl + 1

Microsoft®

Excel®

Advanced Functions and Formulas

Performance Objectives

Upon successful completion of Chapter 2, you will be able to:

1 Create and manage names for ranges of cells

2 Write formulas with the COUNTBLANK, COUNTIF, and COUNTIFS statistical functions

3 Write formulas with the AVERAGEIF and AVERAGEIFS statistical functions

4 Write formulas with the SUMIF and SUMIFS math and trigonometry functions

5 Write formulas with the VLOOKUP and HLOOKUP lookup functions

6 Write formulas with the PPMT financial function

7 Write formulas with the nested IF, AND, and OR logical functions and the IFS logical function

8 Write formulas with the ROUND math and trigonometry function

9 Expand the Formula bar to view longer formulas

To help make complex calculations easier to perform, Excel provides numerous preset formulas called *functions*. These are grouped into thirteen different categories to facilitate calculations in worksheets containing financial, logical, mathematical, statistical, or other types of data. The Insert function dialog box provides options for locating and building formulas with various functions. The structure of a function formula includes an equals sign (=) followed by the name of the function and then the function argument. *Argument* is the term given to the values to be included in the calculation. The structure of the argument is dependent on the type of function being used and can include references to values in a single cell, a range, multiple ranges, or any combination of these.

 Data Files

Before beginning chapter work, copy the EL2C2 folder to your storage medium and then make EL2C2 the active folder.

The online course includes additional training and assessment resources.

Activity 1 **Calculate Statistics and Sums Using**   **6 Parts**
Conditional Formulas for an Insurance Claims Worksheet

You will manage range names in an insurance claims worksheet and use the range names in statistical formulas that count, average, and sum based on single and multiple criteria.

Managing Range Names

Review: Naming and Using a Range

Name Manager

Quick Steps

Modify Range Name and Reference
1. Click Formulas tab.
2. Click Name Manager button.
3. Click range name.
4. Click Edit button.
5. Type new range name in *Name* text box.
6. Type new range address at *Refers to* text box.
7. Click OK.
8. Click Close.

💡 **Hint** The Formulas tab contains a Create from Selection button in the Defined Names group that can be used to automatically create range names for a list or table. Select the list or table and click the button. Excel uses the names in the top row or left-most column as the range names.

Managing Range Names

Recall that a range name is a name assigned to a cell or range of cells. Range names provide the option of referencing a source using a descriptive label, rather than the cell address or range address, when creating a formula, printing a worksheet, or navigating in a worksheet. Creating range names makes the task of managing complex formulas easier and helps others who may work in or edit a worksheet to understand the purpose of a formula more quickly.

By default, a range name is an absolute reference to a cell or range of cells. This means that if the formula is copied or moved to a different location, the references will not change. Later in this chapter, when creating a lookup formula, take advantage of the absolute referencing of a range name when including a group of cells in the formula that stay fixed when the formula is copied. A range name also includes the worksheet reference by default; therefore, typing the range name in the formula automatically references the correct worksheet. For example, assume that cell A3 in Sheet 2 has been named *ProductA* and cell A3 in Sheet 3 has been named *ProductB*. To add the two values, type the formula =*ProductA*+*ProductB* in the formula cell. Notice that the worksheet references do not need to be included.

The Name Manager dialog box, shown in Figure 2.1, is opened by clicking the Name Manager button in the Defined Names group on the Formulas tab or by using the keyboard shortcut Ctrl + F3. The Name Manager dialog box can be used to create, edit, and delete range names. A range name can be edited by changing the name or modifying the range address associated with it. A range name can also be deleted, but extra caution should be used when doing so. Cells that include a deleted range name in the formula will display the error text #*NAME?* Also use the Name Manager dialog box to add new range names to a worksheet.

Figure 2.1 Name Manager Dialog Box

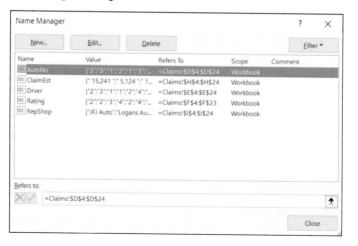

1. Open **ACOctVehRpt**.
2. Save the workbook with the name **2-ACOctVehRpt**.
3. Named ranges have been created for the auto number, driver number, rating, claim estimate, and repair shop data. Modify the range name *Drver* by completing the following steps:
   a. Click the Formulas tab.
   b. Click the Name Manager button in the Defined Names group.
   c. Click *Drver* in the *Name* column and then click the Edit button.
   d. At the Edit Name dialog box with *Drver* selected in the *Name* text box, type DriverNo and then click OK.

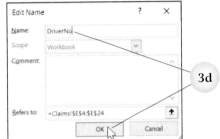

4. Modify the references in the range named *Rating* to include cell F24 by completing following steps:
   a. Click *Rating* at the Name Manager dialog box and then click the Edit button.
   b. At the Edit Name dialog box, click right of the text in the *Refers to* text box (which displays *Claims!$F$4:$F:$23*), press the Backspace key, type 4, and then click OK.

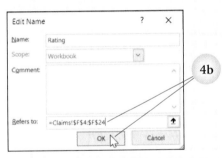

5. Delete the range name *AutoNo* by completing the following steps:
   a. Click *AutoNo* at the Name Manager dialog box and then click the Delete button.
   b. Click OK.
6. Click the Close button.
7. Save **2-ACOctVehRpt**.

Review: Using
Statistical
Functions

 More Functions

Using Statistical Functions

Commonly used statistical functions include AVERAGE, MAX, and MIN. AVERAGE returns the arithmetic mean, MAX returns the largest value, and MIN returns the smallest value in the range. Other common functions, COUNT and COUNTA, return the number of cells based on what is contained in the cells. COUNT is used when the cells contain numbers or dates and COUNTA is used when the cells contain text or a combination of text and numbers. Excel provides additional AVERAGE and COUNT functions, such as the COUNTBLANK function to find counts or averages for a range based on a criterion. The COUNTBLANK function counts the number of empty cells in range.

 Insert Function

Open the Insert Function Dialog box by clicking the Insert Function button in the Formula bar or in the Insert Function group on the Formulas tab or by using the shortcut combination of Shift + F3. At the Insert Function dialog box, change the *Or select a category* option to *Statistical* and then scroll down the list of available functions or click the More Functions button in the Function Library group on the Formulas tab, click the *Statistical* option, and then scroll down the list of available functions.

Using Statistical Functions: COUNTIF and COUNTIFS

 Tutorial

Using Statistical Functions: COUNTIF and COUNTIFS

Quick Steps

Create COUNTIF Formula

1. Make cell active.
2. Click Insert Function button.
3. Change category to *Statistical*.
4. Select *COUNTIF*.
5. Click OK.
6. Enter range or range name in *Range* text box.
7. Enter condition expression or text in *Criteria* text box.
8. Click OK.

Create COUNTIFS Formula

1. Make cell active.
2. Click Insert Function button.
3. Change category to *Statistical*.
4. Select *COUNTIFS*.
5. Click OK.
6. Enter range or range name in *Criteria_range1* text box.
7. Enter condition expression or text in *Criteria1* text box.
8. Enter range or range name in *Criteria_range2* text box.
9. Enter condition expression or text in *Criteria2* text box.
10. Continue adding criteria range expressions and criteria as needed.
11. Click OK.

Use the COUNTIF function to count cells within a range that meet a single criterion or condition. For example, in a grades worksheet, use a COUNTIF function to count the number of students who achieved greater than 75%. The structure of a COUNTIF function is *=COUNTIF(range,criteria)*. The range is where to look for the data. The criteria defines a conditional test that must be passed (what to look for) in order for the cell to be counted. For the grades worksheet example, the formula to count the cells of students who achieved greater than 75% is *=COUNTIF(grades,">75")*, assuming the range name *grades* has been defined. Each time Excel finds a grade greater than 75, the count increases by 1. Notice that the syntax of the argument requires enclosing the criteria in quotation marks. If the Insert Function dialog box is used to create a formula, Excel adds the required syntax automatically. A cell reference may also be used as the criterion. A cell reference is not enclosed in quotation marks and should only contain the exact criterion.

The COUNTIFS function is used to count cells when more than one condition must be met. The formula uses the same structure as COUNTIF but includes additional ranges and criteria within the argument. The structure of a COUNTIFS function is *=COUNTIFS(range1,criteria1,range2,criteria2,. . .)*. For every range (where to look), there is a corresponding criteria or conditional test (what to look for). If all the conditions are met for each range, then the count increases by 1. Figure 2.2 shows a nursing education worksheet with a single-criterion COUNTIF to count the number of nurses (RNs) and a multiple-criteria

Figure 2.2 COUNTIF and COUNTIFS Formulas

	A	B	C	D	E	F	G	H	I	J	K
1				Department of Human Resources							
2				Full-Time Nursing Education Worksheet							
3	Employee Number	Employee Last Name	Employee First Name	Title	Unit	Extension	Years Experience	PD Current?		Nursing Educational Statistical Summary	
4	FT02001	Santos	Susan	RN	Med/Surg	36415	30	Yes		Number of RNs	16
5	FT02002	Daniels	Jasmine	RN	Med/Surg	36415	27	No		Number of LPNs	12
6	FT02003	Walden	Virgina	RN	ICU	34211	22	No			
7	FT02004	Jaffe	Paul	LPN	CSRU	36418	24	Yes		RNs who are current with PD	9
8	FT02005	Salvatore	Terry	LPN	ICU	34211	22	Yes		LPNs who are current with PD	7
9	FT02006	Mander	Kaitlynn	RN	ICU	34211	24	Yes			
10	FT02007	Friesen	Jessica	LPN	ICU	34211	20			formula	
11	FT02008	Lavigne	Gisele	RN	CSRU	36418	20			=COUNTIF(Title,"RN")	
12	FT02009	Gauthier	Jacqueline	RN	PreOp	32881	19				
13	FT02010	Williamson	Forman	RN	CSRU	36418	19	Yes			
14	FT02011	Orlowski	William	RN	Ortho	31198	22	No			
15	FT02012	Kadri	Ahmed	LPN	Ortho	31198	21	No			
16	FT02013	El-Hamid	Lianna	LPN	Med/Surg	36415	20	No			
17	FT02014	Vezina	Ursula	LPN	Ortho	31198	20	No			
18	FT02015	Adams	Sheila	LPN	Med/Surg	36415	20			formula	
19	FT02016	Jorgensen	Macy	RN	Med/Surg	36415				=COUNTIFS(Title,"RN",PDCurrent,"Yes")	
20	FT02017	Pieterson	Eric	RN	ICU	34211					
21	FT02018	Keller	Douglas	RN	ICU	34211	10	No			
22	FT02019	Costa	Michael	RN	Ortho	31198	10	No			
23	FT02020	Li-Kee	Su-Lynn	LPN	PreOp	32881	8	No			
24	FT02021	Besterd	Mary	RN	PreOp	32881	7	Yes			

COUNTIFS to count the number of RNs who are current with their professional development (PD) activities. The formulas shown in Figure 2.2 (on page 34) include range names for which *Title* references the entries in column D and *PDCurrent* references the entries in column H. The ranges do not have to be adjacent but they must have the same number of rows and columns.

Activity 1b Creating COUNTBLANK and COUNTIF Formulas

1. With **2-ACOctVehRpt** open, make cell I25 active.
2. Create a COUNTBLANK function to count any cells in which repair shop information has not been entered by completing the following steps:
   a. Click the Insert Function button in the Formula bar.
   b. At the Insert Function dialog box, click the *Or select a category* option box arrow and then click *Statistical* at the drop-down list. **Note: Skip this step if Statistical is already selected as the category**.
   c. Scroll down the Select a function list box and then click *COUNTBLANK*.
   d. Read the formula description below the function list box and then click OK.
   e. At the Function Arguments dialog box with the insertion point positioned in the *Range* text box type repshop. Recall from Activity 1a that a range name exists for the entries in column I. **Note: If the dialog box is obscuring the view of the worksheet, drag the Function Arguments dialog box title bar left or right**.

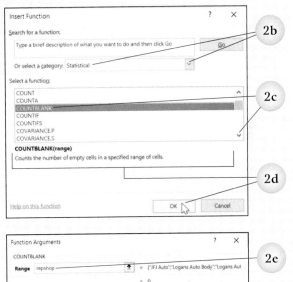

   f. Click OK. Excel returns the value 0 in cell I25 as all the repair shop information has been entered.
3. Click in cell L4.
4. Create a COUNTIF function to count the number of auto insurance claims for which Dunbar Auto is the repair shop by completing the following steps:
   a. Click the Insert Function button in the Formula bar.
   b. With *Statistical* selected in the *Or select a category* option box, scroll down the *Select a function* list box and then click *COUNTIF*.
   c. Read the formula description below the function list box and then click OK.

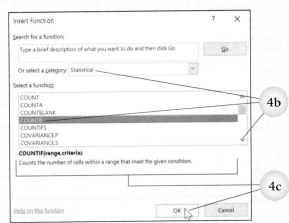

d. At the Function Arguments dialog box with the insertion point positioned in the *Range* text box, type repshop and then press the Tab key.

e. With the insertion point positioned in the *Criteria* text box, type Dunbar Auto and then press the Tab key. When the Tab key is pressed, Excel adds quotation marks around the criteria text.

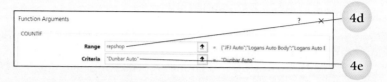

f. Click OK. Excel returns the value *3* in cell L4.

g. Look at the formula in the Formula bar created by the Function Arguments dialog box: *=COUNTIF(RepShop,"Dunbar Auto")*.

5. Make cell L5 active. The repair shop names are in the range K4:K7. Use cell K5 as the cell reference for JFJ Auto by typing the formula =countif(repshop,k5) and then press the Enter key. (When entering a formula, type the cell references and range names in lowercase letters. Excel will automatically display uppercase letters once the formula has been entered.)

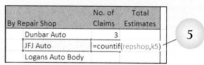

6. Use the fill handle to copy the formula in cell L5 to the range L6:L7. When completed, the COUNTIF formulas will be as follows:

    L6: =COUNTIF(RepShop,K6)
    L7: =COUNTIF(RepShop,K7)

7. Save **2-ACOctVehRpt**.

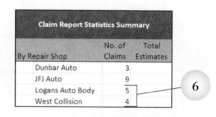

Check Your Work

Activity 1c Creating COUNTIFS Formulas

Part 3 of 6

1. With **2-ACOctVehRpt** open, make cell L10 active.
2. Create a COUNTIFS function to count the number of auto insurance claims for which the repair shop is JFJ Auto and the claims estimate is greater than $5,000 by completing the following steps:

a. Click the Insert Function button in the Formula bar.

b. With *Statistical* selected in the *Or select a category* option box, scroll down the *Select a function* list box and then click COUNTIFS.

c. Read the formula description below the function list box and then click OK.

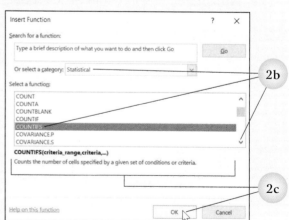

d. At the Function Arguments dialog box with the insertion point positioned in the *Criteria_range1* text box, type repshop and then press the Tab key. After the Tab key is pressed, a *Criteria_range2* text box is added to the dialog box.

e. With the insertion point positioned in the *Criteria1* text box, type k10 as the cell reference for JFJ Auto and then press the Tab key. After the Tab key is pressed, a *Criteria2* text box is added to the dialog box.

f. With the insertion point positioned in the *Criteria_range2* text box, type claimest and then press the Tab key. After the Tab key is pressed, a *Criteria_range3* text box is added to the dialog box.

g. With the insertion point positioned in the *Criteria2* text box, type >5000 and then press the Tab key. When the Tab key is pressed, Excel adds quotation marks around the criteria text.

h. Click OK. Excel returns the value *5* in cell L10.

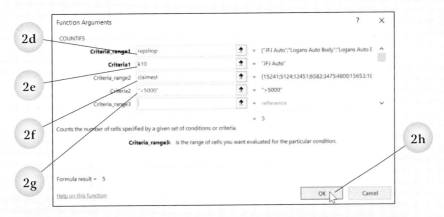

3. Look at the formula in the Formula bar created by the Function Arguments dialog box: *=COUNTIFS(RepShop,K10,ClaimEst,">5000")*.

4. In cell L13, enter a COUNTIFS formula to count the number of claims for which the repair shop is JFJ Auto and the rating is greater than 3 by using the Insert Function dialog box or by typing the following formula into the cell: =countifs(repshop,k13,rating,">3").

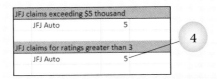

5. Save **2-ACOctVehRpt**.

Quick Steps

**Create AVERAGEIF
Formula**

1. Make cell active.
2. Click Insert Function button.
3. Change category to *Statistical.*
4. Select *AVERAGEIF.*
5. Click OK.
6. Enter range or range name in *Range* text box.
7. Enter condition expression or text in *Criteria* text box.
8. Enter range or range name to average in *Average_range* text box.
9. Click OK.

**Create AVERAGEIFS
Formula**

1. Make cell active.
2. Click Insert Function button.
3. Change category to *Statistical.*
4. Select *AVERAGEIFS.*
5. Click OK.
6. Enter range or range name to average in *Average_range* text box.
7. Enter range or range name in *Criteria_range1* text box.
8. Enter condition expression or text in *Criteria1* text box.
9. Enter range or range name in *Criteria_range2* text box.
10. Enter condition expression or text in *Criteria2* text box.
11. Continue adding criteria range expressions and criteria as needed.
12. Click OK.

Using Statistical Functions: AVERAGEIF and AVERAGEIFS

The AVERAGEIF function is used to find the arithmetic mean of the cells within a specified range that meet a single criterion or condition. The structure of an AVERAGEIF function is *=AVERAGEIF(range,criteria,average_range). Range* is the cells to be tested for the criterion or where to look for the data. *Criteria* is the conditional test that must be passed (what to look for). *Average_range* is the range containing the values to average. If *average_range* is omitted, the cells in the *range* are used to calculate the average. The AVERAGEIFS function is used to average cells that meet multiple criteria using the formula *=AVERAGEIFS(average_ range,criteria_range1,criteria1,criteria_range2,criteria2,. . .).* Notice that the *average_ range* (what to actually average) is at the beginning of the formula. It is followed by pairs of ranges (where to look for the specific condition) and criteria (the conditions that must be met).

Figure 2.3 shows an executive management salary report for a hospital. Average salary statistics are shown below the salary data. In the first two rows of salary statistics, the average total salary is calculated for each of two hospital campuses. In the second two rows of salary statistics, the average total salary is calculated for each campus for executives hired before 2018. The formulas shown in Figure 2.3 include range names for which *Year* references the values in column E, *Campus* references the entries in column F, and *Total* references the values in column I.

Figure 2.3 AVERAGEIF and AVERAGEIFS Formulas

	A	B	C	D	E	F	G	H	I
1				**Columbia River General Hospital**					
2				Executive Management Salary Report					
3				For the fiscal year 2021-2022					
4				**Job Title**	**Year Hired**	**Campus**	**Salary**	**Benefits**	**Total**
5	Ms.	Michelle	Tan	Chief Executive Officer	2001	Sunnyside	$ 231,750	$ 25,894	$ 257,644
6	Mr.	Douglas	Brown	Legal Counsel	2013	Sunnyside	137,975	23,595	161,570
7	Mrs.	Lauren	Quandt	Chief Financial Officer	2016	Portland	164,898	23,474	188,372
8	Dr.	Dana	Pembroke	Medical Director	2018	Portland	167,015	18,937	185,952
9	Mrs.	Gina	Wright	Director of Nursing	2010	Portland	137,945	18,937	156,881
10	Mr.	Fernando	Ortiega	Director of Patient Care Services	2011	Sunnyside	133,598	16,547	150,144
11	Mr.	Joshua	Vitello	Director of Facilities	2020	Sunnyside	130,270	12,828	143,098
12	Miss	Carin	Ledicke	Director of Human Resources	2006	Portland	130,270	12,828	143,098
13	Mr.	William	Formet	Director of Planning	2019	Portland	130,270	12,828	143,098
14	Mr.	Paul	Unraue	Director, Community Relations	1999	Sunnyside	120,270	11,070	131,340
15									
16							$ 1,484,260	$ 176,936	$ 1,661,196
17									
18				Salary Statistics					
19				Average executive total salary at Portland campus			$ 163,480		
20				Average executive total salary at Sunnyside campus			$ 168,759		
21									
22				Average executive total salary at Portland campus hired before 2018			$ 162,784		
23				Average executive total salary at Sunnyside campus hired before 2018			$ 175,175		

formula
=AVERAGEIFS(Total,Campus,"Sunnyside",Year,"<2018")

formula
=AVERAGEIF(Campus,"Portland",Total)

1. With **2-ACOctVehRpt** open, make cell M16 active.
2. Create an AVERAGEIF function to calculate the average auto insurance claim estimate for those claims with a rating of 1 by completing the following steps:
   a. Click the Insert Function button in the Formula bar.
   b. With *Statistical* selected in the *Or select a category* option box, click *AVERAGEIF* in the *Select a function* list box.
   c. Read the formula description below the function list box and then click OK.
   d. At the Function Arguments dialog box with the insertion point positioned in the *Range* text box, type rating and then press the Tab key.
   e. With the insertion point positioned in the *Criteria* text box, type 1 and then press the Tab key.
   f. With the insertion point positioned in the *Average_range* text box, type claimest.
   g. Click OK. Excel returns the value *2691* in cell M16.

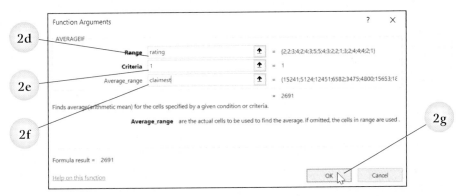

   h. Look at the formula in the Formula bar created by the Function Arguments dialog box:
      =AVERAGEIF(Rating,1,ClaimEst).
3. Apply the Comma format with no digits after the decimal point to cell M16.
4. Make cell M17 active, type the formula =averageif(rating,k17,claimest), and then press the Enter key.
5. Apply the Comma format with no digits after the decimal point to cell M17.
6. With cell M17 active, drag the fill handle into cell M20. When completed, the AVERAGEIF formulas will be as follows:
   M18: *=AVERAGEIF(Rating,K18,ClaimEst)*
   M19: *=AVERAGEIF(Rating,K19,ClaimEst)*
   M20: *=AVERAGEIF(Rating,K20,ClaimEst)*

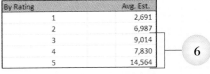

By Rating	Avg. Est.
1	2,691
2	6,987
3	9,014
4	7,830
5	14,564

7. Save **2-ACOctVehRpt**.

Check Your Work

1. With **2-ACOctVehRpt** open, make cell M22 active.
2. Create an AVERAGEIFS function to calculate the average auto insurance claim estimate for those claims with a rating of 2 and a driver number of 1 by completing the following steps:
   a. Click the Insert Function button in the Formula bar.
   b. With *Statistical* selected in the *Or select a category* option box, click *AVERAGEIFS* in the *Select a function* list box.
   c. Read the formula description and then click OK.
   d. At the Function Arguments dialog box with the insertion point positioned in the *Average_range* text box, type claimest and then press the Tab key.
   e. Type rating in the *Criteria_range1* text box and then press the Tab key.
   f. Type 2 in the *Criteria1* text box and then press the Tab key.
   g. Type driverno in the *Criteria_range2* text box and then press the Tab key.
   h. Type 1 in the *Criteria2* text box.
   i. Click OK. Excel returns the value *6272.6667* in cell M22.

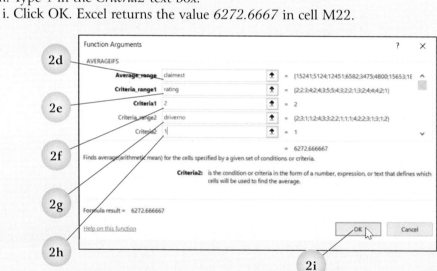

   j. Apply the Comma format with no digits after the decimal point to cell M22.
3. Copy the AVERAGEIFS formula in cell M22 and paste it into cell M23.
4. Edit the formula in cell M23 to change the rating criterion from *2* to *3*. When completed, the AVERAGEIFS formula will be *=AVERAGEIFS(ClaimEst,Rating,3,DriverNo,1)*.
5. Save **2-ACOctVehRpt**.

Check Your Work

Using Math and Trigonometry Functions: SUMIF and SUMIFS

 Math & Trig

Quick Steps

Create SUMIF Formula
1. Make cell active.
2. Click Formulas tab.
3. Click Math & Trig button.
4. Scroll down and click *SUMIF.*
5. Enter range or range name in *Range* text box.
6. Enter condition expression or text in *Criteria* text box.
7. Enter range or range name to add in *Sum_range* text box.
8. Click OK.

Using Math and Trigonometry Functions: SUMIF and SUMIFS

Excel provides several math and trigonometry functions, such as ABS to return the absolute value of a number, SQRT to find the square root of a number, and RAND to return a random number between 0 and 1, to name a few. At the Insert Function dialog box, change the *Or select a category* option to *Math & Trig* or click the Math & Trig button in the Function Library group and then scroll down the list of available functions.

Within the category of math and trigonometry functions, Excel includes SUMIF to add the cells within a range that meet a single criterion or condition and SUMIFS to add the cells within a range that meet multiple criteria or conditions. The structure of the SUMIF function is *=SUMIF(range,criteria,sum_range)*, where *range* is where to look for the data, *criteria* is the conditional statement (the conditions that must be met or what to look for), and *sum_range* is the range containing the values to add. The SUMIFS function is used to add cells that meet multiple criteria using the formula *=SUMIFS(sum_range,criteria_range1,criteria1,criteria_range2,criteria2,. . .)*. Similar to the AVERAGEIFS function, the *sum_range* (what to actually sum) appears at the beginning of the formula. It is followed by pairs of ranges (where to look for the specific conditions) and criteria (the conditions that must be met).

Figure 2.4 shows how the SUMIF and SUMIFS formulas are used in the standard cost worksheet for examination room supplies at a medical clinic. Right of the clinic supplies inventory data, a SUMIF formula adds up the costs of items by supplier number. A SUMIFS formula adds up the costs by supplier number for items that require a minimum stock quantity of more than four. The formulas shown in Figure 2.4 include the range names *Supplier*, which references the entries in column C; *MinQty*, which references the values in column E; and *StdCost*, which references the values in column F.

Figure 2.4 SUMIF and SUMIFS Formulas

Item	Unit	Supplier Number	Price	Minimum Stock Qty	Standard Cost		Exam Room Cost Analysis	
North Shore Medical Clinic								
Clinic Supplies Inventory Units and Price								
Sterile powder-free synthetic gloves, size Small	per 100	101	45.95	4	183.80		**Cost by Supplier**	
Sterile powder-free synthetic gloves, size Medium	per 100	101	45.95	8	367.60		Supplier Number 101	2,061.40
Sterile powder-free synthetic gloves, size Large	per 100	101	45.95	10	459.50		Supplier Number 155	874.33
Sterile powder-free latex gloves, size Small	per 100	101	26.25	4	105.00		Supplier Number 201	2,058.00
Sterile powder-free latex gloves, size Medium	per 100	101	26.25	8	210.00		Supplier Number 350	1,030.80
Sterile powder-free latex gloves, size Large	per 100	101	26.25	10	262.50			
Sterile powder-free vinyl gloves, size Small	per 100	101	21.50	4	86.00			
Sterile powder-free vinyl gloves, size Medium	per 100	101	21.50	8	172.00		**Cost by Supplier with**	
Sterile powder-free vinyl gloves, size Large	per 100	101	21.50	10	215.00		**Minimum Qty over 4**	
Disposable earloop mask	per 50	155	15.61	8	124.88		Supplier Number 101	1,686.60
Disposable patient gown	per dozen	155	17.90	16	286.40		Supplier Number 155	790.80
Disposable patient slippers	per dozen	155	14.27	16	228.32		Supplier Number 201	1,430.00
Cotton patient gown	per dozen	201	143.00	10	1,430.00		Supplier Number 350	859.00
Cotton patient robe	per dozen	201	157.00	4	628.00			
Disposable examination table paper	per roll	155	18.90	8	151.20			
Lab coat, size Small	each	350	42.95	4	171.80			
Lab coat, size Medium	each	350	42.95	8	343.60			
Lab coat, size Large	each	350	42.95	12	515.40			
Disposable shoe cover	per 300	155	47.75	1	47.75			
Disposable bouffant cap	per 100	155	17.89	2	35.78			
TOTAL STANDARD EXAM ROOM SUPPLIES COST:					6,024.53			

formula
=SUMIF(Supplier,"101",StdCost)

formula
=SUMIFS(StdCost,Supplier,"350",MinQty,">4")

Note: In Step 4, check with your instructor before printing to see if two copies of the worksheets for the activities in this chapter need to be printed: one as displayed and another displaying the cell formulas. Save the worksheet before displaying formulas (Ctrl + `) so that column widths can be adjusted as necessary and then close without saving the changes.

1. With **2-ACOctVehRpt** open, make cell M4 active.
2. Create a SUMIF function to add up the auto insurance claim estimates for those claims being repaired at Dunbar Auto by completing the following steps:
   a. Click the Formulas tab.
   b. Click the Math & Trig button in the Function Library group.
   c. Scroll down the drop-down list and then click *SUMIF*.
   d. At the Function Arguments dialog box with the insertion point positioned in the *Range* text box, type repshop and then press the Tab key.
   e. Designate cell K4 as the cell reference for Dunbar Auto by typing k4 in the *Criteria* text box and then press the Tab key.
   f. Type claimest in the *Sum_range* text box.
   g. Click OK. Excel returns the value *16656* in cell M4.

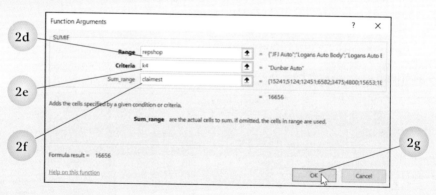

   h. Apply the Comma format with no digits after the decimal point to cell M4.
3. Use the fill handle to copy the formula in cell M4 to the range M5:M7. When completed, the SUMIF formulas will be as follows:

   M5: =SUMIF(RepShop,K5,ClaimEst)
   M6: =SUMIF(RepShop,K6,ClaimEst)
   M7: =SUMIF(RepShop,K7,ClaimEst)
4. Save, print, and then close **2-ACOctVehRpt**.

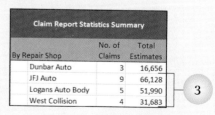

Claim Report Statistics Summary		
By Repair Shop	No. of Claims	Total Estimates
Dunbar Auto	3	16,656
JFJ Auto	9	66,128
Logans Auto Body	5	51,990
West Collision	4	31,683

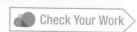

Check Your Work

Using Lookup
Functions

Lookup &
Reference

Using Lookup Functions

The Lookup & Reference functions provide formulas for looking up values in a range and can be found by clicking the Lookup & Reference button in the Function Library group. For example, in a grades worksheet, a letter grade can be generated by looking up the final numerical score in a range of cells that contain the letter grades with corresponding numerical scores. Being able to look up a value automates data entry in large worksheets and, when used properly, can prevent inaccuracies caused by data entry errors.

Excel provides the VLOOKUP and HLOOKUP functions, which refer to vertical and horizontal lookups, respectively. The layout of the lookup range (referred to as a *lookup table*) determines whether to use VLOOKUP or HLOOKUP. VLOOKUP is used more commonly, since most lookup tables are arranged with comparison data in columns (which means Excel searches for the lookup value in a vertical order). HLOOKUP is used when the lookup range contains comparison data in rows (which means Excel searches for the lookup value in a horizontal order).

Using the VLOOKUP Function

The structure of a VLOOKUP function is =*VLOOKUP(lookup_value,table_array,col_index_num,range_lookup)*. Table 2.1 explains all the parameters of a VLOOKUP argument.

The VLOOKUP function is easier to understand when explained using an example. In the worksheet shown in Figure 2.5, VLOOKUP is used to return the starting salary for new hires at a medical center. Each new hire is assigned a salary grid number depending on his or her education and years of work experience. This

Table 2.1 VLOOKUP Argument Parameters

Argument Parameter	Description
lookup_value	The value that Excel should search for in the lookup table. Enter a value or cell reference to a value.
table_array	The range address or range name for the lookup table that Excel should search for. Do not include column headers in the range. Use range names or absolute cell referencing.
col_index_num	The column number from the lookup table that contains the data to be placed in the formula cell.
range_lookup	Enter TRUE to instruct Excel to find an exact or approximate match for the lookup value. If this parameter is left out of the formula, Excel assumes TRUE, which means if an exact match is not found, Excel returns the value for the last category into which the known value fits. For the formula to work properly, the first column of the lookup table must be sorted in ascending order. Enter FALSE to instruct Excel to return only exact matches to the lookup value.

Quick Steps

Create VLOOKUP Formula

1. Make cell active.
2. Click Formulas tab.
3. Click Lookup & Reference button.
4. Click *VLOOKUP*.
5. Enter cell address, range name, or value in *Lookup_value* text box.
6. Enter range or range name in *Table_array* text box.
7. Type column number to return values from in *Col_index_num* text box.
8. Type false or leave blank for TRUE in *Range_lookup* text box.
9. Click OK.

salary grid number determines the new hire's starting salary. The lookup table contains the grid numbers with the corresponding starting salaries. In column E, VLOOKUP formulas automatically insert the starting salary for each new employee based on his or her salary grid rating in column D. In the formula shown in Figure 2.5, a range named *Grid* represents the lookup table in the range G4:H8.

Figure 2.5 VLOOKUP Example

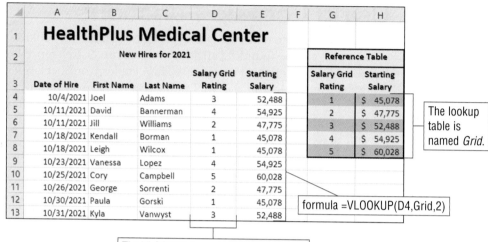

The lookup table is named *Grid*.

formula =VLOOKUP(D4,Grid,2)

The VLOOKUP formula populates the range E4:E13 by matching the salary grid rating number in column D with the corresponding salary grid rating number in the lookup table named *Grid*.

Activity 2 Creating a VLOOKUP Formula

Part 1 of 1

1. Open **PrecisionPrices**.
2. Save the workbook with the name **2-PrecisionPrices**.
3. Create a VLOOKUP formula to find the correct discount value for each product by completing the following steps:
   a. Select the range H4:I8 and name it *DiscTable*. DiscTable is the range name used for the lookup table.
   b. Make cell E4 active and then click the Formulas tab.
   c. Click the Lookup & Reference button in the Function Library group.
   d. Click *VLOOKUP* at the drop-down list.
   e. If necessary, drag the Function Arguments dialog box out of the way so that the first few rows of the product price list and discount table data can be seen.

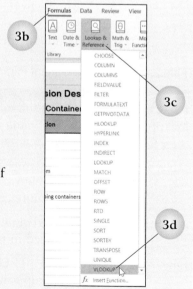

f. With the insertion point positioned in the *Lookup_value* text box, type c4 and then press the Tab key. Product discounts are categorized by letter codes. To find the correct discount, Excel needs to look for the matching category letter code found in cell C4 within the first column of the discount table. Notice that the letter codes in the discount table are listed in ascending order.

g. Type disctable in the *Table_array* text box and then press the Tab key. Using a range name for a reference table is a good idea, since the formula will be copied and absolute references are needed for the cells in the lookup table.

h. Type 2 in the *Col_index_num* text box and then press the Tab key. The discount percentage in column 2 of DiscTable will be placed in cell E4.

i. Type false in the *Range_lookup* text box (Entering *false* instructs Excel to return values for exact matches only. Should a discount category be typed into a cell in column C for which no entry exists in the discount table, Excel will return *#N/A* in the formula cell; this is an alert that an error has occurred in the data entry.)

j. Click OK.

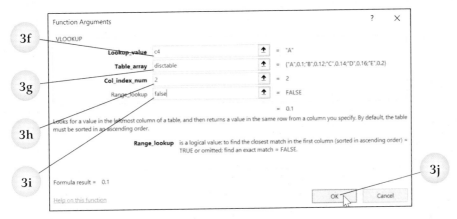

4. Look at the formula in the Formula bar: *=VLOOKUP(C4,DiscTable,2,FALSE)*.
5. Apply the Percent format to cell E4.
6. Make cell F4 active, type the formula =d4-(d4*e4) to calculate the net price, and then press the Enter key.

	C	D	E	F	G	H	I
	and Packaging						
	ducts Price List					**Discount Table**	
	Discount Category	List Price	Discount	Net Price		Discount Category	Discount Percent
	A	18.67		10%	=d4-(d4*e4)	A	10%
	C	22.50				B	12%
	B	14.53				C	14%
	D	5.25				D	16%
	A	18.54				E	20%

6

7. Select the range E4:F4 and then drag the fill handle into row 21.
8. Deselect the range.
9. Print the worksheet.
10. Save and then close **2-PrecisionPrices**.

Check Your Work

Using the HLOOKUP Function

The HLOOKUP function uses the same argument parameters as the VLOOKUP function. Use HLOOKUP when the table being searched for a comparison value is arranged horizontally, like the one shown in the range J3:O4 in Figure 2.6. Excel searches across the table in the first row for a matching value and then returns to the formula cell the value from the same column.

The structure of an HLOOKUP function is =HLOOKUP(*lookup_value,table_array,row_index_num,range_lookup*). The argument parameters are similar to the VLOOKUP parameters described in Table 2.1 on page 43. Excel searches the first row of the table for the lookup value. When a match is found, Excel returns the value from the same column in the row number specified in the *row_index_num* argument.

Figure 2.6 HLOOKUP Example

formula
=HLOOKUP(F4,GradeTable,2)

	A	B	C	D	E	F	G	H	I	J	K	L	M	N	O
1	Math by Janelle Tutoring Service														
2	Student Progress Report														
3	Student Name	Test 1	Test 2	Test 3	Test 4	Total	Grade			Score	0	50	60	70	80	90
4	Dana Rosenthal	51	48	55	50	51.0	D			Grade	F	D	C	B	A	A+
5	Kelsey Williams	75	82	66	72	73.8	B									
6	Hilary Orbet	81	88	79	83	82.8	A									
7	Jose Alvarez	67	72	65	78	70.5	B									
8	Linden Porter	42	51	40	55	47.0	F									
9	Carl Quenneville	65	44	72	61	60.5	C									
10	Andrewa Desmond	55	48	60	50	53.3	D									
11	Kylie Winters	78	82	67	71	74.5	B									
12	Lindsay Cortez	82	78	85	88	83.3	A									

The lookup table is named *GradeTable*.

The HLOOKUP formula populates the range G4:G12 by looking up the total value in column F in the first row in the lookup table (GradeTable). The formula stops at the largest value in the table that is less than or equal to the lookup value. For example, looking for *62.3* would make Excel stop at *60*.

Activity 3 Analyze an Expansion Project Loan   1 Part

You will use a financial function to calculate the principal portion of an expansion loan payment for two lenders. You will then calculate the total loan payments and analyze the results.

Tutorial

Using the PPMT
Financial Function

Tutorial

Review: Using
Financial Functions

Financial

Using the PPMT Financial Function

Financial functions can be used to perform a variety of financial analyses, including loan amortizations, annuity payments, investment planning, depreciation, and so on and can be found by clicking the Financial button in the Function Library group. The PMT function is used to calculate a payment for a loan based on a constant interest rate and constant payments for a set period. Excel provides two related financial functions: PPMT, to calculate the principal portion of the loan payment, and IPMT, to calculate the interest portion.

Quick Steps

Create PPMT Formula

1. Make cell active.
2. Click Formulas tab.
3. Click Financial button.
4. Click *PPMT*.
5. Enter value, cell address, or range name for interest rate in *Rate* text box.
6. Enter number representing payment to find principal for *Per* text box.
7. Enter value, cell address, or range name for total number of payments in *Nper* text box.
8. Enter value, cell address, or range name for amount borrowed in *Pv* text box.
9. Click OK.

Knowing the principal portion of a loan payment is useful in determining the amount of the payment being used to reduce the principal balance owed. The difference between the loan payment and the PPMT value represents the interest cost. The function returns the principal portion of a specific payment for a loan. For example, calculate the principal on the first payment, last payment, or any payment in between. The structure of a PPMT function is *=PPMT(rate,per,nper,pv,fv,type)*, where

- *rate* is the interest rate per period,
- *per* is the period for which to find the principal portion of the payment,
- *nper* is the number of payment periods,
- *pv* is the amount of money borrowed,
- *fv* is the balance at the end of the loan (if left blank, 0 is assumed), and
- *type* is either 0 (payment at end of period) or 1 (payment at beginning of period).

Make sure to be consistent with the units for the interest rate and payment periods. If the interest rate is divided by 12 for a monthly rate, the payment period should also be expressed monthly. For example, multiply the term by 12 if the amortization is entered in the worksheet in years.

Activity 3   Calculating Principal Portions of Loan Payments Using the PPMT Function   Part 1 of 1

1. Open **DExpansion**.
2. Save the workbook with the name **2-DExpansion**.
3. Calculate the principal portion of the first loan payment for two loan proposals to fund a building expansion activity by completing the following steps:
   a. Make cell C10 active.
   b. If necessary, click the Formulas tab.
   c. Click the Financial button in the Function Library group.
   d. Scroll down the drop-down list and then click *PPMT*.
   e. If necessary, move the Function Arguments dialog box to the right side of the screen so that all the values in column C can be seen.

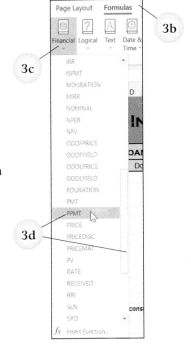

f. With the insertion point positioned in the *Rate* text box, type c4/12 and then press the Tab key. Since the interest rate is stated per annum (per year), dividing the rate by 12 calculates the monthly rate.

g. Type 1 in the *Per* text box to calculate the principal for the first loan payment and then press the Tab key.

h. Type c5*12 in the *Nper* text box and then press the Tab key. Since a loan payment is made each month, the number of payments is 12 times the amortization period.

i. Type c6 in the *Pv* text box. *Pv* refers to present value; in this example, it means the loan amount for which the payments are being calculated. It is positive because it represents cash received by the company.

j. Click OK. Excel returns the value *-1853.05* in cell C10. Payments are shown as negative numbers because they represent cash that is paid out. In this worksheet, negative numbers have been formatted to display in red and enclosed in parentheses.

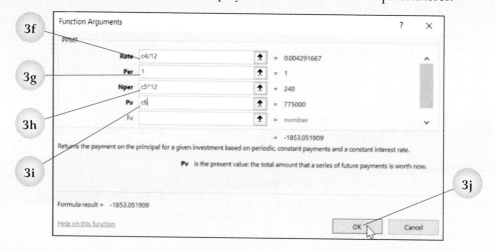

4. Copy and paste the formula from cell C10 into cell E10 and then press the Esc key to remove the scrolling marquee from cell C10.

5. Make cell C12 active, type =c8*12*c5, and then press the Enter key.

3		Victory Trust
4	Interest Rate	5.15%
5	Amortization	20
6	Loan Amount	$ 775.000
7		
8	Monthly Payment	($5,179.09)
9		
10	Monthly Principal Payment (1st payment)	($1,853.05)
11		
12	Total Loan Payments	=c8*12*c5

5

6. Copy and paste the formula from cell C12 into cell E12. Press the Esc key to remove the scrolling marquee from cell C12 and then AutoFit the width of column E. Notice that the loan from Dominion Trust is a better choice for Deering Industries, assuming the company can afford the higher monthly payments. Although the interest rate is higher than that for the Victory Trust loan, the shorter term means the loan will be repaid sooner and at a lesser total cost.

7. Print the worksheet.

8. Save and then close **2-DExpansion**.

You will create formulas to calculate the employee benefit costs and bonuses for ViewRite using logical functions to test multiple conditions.

Using the Nested IF
Logical Function

Review: Using
Logical IF
Functions

  Logical

Using and Nesting Logical Functions

Using conditional logic in a formula requires Excel to perform a calculation based on the outcome of a logical or conditional test. One calculation is performed if the test proves true and another calculation is performed if the test proves false. For example, the following is an IF formula using named ranges that could be used to calculate a salesperson's bonus if his or her sales exceed a target: *=IF(Sales>Target,Bonus,0)*. Excel first tests the value in the cell named *Sales* to see if it is greater than the value in the cell named *Target*. If the condition proves true, then Excel returns the value of the cell named *Bonus*. If the sales value is not greater than the target value, then the condition proves false and Excel places a *0* in the cell. The structure of the IF function is *=IF(logical_test,value_if_true,value_if_false)*. Logical functions can be found by clicking the Logical button in the Function Library group.

Using the Nested IF Logical Function

Quick Steps

Create IF Formula
1. Make cell active.
2. Click Formulas tab.
3. Click Logical button.
4. Click *IF*.
5. Type conditional test argument in *Logical_test* text box.
6. Type argument in *Value_if_true* text box.
7. Type argument in *Value_if_false* text box.
8. Click OK.

Hint If you type a nested IF function directly into a cell, Excel color-codes the parentheses for the different IF functions so you can keep track of them separately.

Hint The number of right parentheses needed to end a nested IF statement equals the number of times IF appears in the formula.

When more than two outcomes are possible or a decision is based on more than one field, a nested IF statement is used. A nested IF function is one IF function inside another. The structure of a nested IF statement is *=IF(logical_test,value_if_true,IF(logical_test,value_if_true,value_if_false))*. Excel evaluates the first *logical_test*. If the answer is true, then depending on what is entered for the *value_if_true*, a calculation is performed and text or numbers are entered; if the *value_if_true* is omitted, a 0 is entered. If the first *logical_test* is not true, then the next *logical_test* is evaluated and if the answer is true, the *value_if_true* is placed in the cell. Excel stops evaluating the formula once the *logical_test* has been answered as true. If the answer is never true, then depending on what is entered as the *value_if_false*, a calculation is performed and text or numbers are entered; if the *value_if_false* is omitted, then a 0 is entered.

For example, assume that a company has three sales commission rates based on the level of sales achieved by the salesperson. If sales are less than $40,000, the salesperson earns a 5% commission; if sales are greater than or equal to $40,000 but less than $80,000, the salesperson earns a 7% commission; and if sales are greater than or equal to $80,000, the salesperson earns a 9% commission. Since there are three possible sales commission rates, a single IF function will not work. To correctly calculate the sales commission rate, two conditional tests must be created. The last level (or in this case, the third commission rate of 9%) is used for the *value_if_false*.

Consider the following formula: *=IF(Sales<40000,Sales*5%,IF(Sales<80000, Sales*7%,Sales*9%))*. This formula includes two IF functions. In the first IF function, the conditional test is to determine if the sales value is less than $40,000 *(Sales<40000)*. If the test proves true (for example, sales are $25,000), then Excel calculates the sales times 5% and returns the result in the active cell. If the test is

Quick Steps

Create AND Formula

1. Make cell active OR nest formula in IF statement *Logical_ test* text box.
2. Type =and(or and(if nesting in IF statement.
3. Type first conditional test argument.
4. Type ,.
5. Type second conditional test argument.
6. Repeat Steps 4–5 for remaining conditions.
7. Type).

Using Logical Functions: Nested IF, AND, and OR

Hint Nest an AND or OR function with an IF function to test multiple conditions.

Quick Steps

Create OR Formula

1. Make cell active OR nest formula in IF statement *Logical_ test* text box.
2. Type =or(or or(if nesting in IF statement.
3. Type first conditional test argument.
4. Type ,.
5. Type second conditional test argument.
6. Repeat Steps 4–5 for remaining conditions.
7. Type).

not true, then Excel reads the next section of the argument, which is the next IF function that includes the conditional test to determine if sales are less than $80,000 (*Sales<80000*). If this second conditional test proves true, then Excel calculates the sales times 7%. If the test proves false, then Excel calculates the sales times 9%. Since these are the only three possible actions, the formula ends. While up to 64 IF functions can be nested, doing this would create a very complex formula. Consider using a VLOOKUP or HLOOKUP to test different conditions.

Any function can be nested inside another function. For example, in the PPMT formula discussed in the previous section, Excel returns a negative value for the principal portion of the payment. The PPMT formula can be nested inside the ABS formula to have the principal payment displayed without a negative symbol. ABS is the function used to return the absolute value of a number (that is, the number without its sign). For example, *=ABS(PPMT(C4/12,1,C5*12,C6))* displays the payment calculated in Activity 3 as *$1,853.05* instead of *-$1,853.05*.

Using Logical Functions: Nested IF, AND, and OR

Other logical functions offered in Excel include AND and OR. These functions use Boolean logic to construct a conditional test in a formula to be either true or false. Table 2.2 describes how each function works to test a statement and provides an example of each function.

Table 2.2 AND and OR Logical Functions

Logical Function	Description	Example
AND	All conditions must be true for a result of *TRUE*. If any are false, the function returns *FALSE*.	*=AND(Sales>Target,NewClients>5)* Returns *TRUE* if both test true Returns *FALSE* if *Sales* is greater than *Target* but *NewClients* is less than 5. Returns *FALSE* if *Sales* is less than *Target* but *NewClients* is greater than 5.
OR	Returns *TRUE* if any of the conditions tests true; returns *FALSE* only when all conditions are false.	*=OR(Sales>Target,NewClients>5)* Returns *TRUE* if *Sales* is greater than *Target* or *NewClients* is greater than 5. Returns *FALSE* only if *Sales* is not greater than *Target* and *NewClients* is not greater than 5.

Using the ROUND Function

ROUND is another example of a function that can easily be nested with other functions. Excel uses the entire number stored in the cell and not just the visible number in any calculations. The function ROUND is used to modify the actual number of characters by rounding the value. The structure of this function is =ROUND(number,num_digits). *Number* can be a number or a formula. The *num_digits* number can be positive or negative. A positive number rounds the decimal value (the numbers right of the decimal point) to the designated number of places. A negative number rounds the numbers left of the decimal point to the nearest ones, tens, hundreds, and so on. Table 2.3 demonstrates how positive and negative *num_digits* are handled.

When nesting the ROUND function, make sure that the original function is working before rounding the final result. In Activity 4a, the nested IF AND formula used to calculate the pension contributions returns some values with three digits after the decimal point. The ROUND function will be added after the IF AND statement.

Table 2.3 Examples of Applying the ROUND Function

Example	Description	Result
=ROUND(1625.09,1)	Rounds *1625.09* to one digit past the decimal point.	*1625.1*
=ROUND(1625.1,0)	Rounds *1625.1* to zero digits past the decimal point.	*1625*
=ROUND(1625,-1)	Rounds *1625* to the nearest tens value.	*1630*

Activity 4a Calculating Pension Costs Using Nested IF, AND, and ROUND Functions   Part 1 of 3

1. Open **VRSalCost**.
2. Save the workbook with the name **2-VRSalCost**.
3. ViewRite contributes 5.575% of an employee's salary into a privately managed company retirement account if the employee works full time and earns more than $50,000 a year. Calculate the pension benefit costs for eligible employees by completing the following steps:
   a. Make cell H6 the active cell.
   b. Click the Formulas tab.
   c. Click the Logical button in the Function Library group and then click *IF* at the drop-down list.
   d. If necessary, drag the Function Arguments dialog box down until all of row 6 can be seen in the worksheet.

e. With the insertion point positioned in the *Logical_test* text box, type and(c6="FT",g6>50000) and then press the Tab key. An AND function is required, since both conditions must be true for the company to contribute to the pension plan. The two conditions—being a full-time (FT) employee and having a salary over $50,000—are separated by a comma. *Note: Excel requires having quotation marks around text when it is used in a conditional test formula.*

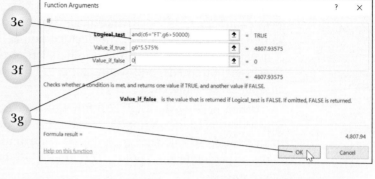

f. Type g6*5.575% in the *Value_if_true* text box and then press the Tab key.

g. Type 0 in the *Value_if_false* text box and then click OK.

h. Look at the formula =IF(AND(C6="FT",G6>50000),G6*5.575%,0) in the Formula bar. Notice that the AND function is nested within the IF function. Since both conditions for the first employee tested true, the pension cost is calculated.

4. With cell H6 selected, increase the number of digits after the display point to three. Use the ROUND function to round the pension amount to the nearest penny by completing the following steps:

   a. Click to the right of the equals sign in the Formula bar.

   b. Type round(and then press the End key to move to the end of the formula.

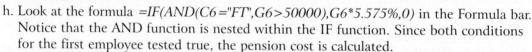

   c. Type ,2) and then press the Enter key.

   d. Select cell H6, decrease the number of digits after the decimal point to two, and then copy the formula in cell H6 to the range H7:H14. Deselect the range. Notice that only the first four employees have pension benefit values. This is because they are the only employees who both work full time and earn over $50,000 a year in salary.

   5. Save **2-VRSalCost**.

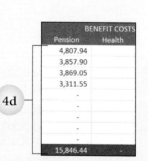

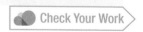

Activity 4b Calculating Health and Dental Costs Using Nested IF and OR Functions   Part 2 of 3

1. With **2-VRSalCost** open, make cell I6 the active cell.
2. ViewRite offers to pay the annual health premiums for employees not covered by other medical plans. The company pays $3,600 per year per employee for family coverage, $2,580 per year per employee for single coverage, and $0 per year if the employee declines coverage. Calculate the cost for each employee who chose to join the health plan by completing the following steps:

   a. This formula requires a nested IF statement, since the result will be *$3,600, $2,580*, or *0* depending on the contents of cell D6. (An OR statement will not work for this formula, since two different health premiums are used.) In cell I6, type =if(d6="Family",3600,if(d6="Single",2580,0)) and then press the Enter key. ***Note: Recall that Excel requires the use of quotation marks around text entries within an IF function***.

    b. Copy the formula in cell I6 to the range I7:I14. Notice the cells in column I for which no values are entered. In column D in the corresponding row, the text *Declined* displays. Excel returned a value of *0* in column I because the conditions *D6="Family"* and *D6="Single"* both proved false.

3. ViewRite has negotiated a flat fee with its dental benefit service provider. The company pays $2,750 per year for each employee, regardless of the type of coverage. However, the service provider requires ViewRite to report each person's coverage as *Family* or *Single* for audit purposes. The dental plan is optional and some employees have declined coverage. Calculate the cost of the dental plan by completing the following steps:

    a. Make cell J6 the active cell.

    b. If necessary, click the Formulas tab.

    c. Click the Logical button and then click *IF* at the drop-down list.

    d. If necessary, drag the Function Arguments dialog box down until all of row 6 can be seen in the worksheet.

    e. With the insertion point positioned in the *Logical_test* text box, type or(e6="Family",e6="Single") and then press the Tab key. An OR function is appropriate for calculating this benefit, since either condition can be true for the company to contribute to the dental plan. The two conditions—being a family or being single—are separated by a comma.

    f. Type *2750* in the *Value_if_true* text box and then press the Tab key.

    g. Type *0* in the *Value_if_false* text box and then click OK.

    h. Look at the formula *=IF(OR(E6="Family", E6="Single"),2750,0)* in the Formula bar. Notice that the OR function is nested within the IF function. Since cell E6 contains neither *Family* nor *Single*, the OR statement tests false and *0* is returned in cell J6.

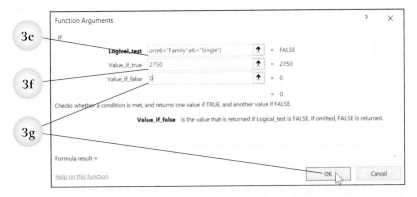

    i. Copy the formula in cell J6 to the range J7:J14 and then deselect the range.

| BENEFIT COSTS | | | Total | Salary + |
Pension	Health	Dental	Benefits	Benefits
4,807.94	3,600.00	-	8,407.94	94,648.94
3,857.90	2,580.00	2,750.00	9,187.90	78,387.90
3,869.05	-	-	3,869.05	73,269.05
3,311.55	2,580.00	2,750.00	8,641.55	68,041.55
-	3,600.00	2,750.00	6,350.00	44,750.00
-	3,600.00	-	3,600.00	43,000.00
-	2,580.00	-	2,580.00	49,180.00
-	-	-	-	49,900.00
-	-	2,750.00	2,750.00	49,754.00
15,846.44	18,540.00	11,000.00	45,386.44	550,931.44

4. Save **2-VRSalCost**.

Check Your Work

Using the IFS Logical Function

An alternative to using a nested IF function is to use an IFS function. The result of the IFS function must test true; in contrast, the last argument of the IF function tests false. If you can change the last argument to test true, then the IFS function can be used instead of a nested IF function. If no condition tests true, then the IFS function returns the error code *#NA*. The IFS function can test up to 127 conditions. Unlike a nested IF function, an IFS function does not require each argument to be enclosed in parentheses. This difference makes the IFS function easier to read.

Quick Steps

Create IFS Formula
1. Make cell active.
2. Click Formulas tab.
3. Click Logical button.
4. Click *IFS*.
5. Type conditional test argument in *Logical_test1* text box.
6. Type argument in *Value_if_true1* text box.
7. Add necessary pairs of *Logical_tests* and *Value_if_true*.
8. Click OK.

The structure of the IFS function is =*IFS(logical_test1,value_if_true1,logical_test2,value_if_true2,...)*. Just as with a nested IF statement, Excel evaluates the first *logical_test*. If the answer is true, then depending on what is entered for the *value_if_true*, a calculation is performed and text or numbers are entered. If the first *logical_test* is not true, then the next *logical_test* is evaluated and if the answer is true, the *value_if_true* is placed in the cell. Excel stops evaluating the formula once the *logical_test* has been answered as true. If the answer is never true, then *#NA* is placed in the cell.

Viewing Long Formulas in the Formula Bar

Formulas containing nested or lengthy functions can get quite long and be difficult to read when viewed in the Formula bar. To make a formula easier to read, place each logical test on a separate line and expand the Formula bar.

To place an argument or logical test on a new line in the Formula bar, place the insertion point immediately before the logical test and then press Alt + Enter. To expand the Formula bar, hover the mouse pointer over the bottom of the bar until the pointer turns into a two-headed arrow, click and hold down the left mouse button, drag the border down until the new size is achieved, and then release the mouse button. Figure 2.7 shows the IFS function for Activity 4c with each argument displayed on a separate line in an expanded Formula bar.

Figure 2.7 IFS Function

Each argument is displayed on a separate line and individual arguments are separated by commas. The IFS function does not require each argument to be enclosed in parentheses.

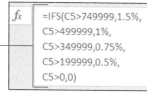

```
=IFS(C5>749999,1.5%,
C5>499999,1%,
C5>349999,0.75%,
C5>199999,0.5%,
C5>0,0)
```

1. With **2-VRSalCost** open, click the Bonus worksheet tab and then click in cell D5.
2. ViewRite offers an employee bonus based on sales. Enter a formula that uses an IFS function using the following data:

Sales	Bonus Percentage
>$749,999	1.5%
>$499,999	1%
>$349,999	0.75%
>$199,999	0.5%
Between $0 and $199,000	0%

Follow these steps to create the formula:
a. If necessary, click the Formulas tab.
b. Click the Logical button and then click *IFS* at the drop-down list.
c. Type c5>749999 in the *Logical_test1* text box and then press the Tab key.
d. Type 1.5% in the *Value_if_true1* text box and then press the Tab key.
e. Type c5>499999 in the *Logical_test2* text box and then press the Tab key.
f. Type 1% in the *Value_if_true2* text box and then press the Tab key.
g. With the insertion point in the *Logical_test3* text box, type c5>349999 and then press the Tab key.

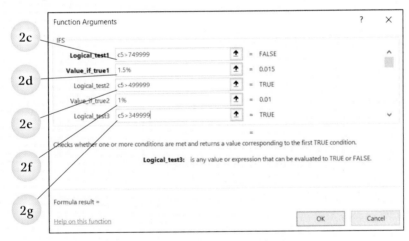

h. Type 0.75% in the *Value_if_true3* text box and then press the Tab key.

i. In the *Logical_test4* text box type c5>199999 and then press the Tab key.

j. Type 0.5% in the *Value_if_true4* text box and then press the Tab key.

k. In the *Logical_test5* text box type c5>0 and then press the Tab key.

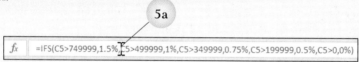

Function Arguments ? ✕

IFS

Value_if_true3	0.75%	↑	= 0.0075
Logical_test4	c5>199999	↑	= TRUE
Value_if_true4	0.5%	↑	= 0.005
Logical_test5	c5>0	↑	= TRUE
Value_if_true5	0%	↑	= 0

= 0.01

Checks whether one or more conditions are met and returns a value corresponding to the first TRUE condition.

Value_if_true5: is the value returned if Logical_test is TRUE.

Formula result = 1.00%

Help on this function   OK   Cancel

l. Type 0% in the *Value_if_true5* text box and then click OK.

3. Look at the formula in the Formula bar created by the Function Arguments dialog box: *=IFS(C5>749999,1.5%,C5>499999,1%,C5>349999,0.75%,C5>199999,0.5%,C5>0,0%)*.

4. Apply the Percent format, increase the number of decimals to two digits after the decimal point, and then drag the fill handle into row 15.

5. View each argument on a separate line and then expand the Formula bar by completing the following steps:

   a. Click in the Formula bar after the second comma between *1.5%* and *C5* and then press Alt + Enter.

   5a

   *f*x =IFS(C5>749999,1.5%,C5>499999,1%,C5>349999,0.75%,C5>199999,0.5%,C5>0,0%)

   b. Click in the Formula bar after the second visible comma between *1%* and *C5* and then press Alt + Enter.

   c. Click in the formula bar after the second visible comma between *0.75%* and *C5* and then press Alt + Enter.

   d. Click in the formula bar after the second visible comma between *0.5%* and *C5* and then press Alt + Enter.

   e. Press the Enter key and then click in cell D5.

   f. Hover the mouse pointer over the bottom of the Formula bar until the pointer turns into a two-headed arrow, click and hold down the left mouse button, drag the bottom of the bar down until all the rows of the formula can be seen, and then release the mouse button.

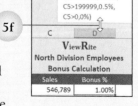

6. Collapse the Formula bar by completing the following steps:

   a. Hover the mouse pointer over the bottom of the Formula bar until the pointer turns into a two-headed arrow.

   b. Click and hold down the left mouse button, drag the bottom of the bar up until only one row is displayed, and then release the mouse button.

7. Save, print and then close **2-VRSalCost**.

Check Your Work

Chapter Summary

- Using range names in formulas makes it easier to manage complex formulas and helps others who work in or edit a worksheet to understand the purpose of a formula more quickly.

- Click the Name Manager button in the Defined Names group on the Formulas tab to open the Name Manager dialog box. Use options at the Name Manager dialog box to create, edit, or delete a range name or edit the cells that a range name references.

- To insert a formula click the Insert Function button in the Formula bar, click the name of the function at the drop-down list, and then enter arguments at the Insert Function dialog box. Alternatively, you can click a button in the Function Library group on the Formulas tab, click the name of the function at the drop-down list, and then enter arguments at the Insert Function dialog box.

- The COUNTBLANK function counts the number of empty cells in a range. The COUNTIF statistical function counts cells within a range that meet a single criterion or condition; the COUNTIFS statistical function counts cells within a range that meet multiple criteria or conditions.

- Find the arithmetic mean of a range of cells that meet a single criterion or condition using the AVERAGEIF statistical function. Use the AVERAGEIFS statistical function to find the arithmetic mean for a range that meet multiple criteria or conditions.

- The math function SUMIF adds cells within a range that meet a single criterion or condition. To add cells within a range based on multiple criteria or conditions, use the SUMIFS math function.

- The Lookup & Reference functions VLOOKUP and HLOOKUP look up data in a reference table and return in the formula cell a value from a column or row, respectively, in the lookup table.

- The PPMT financial function returns the principal portion of a specified loan payment within the term based on an interest rate, total number of payments, and loan amount.

- Using conditional logic in a formula requires Excel to perform a calculation based on the outcome of a logical or conditional test, in which one calculation is performed if the test proves true and another calculation is performed if the test proves false.

- A nested function is one function inside another function. Nest an IF function to test an additional condition.

- Use the ROUND function to modify the number of characters by rounding the value.

- Use the AND logical function to test multiple conditions. Excel returns *TRUE* if all the conditions test true and *FALSE* if any of the conditions tests false.

- The OR logical function also tests multiple conditions. The function returns *TRUE* if any of the conditions tests true and *FALSE* if all the conditions test false.

- The IFS logical function is similar to the IF function, but the IFS function does not require each argument to be enclosed in parentheses and the results of the IFS function must test true.

- To make a formula containing a long function easier to read, place each logical test on a separate line and expand the Formula bar.

Commands Review

FEATURE	RIBBON TAB, GROUP	BUTTON	KEYBOARD SHORTCUT
financial functions	Formulas, Function Library		
Insert Function dialog box	Formulas, Function Library	fx	Shift + F3
logical functions	Formulas, Function Library		
lookup and reference functions	Formulas, Function Library		
math and trigonometry functions	Formulas, Function Library		
Name Manager dialog box	Formulas, Defined Names		Ctrl + F3

Microsoft® Excel®

Working with Tables and Data Features

Performance Objectives

Upon successful completion of Chapter 3, you will be able to:

1 Create a table in a worksheet

2 Expand a table to include new rows and columns

3 Add a calculated column in a table

4 Format a table by applying table styles and table style options

5 Name a table

6 Add a *Total* row to a table and formulas to sum cells

7 Sort and filter a table

8 Use Data Tools to split the contents of a cell into separate columns

9 Remove duplicate records

10 Restrict data entry by creating validation criteria

11 Convert a table to a normal range

12 Create and modify subtotals of data and select data from different outline levels

13 Group and ungroup data

A *table* is a range that can be managed separately from other rows and columns in a worksheet. Data in a table can be sorted, filtered, and totaled as a separate unit. A worksheet can contain more than one table, which allows managing multiple groups of data separately within the same workbook. In this chapter, you will learn how to use the table feature to manage a range. You will use tools to validate data, search for and remove duplicate records, and convert text to a table. You will also convert a table back to a normal range and use data tools such as grouping related records and calculating subtotals.

 Data Files

Before beginning chapter work, copy the EL2C3 folder to your storage medium and then make EL2C3 the active folder.

The online course includes additional training and assessment resources.

<table>
<tr><td>

Activity 1 **Create and Modify a Table in a Billing Summary Worksheet**

4 Parts

You will convert data in a billing summary worksheet to a table and then modify the table by adding a row and calculated columns, applying table styles and sorting and filtering the data.

</td></tr>
</table>

Tutorial

Creating, Formatting, and Naming a Table

Quick Steps

Create Table
1. Select range.
2. Click Quick Analysis button.
3. Click Tables tab.
4. Click Table button.
5. Deselect range.

⊞ Table

Formatting Data as a Table

A table in Excel is similar in structure to a database. Columns are called *fields*. Each field is used to store a single unit of information about a person, place, or object. The first row of a table contains the column headings and is called the *field names row* or *header row*. Each column heading in the table should be unique. Below the field names, data is entered in rows called *records*. A record contains all the field values related to the single person, place, or object that is the topic of the table. No blank rows exist within the table, as shown in Figure 3.1.

To create a table in Excel, enter the data in the worksheet and then define the range as a table using the Table button in the Tables group on the Insert tab, the Format as Table button in the Styles group on the Home tab, Ctrl + T, or the Table button on the Tables tab in the Quick Analysis button at the bottom right of the selected range. Before converting a range to a table, delete any blank rows between the column headings and the data or within the data range.

Figure 3.1 Worksheet with the Range Formatted as a Table

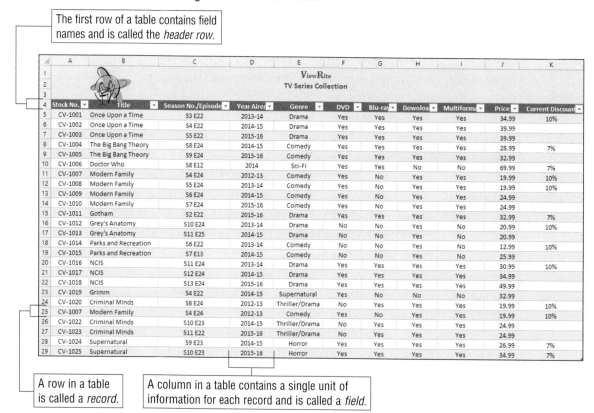

1. Open **BillSumOctWk1**.
2. Save the workbook with the name **3-BillSumOctWk1**.
3. Convert the billing summary data to a table by
   completing the following steps:
   a. Select the range A4:I24.
   b. Click the Insert tab.
   c. Click the Table button in the Tables group.
   d. At the Create Table dialog box with *=$A$4:$I$24*
      selected in the *Where is the data for your table?* text box
      and the *My table has headers* check box selected, click OK.
   e. Deselect the range.
4. Select columns A through I and AutoFit the column widths.
5. Deselect the columns.
6. Save **3-BillSumOctWk1**.

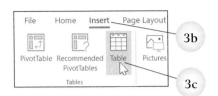

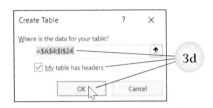

Check Your Work

 Tutorial

Adding a Row
to a Table

 Tutorial

Applying Table
Style Options
and Adding a
Calculated Column

Quick Steps

**Add Calculated
Column**
1. Type formula in first
   record in column.
2. Press Enter key.

Modifying a Table

Once a table has been defined, typing new data in the row immediately below the last row of the table or in the column immediately right of the last column causes the table to automatically expand to include the new entries. Excel displays the AutoCorrect Options button when the table is expanded. Click the button to display a drop-down list with the options *Undo Table AutoExpansion* and *Stop Automatically Expanding Tables*. To add data near a table without having the table expand, leave a blank column or row between the table and the new data.

Typing a formula in the first record of a new table column automatically creates a calculated column. In a calculated column, Excel copies the formula from the first cell to the remaining cells in the column immediately after the formula is entered. The AutoCorrect Options button appears when Excel converts a column to a calculated column. Click the button to display the options *Undo Calculated Column*, *Stop Automatically Creating Calculated Columns*, and *Control AutoCorrect Options*. If the formula is entered by typing the cell references, as in Activity 1b, a normal formula is entered. If the formula is entered by selecting the cells or ranges involved, Excel inserts a structured reference using the column name instead of the cell or range reference. For example, if the formula entered in Activity 1b Step 2b were entered by selecting the cells instead of typing the references, the formula in cell J5 would be =[@[Billable Hours]]*[@Rate] instead of H5*I5.

1. With **3-BillSumOctWk1** open, add a new record to the table by completing the following
   steps:
   a. Make cell A25 active, type RE-522, and then press
      the Tab key. Excel automatically expands the table
      to include the new row and displays the AutoCorrect
      Options button.

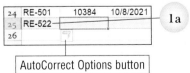

b. With cell B25 active, type the remainder of the record as follows. Press the Tab key to move from column to column in the table.

Client	10512
Date	10/8/2021
Client Name	Connie Melanson
Attorney FName	Kyle
Attorney LName	Williams
Area	Real Estate
Billable Hours	2.5

   c. With cell I25 active, type 250 and then press the Enter key. (If you press the Tab key, a new table row will be created.)

2. Add a calculated column to multiply the billable hours times the rate by completing the following steps:

   a. Make cell J4 active, type Fees Due, and then press the Enter key. Excel automatically expands the table to include the new column.

   b. With cell J5 active, type =h5*i5 and then press the Enter key. Excel creates a calculated column and copies the formula to the rest of the rows in the table.

   c. Double-click the column J boundary to AutoFit the column.

3. Calculate the 6.5% tax owing using a structured reference and a ROUND function that rounds the result to two digits after the decimal point by completing the following steps:

   a. Make cell K4 active, type Taxes Due, and then press the Enter key.

   b. With cell K5 active, type =round(, click in cell J5, type *.065,2), and then press the Enter key. Excel creates a calculated column using a structured reference and copies the formula to the rest of the rows in the table.

   c. Double-click the column K boundary to AutoFit the column.

4. Adjust the centering and fill color of the titles across the top of the table by completing the following steps:

   a. Select the range A1:K1 and then click the Merge & Center button in the Alignment group on the Home tab two times.

   b. Select the range A2:K2 and then press the F4 function key to repeat the command to merge and center row 2 across columns A through K.

   c. Select the range A3:K3 and then press the F4 function key to repeat the command to merge and center row 3 across columns A through K.

5. Save **3-BillSumOctWk1**.

2a

Rate ⌄	Fees Due ⌄
205.00	1,383.75
205.00	666.25
250.00	1,312.50
325.00	1,381.25
325.00	1,056.25
250.00	687.50
325.00	1,625.00
195.00	1,023.75
195.00	828.75
250.00	812.50
325.00	1,462.50
325.00	1,218.75
325.00	1,462.50
205.00	1,076.25
195.00	1,023.75
325.00	1,381.25
325.00	1,218.75
195.00	1,023.75
195.00	682.50
250.00	1,125.00
250.00	625.00

2b

Check Your Work

Applying Table Styles, Table Style Options, and Table Properties

Quick Steps

Change Table Style
1. Make table cell active.
2. If necessary, click Table Tools Design tab.
3. Click style in Table Styles gallery.
   OR
3. Click More button in Table Styles gallery.
4. Click desired style at drop-down gallery.

Add *Total* Row
1. Make table cell active.
2. If necessary, click Table Tools Design tab.
3. Click *Total Row* check box.
4. Click in cell in *Total* row.
5. Click option box arrow.
6. Click function.

Name Table
1. Make table cell active.
2. If necessary, click Table Tools Design tab.
3. Type table name in *Table Name* text box.
4. Press Enter key.

The contextual Table Tools Design tab, shown in Figure 3.2, contains options for formatting the table. Apply a different visual style to a table using the Table Styles gallery. Excel provides several table styles, which are categorized by *Light*, *Medium*, and *Dark* color themes. By default, Excel bands the rows within the table, which means that even-numbered rows are formatted differently from odd-numbered rows. Banding rows or columns makes it easier to read data across a row or down a column in a large table. The banding can be removed from the rows and/or added to the columns. Insert a check mark in the *First Column* or *Last Column* check box in the Table Style Options group to add emphasis to the first or last column in the table by formatting them differently from the rest of the table. Use the *Header Row* check box to show or hide the column headings in the table. Use the *Filter Button* check box to remove the filter arrows from the header row.

Click the *Total Row* check box or click the keyboard shortcut Ctrl + Shift + T to add a total row. Adding a *Total* row causes Excel to add the word *Total* in the leftmost cell of a new row at the bottom of the table. A Sum function is added automatically to the last numeric column in the table. Click in a cell in the *Total* row to display an option box arrow that when clicked displays a pop-up list; a function formula can be selected from this list.

A table name is a unique name used to reference an entire table and helps users easily identify the table if the workbook contains more than one. The table name appears in the *Table Name* text box. To name a table, click in any cell in the table, type the name in the *Table Name* text box in the Properties group on the Table Tools Design tab, and then press the Enter key. To select a table, click its name in the Name box. If a cell within a table is referenced in a formula in another cell outside the table then the name of the table is included in the formula.

Figure 3.2 Table Tools Design Tab

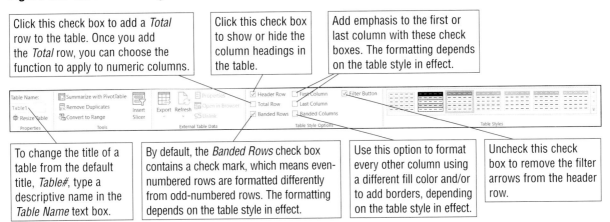

Click this check box to add a *Total* row to the table. Once you add the *Total* row, you can choose the function to apply to numeric columns.

Click this check box to show or hide the column headings in the table.

Add emphasis to the first or last column with these check boxes. The formatting depends on the table style in effect.

To change the title of a table from the default title, *Table#*, type a descriptive name in the *Table Name* text box.

By default, the *Banded Rows* check box contains a check mark, which means even-numbered rows are formatted differently from odd-numbered rows. The formatting depends on the table style in effect.

Use this option to format every other column using a different fill color and/or to add borders, depending on the table style in effect.

Uncheck this check box to remove the filter arrows from the header row.

Activity 1c Formatting a Table and Adding a *Total* Row and a Structured Reference Formula

1. With **3-BillSumOctWk1** open, change the table style by completing the following steps:
   a. Click in any cell in the table to activate the table.
   b. Click the Table Tools Design tab.
   c. Click the More button in the Table Styles gallery.
   d. Click *White, Table Style Medium 15* at the drop-down gallery (first column, third row in the *Medium* section). Notice that the header row stays a dark blue and does not change to black.

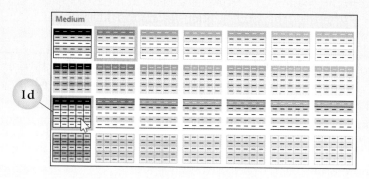

2. Change the table style options to remove the row banding, insert column banding, and emphasize the first column by completing the following steps:
   a. Click the *Banded Rows* check box in the Table Style Options group on the Table Tools Design tab to remove the check mark. All the rows in the table are now formatted the same.
   b. Click the *Banded Columns* check box in the Table Style Options group to insert a check mark. Every other column in the table is now formatted differently.
   c. Click the *First Column* check box in the Table Style Options group to insert a check mark. Notice that a darker fill color and reverse font color are applied to the first column.

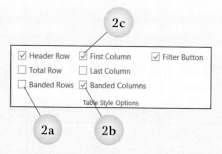

   d. Click the *Header Row* check box in the Table Style Options group to remove the check mark. Notice that the first row of the table (the row containing the column headings) disappears and is replaced with empty cells. The row is also removed from the table range definition.
   e. Click the *Header Row* check box to insert a check mark and redisplay the column headings.
   f. Click in the *Table Name* text box in the Properties group, type OctWk1, and then press the Enter key.

3. Add a *Total* row and add function formulas by completing the following steps:
   a. Click the *Total Row* check box in the Table Style Options group to add a *Total* row to the bottom of the table. Excel formats row 26 as a *Total* row, adds the label *Total* in cell A26, and automatically creates a Sum function in cell K26.
   b. Select the range K5:K26 and then apply comma formatting.
   c. In the *Fees Due* column, make cell J26 active, click the option box arrow that appears just right of the cell, and then click *Sum* at the pop-up list.
   d. Make cell B26 active, click the option box arrow that appears, and then click *Count* at the pop-up list.

None	69.96
Average	66.54
Count	
Count Numbers	89.78
Max	79.22
Min	66.54
Sum	44.36
StdDev	73.13
Var	40.63
More Functions...	
	1,500.04

The *Taxes Due* column automatically sums when a *Total* row is added in Step 3a.

3c

18	FL-385	None		1/7/2021	Lana Moore	Marty		O'Donovan	Separation		5.25	205.00	1,076.25	69.96
19	CL-412	Average		1/8/2021	Hilary Schmidt	Toni		Sullivan	Corporate		5.25	195.00	1,023.75	66.54
20	IN-801	Count		1/8/2021	Paul Sebastian	Rosa		Martinez	Insurance		4.25	325.00	1,381.25	89.78
21	EP-685	Count Numbers		1/8/2021	Frank Kinsela	Rosa		Martinez	Estate		3.75	325.00	1,218.75	79.22
22	CL-412	Max Min		1/8/2021	Hilary Schmidt	Toni		Sullivan	Corporate		5.25	195.00	1,023.75	66.54
23	CL-450	Sum		1/8/2021	Henri Poissant	Toni		Sullivan	Corporate		3.50	195.00	682.50	44.36
24	RE-501	StdDev Var		1/8/2021	Jade Eckler	Kyle		Williams	Real Estate		4.50	250.00	1,125.00	73.13
25	RE-522	More Functions...		1/8/2021	Connie Melanson	Kyle		Williams	Real Estate		2.50	250.00	625.00	40.63
26	Total												23,077.50	1,500.04

3d

4. Click in cell M4 and type Proposed Tax Rate and then press the Enter key.
5. With the insertion point in cell M5 create a structured reference formula that calculates a proposed tax decrease of 15% on the current taxes due by completing the following steps:
   a. Type =round(, click in cell K5, type *0.85,2), and then press the Enter key. Excel creates a structured reference formula using the table name and the column name.
   b. Click in cell M5 and look at the formula *=ROUND(OctWk1[@[Taxes Due]]*0.85,2)* in the Formula bar.
   c. Copy the formula down into cell M25.
   d. Apply Comma formatting and then deselect the range.
6. Click the Page Layout tab and change the *Width* option to *1 page* in the Scale to Fit group.
7. Preview and then print the worksheet.
8. Delete the data in column M.
9. Save **3-BillSumOctWk1**.

 Check Your Work

Sorting and Filtering a Table

By default, Excel displays a filter arrow next to each label in the table header row. Click the filter arrow to display a drop-down list with the same sort and filter options used in Chapter 1.

A table can also be filtered using the Slicer feature. When a Slicer is added, a Slicer pane containing all the unique values for the specified field is opened. Click an option in the Slicer pane to immediately filter the table. Add several Slicer panes to filter by more than one field, as needed.

To insert a Slicer pane, make any cell within the table active, click the Table Tools Design tab if necessary, and then click the Insert Slicer button in the Tools group. Excel opens the Insert Slicers dialog box, which contains a list of the fields

 Tutorial
Sorting a Table

 Tutorial
Filtering a Table

 Tutorial
Filtering a Table with a Slicer

 Slicer

Sort or Filter Table
1. Click filter arrow.
2. Click sort or filter options.
3. Click OK.

Custom Sort Table
1. Click Sort & Filter button.
2. Click *Custom Sort.*
3. Define sort levels.
4. Click OK.

in the table with a check box next to each field. Click to insert a check mark in the check box for each field to be filtered and then click OK. Click the option that the list is to be filtered on. Use the Shift and Ctrl keys to select several adjacent and nonadjacent options respectively or click the Multi-Select button at the top of the Slicer pane.

Activity 1d Sorting and Filtering a Table

1. With **3-BillSumOctWk1** open, filter the table by attorney last name to print a list of billable hours for O'Donovan by completing the following steps:
   a. Click the filter arrow next to *Attorney LName* in cell F4.
   b. Click the *(Select All)* check box to remove the check mark.
   c. Click the *O'Donovan* check box to insert a check mark and then click OK. The table is filtered to display only those records with *O'Donovan* in the *Attorney LName* field. The Sum functions in columns J and K reflect the totals for the filtered records only.
   d. Print the filtered worksheet.

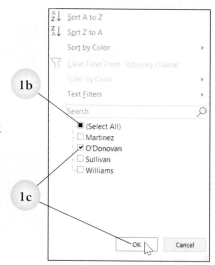

2. Redisplay all the records by clicking the *Attorney LName* filter arrow and then clicking *Clear Filter From "Attorney LName"* at the drop-down list.
3. Click the *Filter Button* check box in the Table Style Options group on the Table Tools Design tab to remove the check mark. Notice that the filter arrows disappear from the header row.
4. Filter the table with Slicers using the area of law by completing the following steps:
   a. With any cell active in the table, click the Insert Slicer button in the Tools group.
   b. At the Insert Slicers dialog box, click the *Area* check box to insert a check mark and then click OK. Excel inserts a Slicer pane in the worksheet with all the areas of law listed.
   c. If necessary, position the mouse pointer at the top of the Area Slicer pane until the pointer changes to a four-headed arrow and then drag the pane to an empty location at the right of the table.

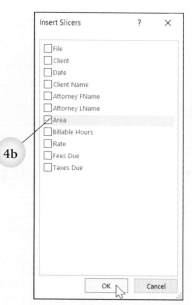

d. Click *Corporate* in the Area Slicer pane to filter the table. Excel filters the table by the *Corporate* area.

e. Click the Multi-Select button in the Slicer pane and then click *Employment*. Excel adds the *Employment* area to the filter.

5. Print the filtered worksheet.

6. Click the Clear Filter button at the top right of the Area Slicer pane to redisplay all the data.

The Area Slicer pane has filtered the table by *Corporate* and *Employment*.

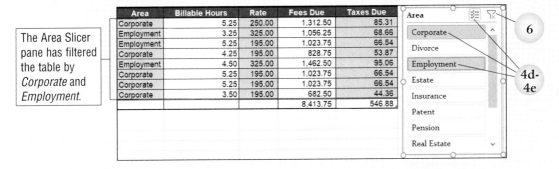

7. Click in the Area Slicer pane and then press the Delete key to remove the Slicer pane.

8. Use the Sort dialog box to sort the table first by attorney last name, then by area of law, and then by client name by completing the following steps:

a. With any cell within the table active, click the Home tab.

b. Click the Sort & Filter button in the Editing group and then click *Custom Sort* at the drop-down list.

c. At the Sort dialog box, click the *Sort by* option box arrow in the *Column* section and then click *Attorney LName* at the drop-down list. The default options for *Sort On* and *Order* are correct since the cell values are to be sorted in ascending order.

d. Click the Add Level button.

e. Click the *Then by* option box arrow and then click *Area* at the drop-down list.

f. Click the Add Level button.

g. Click the second *Then by* option box arrow and then click *Client Name* at the drop-down list.

h. Click OK.

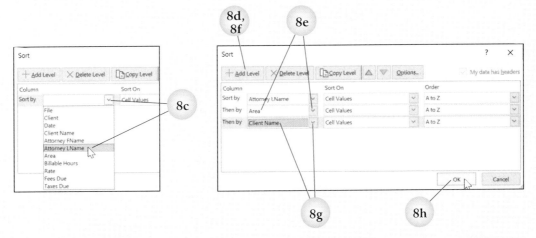

9. Print the sorted table.

10. Save **3-BillSumOctWk1**.

Working with Data Tools

The Data Tools group on the Data tab, shown in Figure 3.3, includes useful features
for working with data in tables.

Separating Data Using Text to Columns

Separating Data
Using Text to
Columns

Text to
Columns

Quick Steps

**Split Text into
Multiple Columns**

1. Insert column(s).
2. Select data to be
   split.
3. Click Data tab.
4. Click Text to
   Columns button.
5. Click Next at first
   dialog box.
6. Select delimiter
   check box.
7. Click Next.
8. Click Finish.

When data in one field needs to be separated in multiple columns, use the Text to
Columns feature. For example, a column that has first and last names in the same
cell can be split so the first name appears in one column and the last name appears
in a separate column. Breaking up the data into separate columns better facilitates
sorting and other data management tasks.

Before using the Text to Columns feature, insert the required number of blank
columns to separate the data immediately right of the column to be split. Select
the column to be split and then click the Text to Columns button to start the
Convert Text to Columns wizard. Work through the three dialog boxes of the
wizard to separate the data.

Figure 3.3 Data Tools Group on the Data Tab

Flash Fill	Consolidate
Remove Duplicates	Relationships
Text to Columns Data Validation	Manage Data Model
	Data Tools

Activity 2a Separating Client Names into Two Columns   Part 1 of 5

1. With **3-BillSumOctWk1** open, save the workbook with the name **3-BillSumOctWk1-2**.
2. Modify the custom sort to sort the table first by date (oldest to newest) and then by client
   (smallest to largest) by completing the following steps:
   a. Click the Sort & Filter button in the Editing group on the Home tab and then click *Custom
      Sort* at the drop-down list.
   b. At the Sort dialog box, click the first *Sort by* option box
      arrow in the *Column* section and then click *Date* at the
      drop-down list.
   c. Click the first *Then by* option box arrow in the *Column*
      section and then click *Client* at the drop-down list.
   d. Click the second *Then by* on the third line and then click
      the Delete Level button.
   e. Click OK.

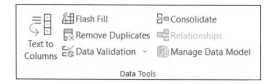

3. Split the client first and last names in column D into two columns by completing the following steps:

   a. Right-click column letter *E* at the top of the worksheet area and then click *Insert* at the shortcut menu to insert a blank column between the *Client Name* and *Attorney FName* columns in the table.

   b. Select the range D5:D25.

   c. Click the Data tab.

   d. Click the Text to Columns button in the Data Tools group.

   e. At the Convert Text to Columns Wizard - Step 1 of 3 dialog box, with *Delimited* selected in the *Choose the file type that best describes your data* section, click Next.

   f. In the *Delimiters* section of the Convert Text to Columns Wizard - Step 2 of 3 dialog box, click the *Space* check box to insert a check mark and then click Next. The *Data preview* section of the dialog box updates after the *Space* check box is clicked to show the names split into two columns.

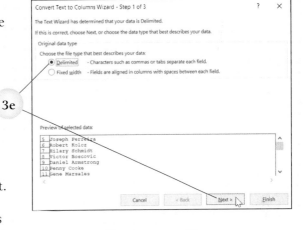

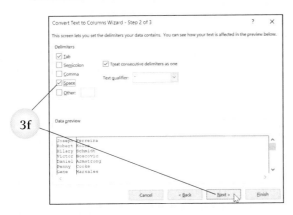

Client FName	Client LName
Joseph	Ferreira
Robert	Kolcz
Hilary	Schmidt
Victor	Boscovic
Daniel	Armstrong
Penny	Cooke
Gene	Marsales
Dana	Fletcher
Alexander	Torrez
Jean	Sauve
Victor	Boscovic
Daniel	Armstrong
Lana	Moore
Sam	Tonini
Hilary	Schmidt
Hilary	Schmidt
Paul	Sebastian
Henri	Poissant
Jade	Eckler
Frank	Kinsela
Connie	Melanson

Client first and last names are split into two columns in Steps 6a–6g.

   g. Click Finish at the last Convert Text to Columns Wizard dialog box to accept the default General data format for both columns.

   h. Deselect the range.

4. Make cell D4 active, change the label to *Client FName*, and then AutoFit the column width.

5. Make cell E4 active, change the label to *Client LName,* and then AutoFit the column width.

6. Save **3-BillSumOctWk1-2**.

Identifying and Removing Duplicate Records

Excel can compare records within a worksheet and automatically delete duplicate rows based on the columns selected that might contain duplicate values. All the columns are selected by default when the Remove Duplicates dialog box, shown in

Identifying and Removing Duplicate Records

Quick Steps

Remove Duplicate Rows
1. Select range or make cell active in table.
2. Click Data tab.
3. Click Remove Duplicates button.
4. Select columns to compare.
5. Click OK two times.

Remove
Duplicates

Figure 3.4, is opened. Click the Unselect All button to remove the check marks from all the columns, click the individual columns to compare, and then click OK. Excel automatically deletes the rows that contain duplicate values, and when the operation is completed, it displays a message with the number of rows that were removed from the worksheet or table and the number of unique values that remain.

Consider conditionally formatting duplicate values first to view the records that will be deleted. To do this, use the *Duplicate Values* option. Access this option by clicking the Conditional Formatting button in the Styles group on the Home tab and then pointing to *Highlight Cells Rules* at the Conditional Formatting drop-down list.

Excel includes the Remove Duplicates button in the Data Tools group on the Data tab and in the Tools group on the Table Tools Design tab. Click Undo to restore any duplicate rows removed by mistake.

Figure 3.4 Remove Duplicates Dialog Box

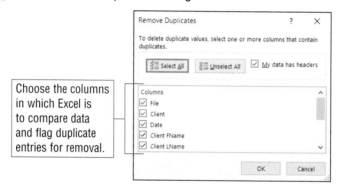

Choose the columns in which Excel is to compare data and flag duplicate entries for removal.

Activity 2b Removing Duplicate Rows

Part 2 of 5

1. With **3-BillSumOctWk1-2** open, remove the duplicate rows in the billing summary table by completing the following steps:
   a. With any cell in the table active, click the Remove Duplicates button in the Data Tools group on the Data tab.
   b. At the Remove Duplicates dialog box with all the columns selected in the *Columns* list box, click the Unselect All button.
   c. In the billing summary table, only one record should be assigned per file per date, since the attorneys record once per day the total hours spent on each file. (Records are duplicates if the same values exist in the two columns that store the file number and date). Click the *File* check box to insert a check mark.
   d. Click the *Date* check box to insert a check mark and then click OK.
   e. Click OK at the Microsoft Excel message box stating that a duplicate value was found and removed and that 20 unique values remain.

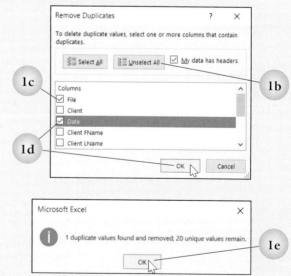

2. Scroll down the worksheet to view the total in cell L25. Compare the total with the printout from Activity 1d, Step 5. Notice that the total of the taxes due is now *1,433.50* compared with *1,500.04* in the printout.

3. Save **3-BillSumOctWk1-2**.

Check Your Work

Tutorial

Validating Data Entry

Validating Data Entry

Data Validation

Quick Steps

Create Data Validation Rule
1. Select range.
2. Click Data tab.
3. Click Data Validation button.
4. Specify validation criteria in Settings tab.
5. Click Input Message tab.
6. Type input message title and text.
7. Click Error Alert tab.
8. Select error style.
9. Type error alert title and message text.
10. Click OK.

Excel's data validation feature allows controlling the type of data that is accepted for entry in a cell. The type of data can be specified, along with parameters that validate whether the entry is within a certain range of acceptable values, dates, times, or text lengths. A list of values can also be set up that displays as a drop-down list when the cell is made active.

To do this, click the Data Validation button in the Data Tools group on the Data tab. At the Data Validation dialog box, shown in Figure 3.5, choose the type of data to be validated in the *Allow* option box on the Settings tab. Additional list or text boxes appear in the dialog box depending on the option chosen in the *Allow* drop-down list.

If a custom number format adds punctuation or text that appears in a cell, ignore the added characters when validating or restricting data entry. For example, a cell that contains the number *1234*, has a custom number format "*PD-*"*####*, and displays as *PD-1234* has a text length equal to four characters.

In addition to defining acceptable data entry parameters, there is the option of adding an input message and an error alert message to the range. Customized text can be added to define these messages.

When a cell to which data validation rules apply is made active, an input message displays. This kind of message is informational in nature. An error alert message appears when incorrect data is entered in a cell. There are three styles of error alerts, and a description and example of each type is provided in Table 3.1. If an error alert message has not been defined, Excel displays the Stop error alert with this default error message: *The value you entered is not valid. A user has restricted values that can be entered into this cell.*

Figure 3.5 Data Validation Dialog Box with the Settings Tab Selected

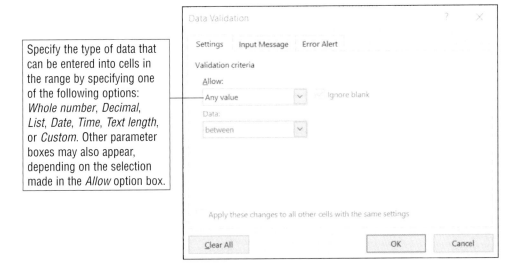

Specify the type of data that can be entered into cells in the range by specifying one of the following options: *Whole number, Decimal, List, Date, Time, Text length,* or *Custom.* Other parameter boxes may also appear, depending on the selection made in the *Allow* option box.

Table 3.1 Data Validation Error Alert Message Styles

Error Alert Icon	Error Alert Style	Description	Message Box Example
⊗	Stop	Prevents the data from being entered into the cell. The error alert message box provides three buttons to ensure that new data is entered.	*Date is outside accepted range.* ✕ ⊗ Please enter a date from October 4 to October 8, 2021. [Retry] [Cancel] [Help]
⚠	Warning	Does not prevent the data from being entered into the cell. The error alert message box provides four buttons below the prompt *Continue?*	*Check number of hours* ✕ ⚠ The hours you have entered are greater than 8. Continue? [Yes] [No] [Cancel] [Help]
ⓘ	Information	Does not prevent the data from being entered into the cell. The error alert message box provides three buttons below the error message.	*Verify hours entered* ✕ ⓘ The hours you have entered are outside the normal range. [OK] [Cancel] [Help]

Activity 2c Restricting Data Entry to Dates within a Range

Part 3 of 5

1. With **3-BillSumOctWk1-2** open, create a validation rule, input message, and error alert for dates in the billing summary worksheet by completing the following steps:
   a. Select the range C5:C24.
   b. Click the Data Validation button in the Data Tools group on the Data tab.
   c. With Settings the active tab in the Data Validation dialog box, click the *Allow* option box arrow (displays *Any value*) and then click *Date* at the drop-down list. Validation options are dependent on the *Allow* setting. When *Date* is chosen, Excel adds *Start date* and *End date* text boxes to the *Validation criteria* section.
   d. With *between* selected in the *Data* option box, click in the *Start date* text box and then type 10/4/2021.
   e. Click in the *End date* text box and then type 10/8/2021. (Since the billing summary worksheet is for the work week of October 4 to 8, 2021, entering this validation criteria will ensure that only dates between the start date and end date are accepted.)
   f. Click the Input Message tab.
   g. Click in the *Title* text box and then type Billing Date.
   h. Click in the *Input message* text box and then type This worksheet is for the week of October 4 to October 8 only.
   i. Click the Error Alert tab.

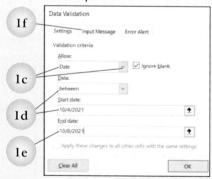

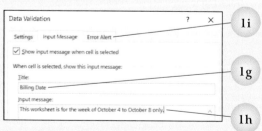

Chapter 3 | Working with Tables and Data Features

j. With *Stop* selected in the *Style* option box, click in the *Title* text box and then type Date is outside accepted range.

k. Click in the *Error message* text box and then type Please enter a date from October 4 to October 8, 2021.

l. Click OK. Since the range is active for which the data validation rules apply, the input message box appears.

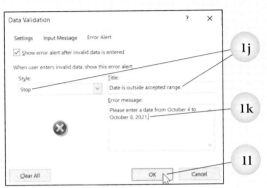

m. Deselect the range.

2. Add a new record to the table to test the date validation rule by completing the following steps:

a. Right-click row number *25* and then click *Insert* at the shortcut menu to insert a new row into the table.

b. Make cell A25 active, type PL-348, and then press the Tab key.

c. Type 10420 in the *Client* column and then press the Tab key. The input message title and text appear when the *Date* column is made active.

d. Type 10/15/2021 and then press the Tab key. Since the date entered is invalid, the error alert message box appears.

e. Click the Retry button.

f. Type 10/8/2021 and then press the Tab key.

g. Enter the data in the remaining fields as follows (pressing the Tab key to move from column to column and pressing the Enter key after the fees due calculation is done):

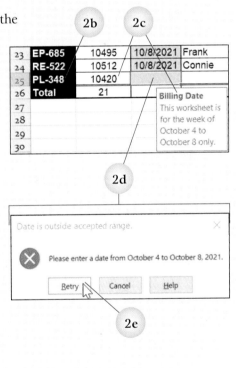

Client FName	Alexander
Client LName	Torrez
Attorney FName	Rosa
Attorney LName	Martinez
Area	Patent
Billable Hours	2.25
Rate	325.00

3. Save **3-BillSumOctWk1-2**.

1. With **3-BillSumOctWk1-2** open, create a list of values allowed in a cell by completing the following steps:
   a. Select the range J5:J25.
   b. Click the Data Validation button in the Data Tools group on the Data tab.
   c. If necessary, click the Settings tab.
   d. Click the *Allow* option box arrow and then click *List* at the drop-down list.
   e. Click in the *Source* text box and then type 195.00,205.00,250.00,325.00.
   f. Click OK.

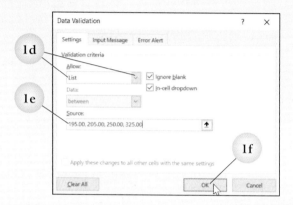

   g. Deselect the range.
2. Add a new record to the table to test the rate validation list by completing the following steps:
   a. Right-click row number *26* and then click *Insert* at the shortcut menu to insert a new row in the table.
   b. Make cell A26 active and then type data in the fields as follows (pressing the Tab key to move from column to column):

File	IN-745
Client	10210
Date	10/8/2021
Client FName	Victor
Client LName	Boscovic
Attorney FName	Rosa
Attorney LName	Martinez
Area	Insurance
Billable Hours	1.75

   c. At the *Rate* field, the validation list becomes active and an option box arrow appears at the right of the cell. Type 225.00 and then press the Tab key to test the validation rule. Since no error alert message was entered, the default message appears.
   d. Click the Cancel button. The value is cleared from the field.
   e. Make cell J26 the active cell, click the option box arrow at the right of the cell, click *325.00* at the drop-down list.
3. Save **3-BillSumOctWk1-2**.

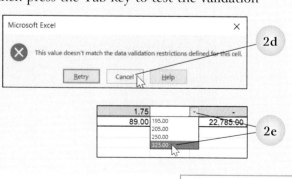

Check Your Work

1. With **3-BillSumOctWk1-2** open, create a validation rule to ensure that all client identification numbers are five characters (to be compatible with the firm's accounting system) by completing the following steps:
   a. Select the range B5:B26 and then click the Data Validation button in the Data Tools group on the Data tab.
   b. With the Settings tab active, click the *Allow* option box arrow and then click *Text length* at the drop-down list.
   c. Click the *Data* option box arrow and then click *equal to* at the drop-down list.
   d. Click in the *Length* text box and then type 5.
   e. Click OK.

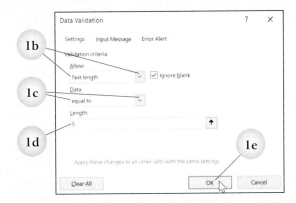

   f. Deselect the range.
2. Add a new record to the table to test the client identification validation rule by completing the following steps:
   a. Right-click row number 27 and then click *Insert* at the shortcut menu.
   b. Make cell A27 active, type FL-325, and then press the Tab key.
   c. Type 1010411 in cell B27 and then press the Tab key. Since this value is greater than the number of characters allowed in the cell, the default error message appears.
   d. Click the Retry button.
   e. Delete the selected text, type 1010, and then press the Tab key. Since this value is less than the specified text length, the default error message appears again. (Using a Text Length validation rule ensures that all entries in the range have the same number of characters. This rule is useful for validating customer numbers, employee numbers, inventory numbers, or any other data that requires a consistent number of characters.)
   f. Click the Cancel button, type 10104, and then press the Tab key. Since this entry is five characters in length, Excel moves to the next field.
   g. Enter the remaining fields as follows:

Date	10/8/2021
Client FName	Joseph
Client LName	Ferreira
Attorney FName	Marty
Attorney LName	O'Donovan
Area	Divorce
Billable Hours	5.75
Rate	205.00

3. Save and then print **3-BillSumOctWk1-2**.

You will open a billing summary workbook and convert the billing summary table to a normal range, sort the rows by the attorney names, and then add subtotals to display total fees due, a count of fees, and the average billable hours and fees due for each attorney.

 Tutorial

Converting a Table to a Normal Range and Subtotaling Related Data

 Convert to Range

 Subtotal

Quick Steps

Convert Table to Range
1. Make table cell active.
2. Click Table Tools Design tab.
3. Click Convert to Range button.
4. Click Yes.

Create Subtotal
1. Select range.
2. Click Data tab.
3. Click Subtotal button.
4. Select field to group by in *At each change in* option box.
5. Select function in *Use function* option box.
6. Select field(s) to subtotal in *Add subtotal to* list box.
7. Click OK.

Converting a Table to a Normal Range and Subtotaling Related Data

A table can be converted to a normal range using the Convert to Range button in the Tools group on the Table Tools Design tab. Convert a table to a range to use the Subtotal feature or when the data no longer needs to be treated as a table, independent of the data in the rest of the worksheet. Remove some or all the table styles before converting the table to a range. Use the Clear button in the Table Styles gallery or click the individual options in the Table Style Options group to remove any unwanted formatting.

A range of data with a column that has multiple rows with the same field value can be grouped and subtotals can be created for each group automatically by using the Subtotal button in the Outline group on the Data tab. For example, a worksheet with multiple records with the same department name in a field can be grouped by department name and a subtotal of a numeric field can be calculated for each department. Choose from a list of functions for the subtotal, such as Average and Sum. Before creating subtotals, sort the data by the fields in which the records are to be grouped. Remove any blank rows within the range that is to be grouped and subtotaled.

Excel displays a new row with a summary total when the field value for the specified subtotal column changes. A grand total is also automatically included at the bottom of the range. Excel displays the subtotals with buttons along the left of the worksheet area. These buttons are used to show or hide the details for each group using the Outline feature. Excel can create an outline with up to eight levels.

Figure 3.6 illustrates the data that will be grouped and subtotaled in Activity 3a; the data is displayed with the worksheet at level 2 of the outline. Figure 3.7 shows the same worksheet with two attorney groups expanded to show the detail records.

Figure 3.6 Worksheet with Subtotals by Attorney Last Name Displayed at Level 2 of Outline

outline level buttons

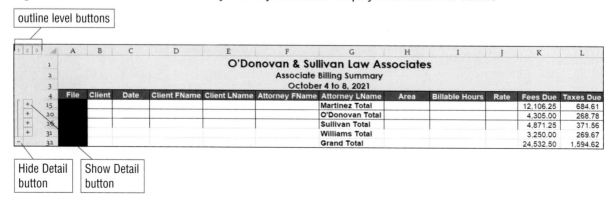

Hide Detail button

Show Detail button

Figure 3.7 Worksheet with Subtotals by Attorney Last Name with Martinez and Sullivan Groups Expanded

File	Client	Date	Client FName	Client LName	Attorney FName	Attorney LName	Area	Billable Hours	Rate	Fees Due	Taxes Due
				O'Donovan & Sullivan Law Associates							
				Associate Billing Summary							
				October 4 to 8, 2021							
IN-745	10210	10/5/2021	Victor	Boscovic	Rosa	Martinez	Insurance	4.25	325.00	1,381.25	68.66
IN-745	10210	10/7/2021	Victor	Boscovic	Rosa	Martinez	Insurance	4.50	325.00	1,462.50	89.94
IN-745	10210	10/8/2021	Victor	Boscovic	Rosa	Martinez	Insurance	1.75	325.00	568.75	52.81
EL-632	10225	10/5/2021	Daniel	Armstrong	Rosa	Martinez	Employment	3.25	325.00	1,056.25	95.06
EL-632	10225	10/7/2021	Daniel	Armstrong	Rosa	Martinez	Employment	4.50	325.00	1,462.50	76.62
PL-512	10290	10/7/2021	Sam	Tonini	Rosa	Martinez	Pension	3.75	325.00	1,218.75	69.96
IN-801	10346	10/8/2021	Paul	Sebastian	Rosa	Martinez	Insurance	4.25	325.00	1,381.25	66.54
PL-348	10420	10/6/2021	Alexander	Torrez	Rosa	Martinez	Patent	5.00	325.00	1,625.00	47.53
PL-348	10420	10/8/2021	Alexander	Torrez	Rosa	Martinez	Patent	2.25	325.00	731.25	73.13
EP-685	10495	10/8/2021	Frank	Kinsela	Rosa	Martinez	Estate	3.75	325.00	1,218.75	44.36
						Martinez Total				12,106.25	684.61
						O'Donovan Total				4,305.00	268.78
CL-412	10125	10/4/2021	Hilary	Schmidt	Toni	Sullivan	Corporate	5.25	250.00	1,312.50	36.97
CL-412	10125	10/8/2021	Hilary	Schmidt	Toni	Sullivan	Corporate	5.25	195.00	1,023.75	85.31
CL-521	10334	10/6/2021	Gene	Marsales	Toni	Sullivan	Corporate	4.25	195.00	828.75	89.78
CL-501	10341	10/6/2021	Dana	Fletcher	Toni	Sullivan	Employment	5.25	195.00	1,023.75	105.63
CL-450	10358	10/8/2021	Henri	Poissant	Toni	Sullivan	Corporate	3.50	195.00	682.50	53.87
						Sullivan Total				4,871.25	371.56
						Williams Total				3,250.00	269.67
						Grand Total				24,532.50	1,594.62

Activity 3a Converting a Table to a Normal Range and Subtotaling Related Data   Part 1 of 4

1. With **3-BillSumOctWk1-2** open, save the workbook with the name **3-BillSumOctWk1-3**.
2. Remove style options and convert the table to a normal range to group and subtotal the records by completing the following steps:
   a. Click in any cell in the table and then click the Table Tools Design tab.
   b. Click the *Total Row* check box in the Table Style Options group to remove the *Total* row from the table. The Subtotal feature includes a grand total automatically, so the *Total* row is no longer needed.
   c. Click the *Banded Columns* check box in the Table Style Options group to remove the banded formatting.
   d. Click the Convert to Range button in the Tools group.
   e. Click Yes at the Microsoft Excel message box asking if you want to convert the table to a normal range.

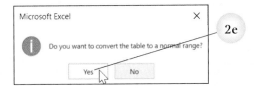

3. Sort the data by the fields to be subtotaled and grouped by completing the following steps:
   a. Select the range A4:L27.
   b. Click the Sort & Filter button in the Editing group on the Home tab and then click *Custom Sort* at the drop-down list.

c. At the Sort dialog box, define three levels to group and sort the records as follows:

Column	Sort On	Order
Attorney LName	Cell Values	A to Z
Client	Cell Values	Smallest to Largest
Date	Cell Values	Oldest to Newest

d. Click OK.

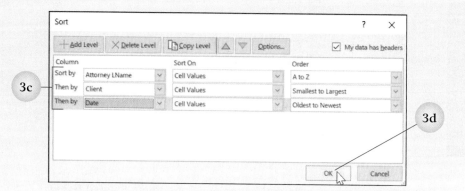

4. Create a subtotal for the fees and taxes due at each change in attorney last name by completing the following steps:

a. With the range A4:L27 still selected, click the Data tab.

b. Click the Subtotal button in the Outline group.

c. At the Subtotal dialog box, click the *At each change in* option box arrow (which displays *File*), scroll down the list, and then click *Attorney LName*.

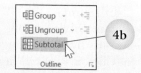

d. Click the *Fees Due* check box in the *Add subtotal to* list box to add a checkmark. Excel adds subtotals to the *Fees Due* and *Taxes Due* columns.

e. With *Use function* set to *Sum*, click OK.

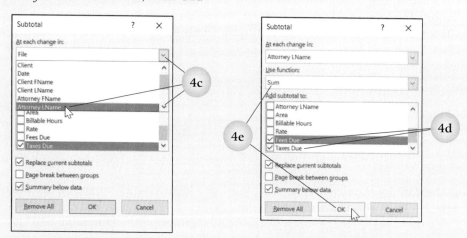

f. Deselect the range.

5. Select columns A through L and AutoFit the column widths. Deselect the columns.

6. Print the worksheet.

7. Save **3-BillSumOctWk1-3**.

Check Your Work

1. With **3-BillSumOctWk1-3** open, show and hide levels in the outlined worksheet by completing the following steps:

    a. Click the level 1 button at the top left of the worksheet area below the Name text box. Excel collapses the worksheet to display only the grand total of the *Fees Due* and *Taxes Due* columns.

    b. Click the level 2 button to display the subtotals by attorney last names. Notice that a button with a plus symbol (+) displays next to each subtotal in the *Outline* section at the left of the worksheet area. The button with the plus symbol is the Show Detail button and the button with the minus symbol (−) is the Hide Detail button. Compare your worksheet with the one shown in Figure 3.6 (on page 76).

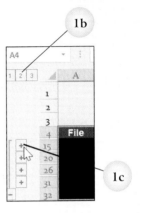

    c. Click the Show Detail button (which displays as a plus symbol) next to the row with the Martinez subtotal. The detail rows for the group of records for Martinez are displayed.

    d. Click the Show Detail button next to the row with the Sullivan subtotal.

    e. Compare your worksheet with the one shown in Figure 3.7 (on page 77).

    f. Click the level 3 button to display all the detail rows.

2. Save **3-BillSumOctWk1-3**.

Modifying Subtotals

Modify subtotals to include more than one type of calculation. For example, if subtotals are inserted that sum data, subtotals that count and average the same data can be added. When a new subtotal is added, it is placed above the existing subtotal or subtotals.

To add a subtotal to a data range that already has one or more subtotals, select a cell in the range that has been subtotaled and then click the Subtotal button in the Outline group on the Data tab. Select the field to insert the new subtotal at the *At each change in* drop-down list, select a function for the new subtotal at the *Use function* drop-down list, click the check box to insert a check mark for the field to which you are adding a subtotal, click the *Replace current subtotals* check box to remove the check mark, and then click OK.

To replace all the subtotals, click in a cell in the range; display the Subtotal dialog box; select the location, function, and field or fields for the replacement; verify that the *Replace current subtotals* check box contains a check mark; and then click OK.

To remove all the subtotals, select a cell in the range that has been subtotaled, click the Subtotal button, and then click the Remove All button.

Selecting Data from Different Outline Levels

🔍 Find & Select

By default, when a subtotal or grand total is selected in a collapsed outline, the underlying data is also selected. To select only specific subtotals and/or grand totals, click the Find & Select button in the Editing group on the Home tab, click the *Go To Special* option to display the Go To Special dialog box, click the *Visible cells only* radio button to insert a bullet, and then click OK. After you have selected the visible subtotals, you can copy them to a new range or format the cells containing them.

Quick Steps

Select Visible Cells Only
1. Click Find & Select button.
2. Click *Go to Special* option.
3. Click *Visible cells only* radio button.
4. Click OK.

Activity 3c Modifying and Formatting Subtotals

Part 3 of 4

1. With **3-BillSumOctWk1-3** open, add a subtotal to count the number of billable records for each attorney for the week by completing the following steps:
   a. Select the range A4:L32 and then click the Subtotal button in the Outline group on the Data tab. The Subtotal dialog box opens with the settings used for the subtotals created in Activity 3a.
   b. Click the *Replace current subtotals* check box to remove the check mark. With this check box cleared, Excel adds another subtotal row to each group.
   c. Click the *Use function* option box arrow and then click *Count* at the drop-down list.
   d. Click the *Fees Due* check box in the *Add subtotal to* list box to remove the check mark.
   e. With *Attorney LName* still selected in the *At each change in* list box and *Taxes Due* still selected in the *Add subtotal to* list box, click OK. Excel adds a new subtotal row to each group with the count of records displayed.

2. Add a subtotal to calculate the average billable hours and average fees due for each attorney by completing the following steps:
   a. With the data range still selected, click the Subtotal button.
   b. Click the *Use function* option box arrow and then click *Average* at the drop-down list.
   c. Click the *Billable Hours*, *Fees Due*, and *Taxes Due* check boxes in the *Add subtotal to* list box to insert check marks in the *Billable Hours* and *Fees Due* check boxes and to remove the check mark from the *Taxes Due* check box.
   d. Click OK. Excel adds a new subtotal row to each group with the average billable hours and average fees due for each attorney.

Attorney LName	Area	Billable Hours	Rate	Fees Due	Taxes Due
Martinez	Insurance	4.25	325.00	1,381.25	68.66
Martinez	Insurance	4.50	325.00	1,462.50	89.94
Martinez	Insurance	1.75	325.00	568.75	52.81
Martinez	Employment	3.25	325.00	1,056.25	95.06
Martinez	Employment	4.50	325.00	1,462.50	76.62
Martinez	Pension	3.75	325.00	1,218.75	69.96
Martinez	Insurance	4.25	325.00	1,381.25	66.54
Martinez	Patent	5.00	325.00	1,625.00	47.53
Martinez	Patent	2.25	325.00	731.25	73.13
Martinez	Estate	3.75	325.00	1,218.75	44.36
Martinez Average		3.73		1,210.63	
Martinez Count					10
Martinez Total				12,106.25	684.61

The averages of the *Billable Hours* and *Fees Due* columns are added to the subtotals for all the attorneys in Steps 2a–2c. The data for the Martinez group is shown.

3. Format the average, count, total, and grand total subtotals by completing the following steps:
   a. Click the level 4 outline button.
   b. Select the range G15:L42, click the Home tab, and then click the Find & Select button in the Editing group.
   c. Click the *Go To Special* option.
   d. Click the *Visible cells only* radio button and then click OK.
   e. Apply bold formatting and the *White, Background 1, Darker 15%* fill (first column, third row). **Note that you will have to click the Bold button twice to apply Bold formatting**.
   f. Click the level 5 outline button.
   g. Deselect the range.
4. Click the Page Layout tab and scale the height of the worksheet to 1 page.
5. Save the revised workbook with the name **3-BillSumOctWk1-3c**.
6. Print and then close **3-BillSumOctWk1-3c**.

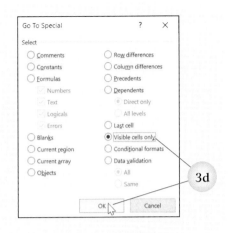

Check Your Work

Grouping and Ungrouping Data

 Group

 Ungroup

Quick Steps

Group Data by Rows
1. Select range to be grouped within outlined worksheet.
2. Click Data tab.
3. Click Group button.
4. Click OK.

Ungroup Data by Rows
1. Select grouped range within outlined worksheet.
2. Click Data tab.
3. Click Ungroup button.
4. Click OK.

Grouping and Ungrouping Data

Use the Group and Ungroup buttons in the Outline group on the Data tab to further collapse and expand subgroups of records at various levels or use the keyboard shortcuts Shift + Alt + Right Arrow key to group data and Shift + Alt + Left Arrow key to ungroup data. For example, in an outlined worksheet with detailed rows displayed, a group of records can be further grouped by selecting a group of records and clicking the Group button to open the Group dialog box, shown in Figure 3.8. Clicking OK with *Rows* selected adds a further group feature to the selection. Selecting records that have been grouped and clicking the Ungroup button removes the group feature added to the selection and removes the Hide Detail button.

Columns can also be grouped and ungrouped. The outline section with the level numbers and the Show Detail and Hide Detail buttons displays across the top of the worksheet area. For example, in a worksheet in which two columns are used to arrive at a formula, the source columns can be grouped and the details hidden so that only the formula column with the calculated results is displayed in an outlined worksheet.

Figure 3.8 Group Dialog Box

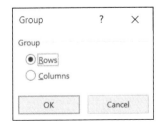

1. Open **3-BillSumOctWk1-3**. Group client data within the Martinez attorney group by completing the following steps:
   a. Select the range A5:L7. These three rows contain billing information for client 10210.
   b. Click the Group button in the Outline group on the Data tab. (Click the button and not the button arrow.)
   c. At the Group dialog box with *Rows* selected, click OK. Excel adds a fourth outline level to the worksheet and a Hide Detail button below the last row of the grouped records in the Outline section.
   d. Select the range A12:L13, click the Group button, and then click OK at the Group dialog box.
   e. Deselect the range.

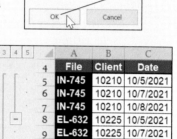

2. Experiment with the Hide Detail buttons in the Martinez group by hiding the detail for client 10210 and then hiding the detail for client 10420.
3. Redisplay the detail rows by clicking the Show Detail button for each client.
4. Select the range A5:L7, click the Ungroup button (click the button and not the button arrow), and then click OK at the Ungroup dialog box.

These records are grouped in Step 1d.

	A	B	C
4	**File**	**Client**	**Date**
5	**IN-745**	10210	10/5/2021
6	**IN-745**	10210	10/7/2021
7	**IN-745**	10210	10/8/2021
8	**EL-632**	10225	10/5/2021
9	**EL-632**	10225	10/7/2021
10	**PL-512**	10290	10/7/2021
11	**IN-801**	10346	10/8/2021
12	**PL-348**	10420	10/6/2021
13	**PL-348**	10420	10/8/2021
14	**EP-685**	10495	10/8/2021

5. Select the range A12:L13, click the Ungroup button, and then click OK at the Ungroup dialog box.
6. Select the range A5:L14, click the Ungroup button, and then click OK at the Ungroup dialog box. Notice that the Hide Detail button is removed for the entire Martinez group.
7. Deselect the range and then click the level 4 button at the top of the outline section. Notice that the data for the Martinez records do not collapse like the others, since they are no longer grouped.
8. Save the revised workbook with the name **3-BillSumOctWk1-3d**.
9. Print and then close **3-BillSumOctWk1-3d**.

Chapter Summary

- A table in Excel is a range of cells similar in structure to a database in which there are no blank rows and the first row of the range contains column headings.

- Columns in a table are called *fields* and rows are called *records*. The first row of a table contains the column headings and is called the *field names row* or *header row*.

- Define a range as a table using the Table button in the Tables group on the Insert tab. Type data in adjacent rows and columns and the table will expand automatically to include them.

- Typing a formula in the first record of a new column causes Excel to define the column as a calculated column and to automatically copy the formula to the remaining cells in the column.

- The contextual Table Tools Design tab contains options for formatting tables.
- The Table Styles gallery contains several options for changing the visual appearance of a table.
- Banding rows or columns formats every other row or column differently to make reading a large table easier.
- Insert check marks in the *First Column* and *Last Column* check boxes in the Table Style Options group to add emphasis to the first column or last column in a table.
- The row containing column headings in a table can be shown or hidden using the *Header Row* option in the Table Style Options group.
- Adding a *Total* row to a table causes Excel to add the word *Total* in the leftmost column and to create a Sum function in the last numeric column in the table. Additional functions can be added by clicking in a column in the *Total* row and selecting a function from the pop-up list.
- By default, Excel displays a filter arrow next to each label in the table header row. Use these arrows to filter and sort the table.
- Slicers are used to filter data in a table using a Slicer pane, which contains all the items in the designated field.
- A column containing text that can be split can be separated into multiple columns using the Text to Columns feature. The Convert Text to Columns wizard contains three dialog boxes that define how to split the data.
- Use options at the Remove Duplicates dialog box to compare records within a worksheet and automatically delete rows that contain duplicate values.
- Data can be validated as it is being entered into a worksheet, and invalid data can be prevented from being stored or a warning can be issued stating that data has been entered that does not conform to the parameters.
- Define the validation criteria for a cell entry at the Settings tab in the Data Validation dialog box. Data can be allowed based on values, dates, times, and text lengths or restricted to values within a drop-down list.
- Define a message that pops up when a cell for which data is restricted becomes active at the Input Message tab in the Data Validation dialog box.
- Define the type of error alert to display and the content of the error message at the Error Alert tab in the Data Validation dialog box.
- Convert a table to a normal range using the Convert to Range button in the Tools group on the Table Tools Design tab. Convert a table to a range to use the Subtotal feature or when a range of cells no longer needs to be treated independently from the rest of the worksheet.
- Sort a worksheet by column(s) to group data for subtotals before opening the Subtotals dialog box.
- A range of data with a column that has multiple rows with the same field value can be grouped and subtotals created for each group automatically by using the Subtotal button in the Outline group on the Data tab.
- Excel adds a subtotal automatically at each change in content for the column specified as the subtotal field. A grand total is also automatically added to the bottom of the range.
- Display more than one subtotal row for a group to calculate multiple functions, such as Sum and Average.

- A subtotaled range is outlined and record details can be collapsed or expanded using the level number, Hide Detail, and Show Detail buttons.
- To select only specific subtotals and/or grand totals, click the Find & Select button in the Editing group on the Home tab, click the *Go To Special* option to display the Go To Special dialog box, click the *Visible cells only* radio button to insert a bullet, and then click OK.
- When a worksheet is outlined, use the Group and Ungroup buttons in the Outline group on the Data tab to manage the display of individual groups.

Commands Review

FEATURE	RIBBON TAB, GROUP	BUTTON	KEYBOARD SHORTCUT
convert table to range	Table Tools Design, Tools		
create table	Insert, Tables		Ctrl + T
group data	Data, Outline		Shift + Alt + Right Arrow key
remove duplicates	Data, Data Tools OR Table Tools Design, Tools		
sort and filter table	Home, Editing		
subtotals	Data, Outline		
table styles	Table Tools Design, Table Styles		
text to columns	Data, Data Tools		
Total row	Table Tools Design, Table Style Options		Ctrl + Shift + T
ungroup	Data, Outline		Shift + Alt + Left Arrow key
validate data	Data, Data Tools		
visible cells only	Home, Editing		Ctrl + G

Microsoft®

Excel®

Summarizing and Consolidating Data

CHAPTER

4

Performance Objectives

Upon successful completion of Chapter 4, you will be able to:

1 Summarize data by creating formulas with range names that reference cells in other worksheets

2 Summarize data by creating 3-D references

3 Create formulas that link to cells in other worksheets or workbooks

4 Edit a link to a source workbook

5 Edit or break a link to an external source

6 Use the Consolidate feature to summarize data from multiple worksheets in a master worksheet

7 Create, edit, and format a PivotTable

8 Filter a PivotTable using Slicers and Timelines

9 Create and format a PivotChart

10 Create and format Sparklines

While working with Excel, you may find it useful to summarize and report data from various worksheets. Data can be summarized by creating formulas that reference cells in other areas of the same worksheet or workbook, or by linking to cells in other worksheets or workbooks. The Consolidate feature can also be used to summarize data and consolidate it into a master worksheet. Once the data has been summarized, consider presenting or analyzing the data by creating and formatting a PivotTable or PivotChart. Also consider creating Sparklines, which are miniature charts inserted into cells that reveal trends or other patterns in the data. Timelines allow the filtering of a PivotTable or PivotChart using a specified timeframe. In this chapter, you will learn how to summarize and filter data using a variety of methods and then present visually summarized data for analysis.

 Data Files

Before beginning chapter work, copy the EL2C4 folder to your storage medium and then make EL2C4 the active folder.

The online course includes additional training and assessment resources.

<table>
<tr><td>

Activity 1 **Calculate Park Attendance Totals**

5 Parts

</td></tr>
<tr><td>

You will calculate total park attendance at three national parks by using data stored in separate worksheets and linking to a cell in another workbook. You will also edit a linked workbook and update and remove the link in the destination file.

</td></tr>
</table>

Summarizing
Data in Multiple
Worksheets Using
Range Names

Quick Steps

**Sum Multiple
Worksheets Using
Range Names**
1. Make formula cell
   active.
2. Type =sum(.
3. Type first range
   name.
4. Type comma ,.
5. Type second range
   name.
6. Type comma ,.
7. Continue typing
   range names
   separated by
   commas until
   finished.
8. Type).
9. Press Enter key.

Summarizing Data in Multiple Worksheets Using Range Names and 3-D References

A workbook that has been organized with data in separate worksheets can be summarized by creating formulas that reference cells in other worksheets. When a formula is created that references a cell in the same worksheet, the sheet name does not need to be included in the reference. For example, the formula *=A3+A4* causes Excel to add the value in cell A3 in the active worksheet to the value in cell A4 in the active worksheet. However, when a formula is created that references a cell in a different worksheet, the sheet name must be included in the formula.

Assume that Excel is to add the value in cell A3 that resides in Sheet2 to the value in cell A3 that resides in Sheet3 in the workbook. To do this, include the worksheet name in the formula by typing *=Sheet2!A3+Sheet3!A3* into the formula cell. This formula contains both worksheet references and cell references. The worksheet reference precedes the cell reference and is separated from the cell reference with an exclamation point. Without a worksheet reference, Excel assumes the cells are in the active worksheet.

A formula that references the same cell in a range that extends over two or more worksheets is often called a *3-D reference*. For a formula that includes a 3-D reference, the 3-D reference can be typed directly in a cell or entered using a point-and-click approach. Formulas that include 3-D references are sometimes referred to as *3-D formulas*.

As an alternative, consider using range names to simplify formulas that summarize data in multiple worksheets. Recall from Chapter 2 that a range name includes the worksheet reference by default; therefore, typing the range name in the formula automatically references the correct worksheet. Another advantage to using a range name is that the name can describe the worksheet with the source data. When range names are used, the two worksheets do not have to be made identical in organizational structure.

Activity 1a **Summarizing Data in Multiple Worksheets Using Range Names**

Part 1 of 5

1. Open **MayEntries**.
2. Save the workbook with the name **4-MayEntries**.
3. Click each sheet tab and review the data. Attendance data for each park is entered as a separate worksheet.

4. In the workbook, range names have already been created. Check each range name to find out what it references.

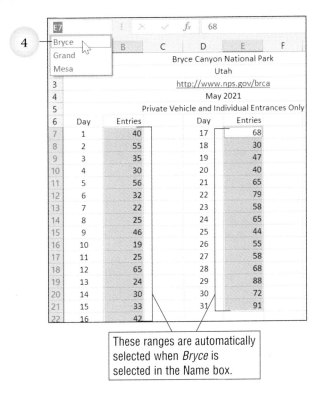

These ranges are automatically selected when *Bryce* is selected in the Name box.

5. Create a formula to add the total attendance for May at all three parks by completing the following steps:
   a. Click the AttendanceSummary tab to activate the worksheet.
   b. If necessary, make cell F7 active, type =sum(bryce,grand,mesa), and then press the Enter key. Notice that in a SUM formula, multiple range names are separated with commas. Excel returns the result *10460* in cell F7 of the AttendanceSummary worksheet.

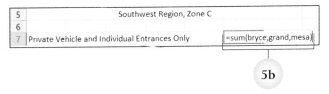

5b

   c. Apply the Comma format with no digits after the decimal point to cell F7.
6. Save and then close **4-MayEntries.**

> Check Your Work

   A disadvantage to using range names emerges when several worksheets need to be summarized because the range name references must be created in each worksheet. If several worksheets need to be summarized, a more efficient method is to use a 3-D reference. Generally, when using a 3-D reference, it is a good idea to set up the data in each worksheet in identical cells. In Activity 1b, you will calculate the same attendance total for the three parks using a 3-D reference instead of range names.

1. Open **MayEntries**.
2. Save the workbook with the name **4-3D-MayEntries**.
3. Calculate the attendance total for the three parks using a point-and-click approach to create a 3-D reference by completing the following steps:

    a. In the AttendanceSummary worksheet, make cell F7 active and then type =sum(.

    b. Click the BryceCanyon sheet tab.

    c. Press and hold down the Shift key, click the MesaVerde sheet tab, and then release the Shift key. (Holding down the Shift key while clicking a sheet tab selects all the worksheets from the first sheet tab to the last sheet tab clicked.) Notice in the Formula bar that the formula reads =sum('BryceCanyon:MesaVerde'!

    d. With BryceCanyon the active worksheet, select the range B7:B22, press and hold down the Ctrl key, select the range E7:E21, and then release the Ctrl key.

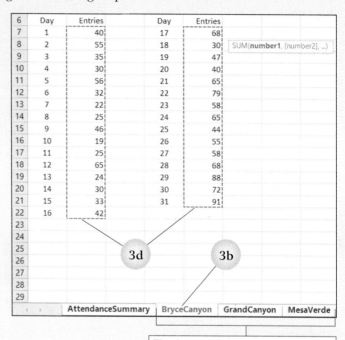

    e. Type) and then press the Enter key. Excel returns the value *10460* in cell F7 in the AttendanceSummary worksheet.

    f. Apply the Comma format with no digits after the decimal point to cell F7.
4. With cell F7 the active cell, compare your formula with the one shown in Figure 4.1.
5. Save and then close **4-3D-MayEntries**.

Check Your Work

Figure 4.1 3-D Formula Created in Activity 1b

This 3-D formula is created in Activity 1b, Step 3, using a point-and-click approach.

	A	B	C	D	E	F	G	H	I	J
1			National Park Service							
2			U.S. Department of the Interior							
3			May 2021							
4			Attendance Summary							
5			Southwest Region, Zone C							
6										
7	Private Vehicle and Individual Entrances Only					10,460				

F7 fx =SUM(BryceCanyon:MesaVerde!B7:B22,BryceCanyon:MesaVerde!E7:E21)

Tutorial

Linking Data

Summarizing Data by Linking to Ranges in Other Worksheets or Workbooks

Quick Steps

Create Link to External Source
1. Open source workbook.
2. Open destination workbook.
3. Arrange windows as desired.
4. Make formula cell active in destination workbook.
5. Type =.
6. Click to activate source workbook.
7. Click source cell.
8. Press Enter key.

Using a method similar to that used in Activity 1a or Activity 1b, data can be summarized in one workbook by linking to a cell, range, or range name in another worksheet or workbook. When data is linked, a change made in the source cell (the cell in which the original data is stored) is updated in any other cell to which the source cell has been linked. A link is established by creating a formula that references the source data. For example, entering the formula =*Sheet1!B10* into a cell in Sheet2 creates a link. The cell in Sheet2 displays the value in the source cell. If the data in cell B10 in Sheet1 is changed, the value in the linked cell in Sheet2 also changes.

As an alternative to creating a formula, copy the source cell to the Clipboard task pane. Make the destination cell active, click the Paste button arrow in the Clipboard group, and then click the Paste Link button in the *Other Paste Options* section of the drop-down gallery. Excel creates the link formula using an absolute reference to the source cell.

Linking to a cell in another workbook incorporates external references and requires adding a workbook name reference to the formula. For example, linking to cell A3 in a sheet named *ProductA* in a workbook named *Sales* requires entering =*[Sales.xlsx]ProductA!A3* in the cell. Notice that the workbook reference is entered first in square brackets. The workbook in which the external reference is added is called the *destination workbook*. The workbook containing the data that is linked to the destination workbook is called the *source workbook*. In Activity 1c, you will create a link to an external cell containing the attendance total for tour group entrances for the three parks.

The point-and-click approach to creating a linked external reference creates an absolute reference to the source cell. Delete the dollar symbols ($) in the cell reference if the formula is to be copied and the source cell needs to be relative. Note that the workbook and worksheet references remain absolute regardless.

Activity 1c   Summarizing Data by Linking to Another Workbook   Part 3 of 5

1. Open **4-MayEntries**.
2. Open **MayGroupSales**. This workbook contains tour group attendance data for the three national parks. Tour groups are charged a flat-rate entrance fee, so their attendance values represent bus capacities rather than the actual numbers of patrons on the buses.
3. Click the View tab, click the Arrange All button in the Window group, click *Vertical* in the *Arrange* section of the Arrange Windows dialog box, and then click OK.
4. In the worksheet used in Activity 1a, create a linked external reference to the total attendance in the worksheet with the commercial tour vehicle attendance data by completing the following steps:
   a. Click in **4-MayEntries** to make the workbook active. Make sure the active worksheet is AttendanceSummary.
   b. Make cell A9 active, type Commercial Tour Vehicles Only, and then press the Enter key.
   c. Make cell F9 active and then type =.

d. Click the **MayGroupSales** title bar to activate the workbook and then click in cell F7. Notice that the formula being entered into the formula cell contains a workbook reference and a worksheet reference in front of the cell reference.

e. Press the Enter key.

f. Apply the Comma format with no digits after the decimal point to cell F9.

g. With cell F9 active, compare your worksheet with the 4-MayEntries worksheet shown below.

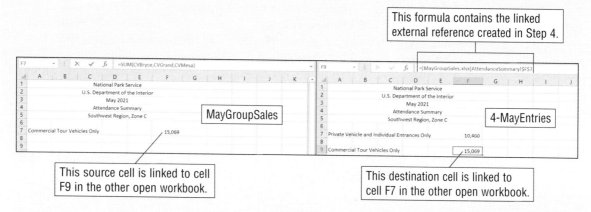

This formula contains the linked external reference created in Step 4.

This source cell is linked to cell F9 in the other open workbook.

This destination cell is linked to cell F7 in the other open workbook.

5. Click the Maximize button in the **4-MayEntries** title bar.

6. Make cell A11 active, type Total Attendance, and then press the Enter key.

7. Make cell F11 active and then create a formula to add the values in cells F7 and F9.

8. Print the AttendanceSummary worksheet in **4-MayEntries**. *Note: If you submit your work as hard copy, check with your instructor to see if you need to print two copies of the worksheet, with one copy displaying the cell formulas.*

9. Save and then close **4-MayEntries**.

10. Close **MayGroupSales**. Click Don't Save if prompted to save changes.

 Check Your Work

Maintaining External References

Quick Steps

Edit Link to External Source
1. Open destination workbook.
2. Click Data tab.
3. Click Edit Links button.
4. Click link.
5. Click Change Source button.
6. Navigate to drive and/or folder.
7. Double-click source workbook file name.
8. Click Close button.
9. Save and close destination workbook.

 Edit Links

In Excel, an *external reference* is a link to a cell or cells in another workbook. The reference includes a path to the specific drive or folder where the source workbook is located. If the source workbook is moved or the workbook name is changed, the link will no longer work. By default, when a linked workbook is opened, the automatic updates feature is disabled and Excel displays a security warning message in the Message bar area above the workbook. From the message bar, the content can be enabled so that links can be updated.

Links can be edited or broken at the Edit Links dialog box, shown in Figure 4.2. Open the dialog box by clicking the Edit Links button in the Queries & Connections group on the Data tab. If more than one link is present in the workbook, begin by clicking the link to be changed in the *Source* list. Click the Change Source button to open the Change Source dialog box and navigate to the drive and/or folder in which the source workbook was moved or renamed. Click the Break Link button to permanently remove the linked reference and convert the linked cells to their existing values. Links cannot be restored using the Undo feature. If a broken link needs to be restored, the linked formula will have to be recreated.

Figure 4.2 Edit Links Dialog Box

Break Link to External
Reference
1. Open destination
   workbook.
2. Click Data tab.
3. Click Edit Links
   button.
4. Click link.
5. Click Break Link
   button.
6. Click Break Links
   button.
7. Click Close button.
8. Save and close
   destination
   workbook.

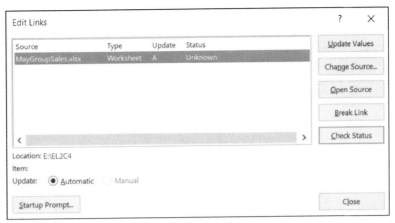

Activity 1d Editing Source Data and Updating an External Link

Part 4 of 5

1. Open **MayGroupSales** and maximize the screen.
2. Save the workbook with the name **4-Source**.
3. Edit the attendance data value at each park by completing the following steps:
   a. Click the BryceCanyon sheet tab.
   b. Make cell B8 active and then change the value from *55* to *361*.
   c. Click the GrandCanyon sheet tab.
   d. Make cell B20 active and then change the value from *275* to *240*.
   e. Click the MesaVerde sheet tab.
   f. Make cell E21 active and then change the value from *312* to *406*.
4. Click the AttendanceSummary tab. Note that the updated value in cell F7 is *15,434*.
5. Save and then close **4-Source**.
6. Open **4-MayEntries**. Notice the security warning in the Message bar above the worksheet area that states that the automatic update of links has been disabled. Instruct Excel to allow automatic updates for this workbook (since you are sure the content is from a trusted source) by clicking the Enable Content button next to the message. *Note: If a Security Warning dialog box appears asking if you want to make the file a trusted document, click No*.

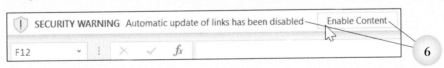

7. Edit the link to retrieve the data from the workbook you revised in Steps 2–5 by completing the following steps:
   a. Click the Data tab.
   b. Click the Edit Links button in the Queries & Connections group.

c. At the Edit Links dialog box, click the Change Source button.

d. If necessary, navigate to the EL2C4 folder. At the Change Source: MayGroupSales.xlsx dialog box, double-click *4-Source* in the file list box. Excel returns to the Edit Links dialog box and updates the source workbook file name and path.

e. Click the Close button.

These are the updated source workbook file name and path edited in Steps 7a–7d.

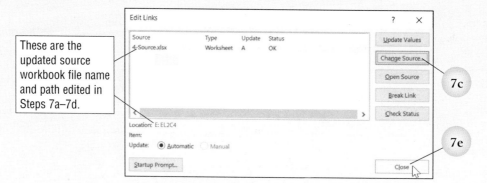

8. Click in cell F9 in the AttendanceSummary worksheet to view the updated linked formula. Notice that the workbook reference in the formula is *[4-Source. xlsx]* and the drive and path are included in the formula. (Your drive and/or path may

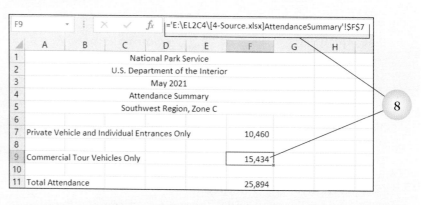

vary from the one shown. If the entire formula is not shown, click the Expand Formula bar down arrow to show the entire formula and then click the Collapse Formula bar up arrow to return the formula bar to one line.)

9. Print the AttendanceSummary worksheet.

10. Save and then close **4-MayEntries**.

Activity 1e Removing a Linked External Reference

Part 5 of 5

1. Open **4-MayEntries**.

2. At the Microsoft Excel message box that states that the workbook contains links to external sources, read the message text and then click the Update button to update the links. *Note: Depending on the system settings on the computer you are using, this message may not appear. Proceed to Step 3.*

3. Remove the linked external reference to attendance values for commercial tour vehicles by completing the following steps:
   a. With the Data tab active, click the Edit Links button in the Queries & Connections group.
   b. Click the Break Link button at the Edit Links dialog box.
   c. Click the Break Links button at the Microsoft Excel message box warning that breaking links permanently converts formulas and external references to their existing values and asking if you are sure you want to break the links.

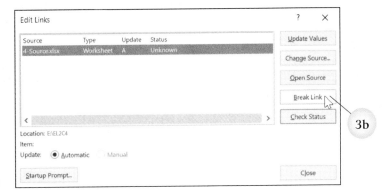

   d. Click the Close button at the Edit Links dialog box with no links displayed.
4. In the AttendanceSummary worksheet with cell F9 active, look in the Formula bar. Notice that the linked formula has been replaced with the latest cell value, *15434*.
5. Save and then close **4-MayEntries**.
6. Reopen **4-MayEntries**. Notice that since the workbook no longer contains a link to an external reference, the security warning no longer appears in the Message bar.
7. Close **4-MayEntries**. Click Don't Save if prompted to save changes.

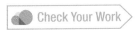

Activity 2 **Calculate Total Fees Billed by Three Dentists**   **1 Part**

You will use the Consolidate feature to summarize the total dental fees billed by treatment category for three dentists.

Summarizing Data Using the Consolidate Feature

Consolidate

Summarizing Data Using the Consolidate Feature

The Consolidate feature is another tool that can be used to summarize data from multiple worksheets into a master worksheet. The worksheets can be located in the same workbook as the master worksheet or in a separate workbook. Open the Consolidate dialog box, shown in Figure 4.3, by clicking the Consolidate button in the Data Tools group on the Data tab.

Quick Steps

Consolidate Data

1. Make starting cell active.
2. Click Data tab.
3. Click Consolidate button.
4. If necessary, change function.
5. Enter first range in *Reference* text box.
6. Click Add button.
7. Enter next range in *Reference* text box.
8. Click Add button.
9. Repeat Steps 7–8 until all ranges have been added.
10. If necessary, click *Top row* and/or *Left column* check boxes.
11. If necessary, click *Create links to source data* check box.
12. Click OK.

Figure 4.3 Consolidate Dialog Box

When the Consolidate dialog box opens, the Sum function is selected by default. Change to a different function, such as Count or Average, using the *Function* drop-down list. In the *Reference* text box, type the range name or use the Collapse Dialog button to navigate to the cells to be consolidated. If the cells are in another workbook, use the Browse button to navigate to the drive and/or folder and locate the file name. Once the correct reference is inserted in the *Reference* text box, click the Add button. Continue adding references for all the units of data to be summarized.

In the *Use labels in* section, click to insert a check mark in the *Top row* or *Left column* check boxes to indicate where the labels are located in the source ranges. Insert a check mark in the *Create links to source data* check box to instruct Excel to update the data automatically when the source ranges change. Make sure enough empty cells are available to the right of and below the active cell when the Consolidate dialog box is opened, since Excel populates the rows and columns based on the size of the source data.

Activity 2 Summarizing Data Using the Consolidate Feature

Part 1 of 1

1. Open **NADQ1Fees**.
2. Save the workbook with the name **4-NADQ1Fees**.
3. The workbook is organized with the first-quarter fees for each of three dentists entered in separate worksheets. Range names have been defined for each dentist's first-quarter earnings. Review the workbook structure by completing the following steps:
   a. Click the Name box arrow and then click *Popovich* at the drop-down list. Excel makes the Popovich worksheet active and selects the range A2:E12.
   b. Deselect the range.
   c. Display the defined range for the range name *Vanket* and then deselect the range.
   d. Display the defined range for the range name *Jones* and then deselect the range.
4. Use the Consolidate feature to total the fees billed by treatment category for each month by completing the following steps:
   a. Make FeeSummary the active worksheet.
   b. Make cell A4 active, if necessary, and then click the Data tab.
   c. Click the Consolidate button in the Data Tools group.

d. With *Sum* selected in the *Function* option box at the Consolidate dialog box and with the insertion point positioned in the *Reference* text box, type Popovich and then click the Add button.

e. With the text *Popovich* selected in the *Reference* text box, type Vanket and then click the Add button.

f. With the text *Vanket* selected in the *Reference* text box, type Jones and then click the Add button.

g. Click the *Top row* and *Left column* check boxes in the *Use labels in* section to insert check marks.

h. Click OK.

5. Deselect the consolidated range in the FeeSummary worksheet.

6. AutoFit the width of each column in the FeeSummary worksheet.

7. Use the Format Painter to apply the formatting options for the column headings and the *Total* row from any of the three dentist worksheets to the FeeSummary worksheet.

8. Print the FeeSummary worksheet.

9. Save and then close **4-NADQ1Fees**.

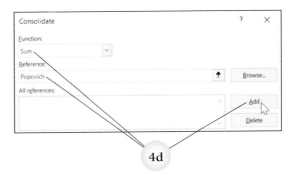

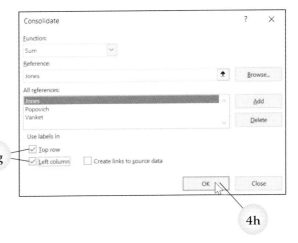

Check Your Work

Activity 3 | **Analyze Fitness Equipment Sales Data in a PivotTable and PivotChart**   **8 Parts**

You will create and edit PivotTables and PivotCharts to analyze fitness equipment sales by region, product, manufacturer, and salesperson. You will change the PivotTable summary function and filter PivotTables using Slicers and a Timeline.

Creating PivotTables

Quick Steps

Create PivotTable
1. Select source range.
2. Click Insert tab.
3. Click PivotTable button.
4. Click OK.
5. Add fields as needed using PivotTable Fields task pane.
6. Modify and/or format as required.

 PivotTable

A PivotTable is an interactive table that allows large worksheets to be manipulated in different ways. It organizes and summarizes data based on fields (column headings) and records (rows). A numeric column is selected and then grouped by the rows and columns category; the data is summarized using a function such as Sum, Average, or Count. PivotTables are useful management tools, since they allow data to be analyzed in a variety of scenarios by filtering a row or column category and instantly seeing the change in results. The interactivity of a PivotTable allows a variety of scenarios to be examined with just a few mouse clicks. Create a PivotTable using the PivotTable button in the Tables group on the Insert tab.

Before creating a PivotTable, examine the source data and determine the following elements:

- Which rows and columns will define how to format and group the data?
- Which numeric field contains the values to be grouped?
- Which summary function will be applied to the values? For example, should the values be summed, averaged, or counted?
- Should it be possible to filter the report as a whole, as well as by columns or rows?
- Should the PivotTable be beside the source data or in a new sheet?
- How many reports should be extracted from the PivotTable by filtering fields?

Creating, Modifying, and Filtering a Recommended PivotTable

Creating a Recommended PivotTable

Click the Recommended PivotTables button to show different PivotTable previews. After the PivotTable is created, it can then be edited and formatted further if required. (You will learn how to format a PivotTable in Activity 3c.)

Recommended PivotTables

To have Excel analyze the data and create a PivotTable using a recommended view, select the source range, click the Insert tab, change the source data if required, and then click the Recommended PivotTables button in the Tables group. Click a PivotTable in the left panel of the Recommended PivotTables dialog box to preview it. Click OK to insert the selected PivotTable.

Building a PivotTable

Building a PivotTable

To build a PivotTable using the PivotTable button in the Tables group on the Insert tab, select the source range or make sure the active cell is positioned within the list range, click the Insert tab, and then click the PivotTable button in the Tables group. At the Create PivotTable dialog box, confirm that the source range is correct and then select whether to place the PivotTable in the existing worksheet or a new worksheet. Figure 4.4 presents the initial PivotTable and PivotTable Fields task pane, in which the report layout is defined. Each column or row heading in the source range becomes a field in the PivotTable Fields task pane list. A PivotTable can also be created by using the Blank PivotTable button in the Tables tab on the Quick Analysis button.

Build a PivotTable by selecting fields in the PivotTable Fields task pane. Click the check box next to a field to insert a check mark and add it to the PivotTable. By default, non-numeric fields are added to the *Rows* box and numeric fields are added to the *Values* box in the layout section of the pane. Once a field has been added, it can be moved to a different box by dragging the field header or clicking the field to display a shortcut menu. As each field is added, the PivotTable updates to show the results. Check and uncheck the various field check boxes to view the data in different scenarios. Figure 4.5 displays the PivotTable built in Activity 3b.

Figure 4.4 PivotTable and PivotTable Fields Task Pane Used to Define the Report Layout

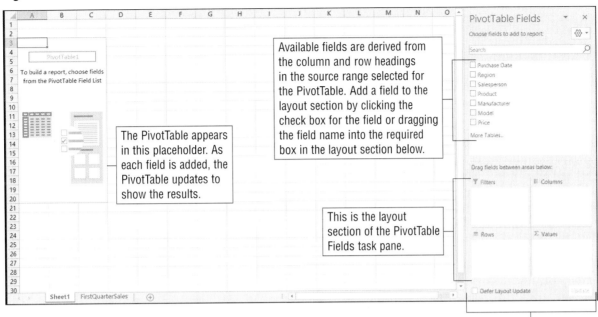

Available fields are derived from the column and row headings in the source range selected for the PivotTable. Add a field to the layout section by clicking the check box for the field or dragging the field name into the required box in the layout section below.

The PivotTable appears in this placeholder. As each field is added, the PivotTable updates to show the results.

This is the layout section of the PivotTable Fields task pane.

When a field is added to the report, Excel adds the header of the field to the corresponding list box in the layout section.

Figure 4.5 PivotTable for Activity 3b

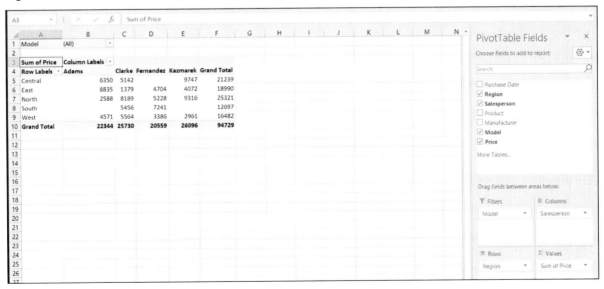

Sum of Price	Column Labels				
Row Labels	Adams	Clarke	Fernandez	Kazmarek	Grand Total
Central	6350	5142		9747	21239
East	8835	1379	4704	4072	18990
North	2588	8189	5228	9316	25321
South		5456	7241		12697
West	4571	5564	3386	2961	16482
Grand Total	22344	25730	20559	26096	94729

1. Open **PFSales**.
2. Save the workbook with the name **4-PFSales**.
3. Create a PivotTable to summarize the price by product by completing the following steps:
   a. A range has been defined to select the list data. Click the Name box arrow and then click *FirstQ* at the drop-down list.
   b. Click the Insert tab.
   c. Click the Recommended PivotTables button in the Tables group.

   d. Click the <u>Change Source Data</u> hyperlink at the bottom of the Recommended PivotTables dialog box to expand the range.

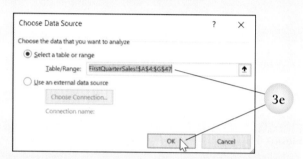

   e. At the Choose Data Source dialog box, with *FirstQuarterSales!$A$4:$G$47* entered in the *Table/Range* text box, click OK.
   f. Click the second PivotTable scenario in the left column to select the *Sum of Price by Product* PivotTable.
   g. Click OK to insert the PivotTable in a new worksheet.

4. Apply the Comma format with no digits after the decimal point to the range B4:B9.
5. Rename the worksheet *PriceByProduct*.
6. Save **4-PFSales**.

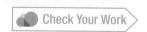

Check Your Work

1. With **4-PFSales** open, make the FirstQuarterSales worksheet active. The FirstQ range should still be selected.
2. Create a PivotTable to summarize fitness equipment sales by region and salesperson, as shown in Figure 4.5 (on page 97), by completing the following steps:
   a. Click the Insert tab.
   b. Click the PivotTable button in the Tables group.
   c. At the Create PivotTable dialog box, with *FirstQuarterSales!$A$4:$G$47* entered in the *Table/Range* text box and *New Worksheet* selected for *Choose where you want the PivotTable report to be placed*, click OK.
   d. Click the *Region* check box in the PivotTable Fields task pane. *Region* is added to the *Rows* list box in the layout section of the task pane and the report updates to show one row per region with a filter arrow at the top of the column and a *Grand Total* row automatically added to the bottom of the table. Since *Region* is a non-numeric field, Excel automatically places it in the *Rows* list box.
   e. Click the *Salesperson* check box in the PivotTable Fields task pane. Excel automatically adds *Salesperson* to the *Rows* list box in the layout section.
   f. Click the *Salesperson* field header in the *Rows* list box in the layout section and then click *Move to Column Labels* at the pop-up list. Notice that the layout of the report now displays one row per region and one column per salesperson.

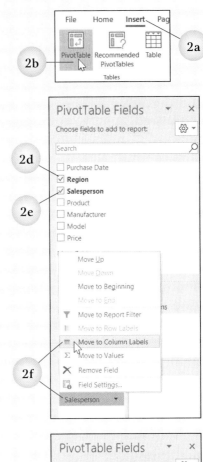

   g. Hover the mouse pointer over *Model* in the PivotTable Fields task pane, click and hold down the left mouse button, drag the field into the *Filters* list box in the layout section, and then release the mouse button. Notice that *Model* is added as a filter at the top left of the PivotTable in the range A1:B1.
   h. Click the *Price* check box in the PivotTable Fields task pane. Since the field is numeric, Excel automatically adds it to the *Values* list box in the layout section and the report updates to show the Sum function applied to the grouped values in the PivotTable. Compare your results with the PivotTable shown in Figure 4.5.
3. Rename the worksheet *SalesByRegion*.
4. Save **4-PFSales**.

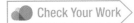
Check Your Work

Formatting and Filtering a PivotTable

When the active cell is positioned inside a PivotTable, the contextual PivotTable Tools Analyze and PivotTable Tools Design tabs become available. The formatting features on the PivotTable Tools Design tab, shown in Figure 4.6, are similar to those on the Table Tools Design tab, which was discussed in Chapter 3.

To filter a PivotTable, click the filter arrow next to Row Labels or Column Labels, click the *(Select All)* check box to remove all the check marks next to the items, and then click the check boxes for the items to show in the PivotTable. Click OK. The PivotTable filters the data to show the items that were checked and the filter arrow changes to indicate that a filter is applied. If a field has been placed in the *Filters* list box, click the filter arrow next to *(All)*, click the *Select Multiple Items* check box, click the *(All)* check box to remove all the check marks next to the items, and then click the check boxes for the items to show in the PivotTable. Click OK.

Figure 4.6 PivotTable Tools Design Tab

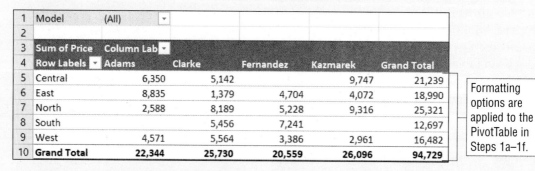

Activity 3c Formatting and Filtering a PivotTable

Part 3 of 8

1. With **4-PFSales** open and the SalesByRegion worksheet active, apply formatting options to the PivotTable to improve the appearance of the report by completing the following steps:
   a. With the active cell positioned in the PivotTable, click the PivotTable Tools Design tab.
   b. Click the More button in the PivotTable Styles gallery.
   c. Click *Light Orange, Pivot Style Medium 10* at the drop-down gallery (third column, second row of the *Medium* section).
   d. Click the *Banded Rows* check box in the PivotTable Style Options group to insert a check mark. Excel adds border lines between the rows in the PivotTable. Recall from Chapter 3 that banding rows or columns adds a fill color or border style, depending on the style that has been applied to the PivotTable.
   e. Apply the Comma format with no digits after the decimal point to the range B5:F10.
   f. Change the width of columns B through F to 12 characters.

	Model	(All)				
1	Model	(All)				
2						
3	Sum of Price	Column Lab				
4	Row Labels	Adams	Clarke	Fernandez	Kazmarek	Grand Total
5	Central	6,350	5,142		9,747	21,239
6	East	8,835	1,379	4,704	4,072	18,990
7	North	2,588	8,189	5,228	9,316	25,321
8	South		5,456	7,241		12,697
9	West	4,571	5,564	3,386	2,961	16,482
10	Grand Total	22,344	25,730	20,559	26,096	94,729

Formatting options are applied to the PivotTable in Steps 1a–1f.

   g. To stop Excel from using AutoFit to adjust the column widths after the cell content has been updated, right-click in the PivotTable and then click *PivotTable Options* at the shortcut menu. The PivotTable Options dialog box opens.

h. On the Layout & Format tab of the PivotTable Options dialog box, click the *Autofit column widths on update* check box to remove the check mark.

i. Click OK.

2. Filter the PivotTable to view sales for a group of product model numbers by completing the following steps:

a. Click the filter arrow next to *(All)* in cell B1.

b. Click the *Select Multiple Items* check box to insert a check mark and turn on the display of check boxes next to all the model numbers in the drop-down list.

c. Click the *(All)* check box to remove the check marks next to all the model numbers.

d. Click the check boxes for those model numbers that begin with *CX* to insert check marks. This selects all six models from Cybex.

e. Click OK.

f. Print the filtered PivotTable.

g. Click the filter arrow next to *(Multiple Items)* in cell B1, click the *(All)* check box to select all the model numbers in the drop-down list, and then click OK.

h. Experiment with the column labels and the row labels filter arrows to filter the PivotTable by region or salesperson.

i. Make sure all the filters are cleared. **Note: To remove all filters, click the (All) check box to insert a check mark**.

3. Save **4-PFSales**.

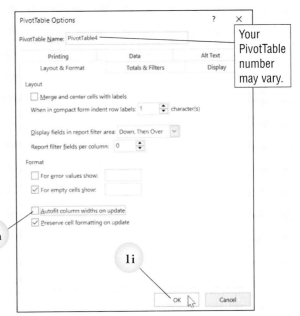

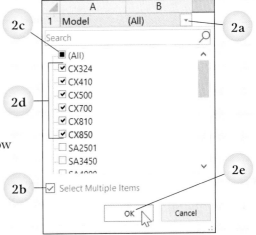

Check Your Work

Changing the PivotTable Summary Function

By default, Excel uses the Sum function to summarize the numeric value added to a PivotTable. To change Sum to another function, click any numeric value within the PivotTable or click the cell containing *Sum of [Fieldname]* at the top left of the PivotTable. Click the PivotTable Tools Analyze tab and then click the Field Settings button in the Active Field group. This opens the Value Field Settings dialog box, where a function other than Sum can be chosen. Alternatively, right-click any numeric value within the PivotTable, point to *Summarize Values By* at the shortcut menu, and then click a function name.

 Field Settings

1. With **4-PFSales** open, save the workbook with the name **4-PFAvgSales**.
2. With the SalesByRegion worksheet active, change the function for the *Price* field from Sum to Average by completing the following steps:
   a. Make cell A3 the active cell in the PivotTable. This cell contains the label *Sum of Price*.
   b. Click the PivotTable Tools Analyze tab.
   c. Click the Field Settings button in the Active Field group.
   d. At the Value Field Settings dialog box with the Summarize Values By tab active, click *Average* in the *Summarize value field by* list box.
   e. Click OK.

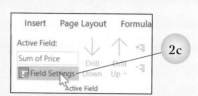

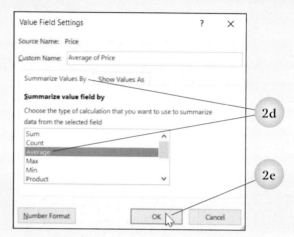

3. Change the page layout to Landscape orientation and then print the revised PivotTable.
4. Save and then close **4-PFAvgSales**.

Filtering a PivotTable Using Slicers

Recall from Chapter 3 that Slicers allow you to filter without using a filter arrow. When Slicers are added to a PivotTable or PivotChart, a Slicer pane containing all the unique values for the specified field is added to the window.

To insert a Slicer pane, make any cell within the PivotTable active, click the PivotTable Tools Analyze tab, and then click the Insert Slicer button in the Filter group. Excel opens the Insert Slicers dialog box, which contains a list of the fields in the PivotTable with a check box next to each field. Click to insert a check mark in the check box for each field to which a Slicer pane is to be added and then click OK.

Click to select one item that Excel should use to filter the list. To select more items, click the Multi-Select button at the top of the Slicer pane. Other ways to select items are to press and hold down the Ctrl key, click each additional item, and then release the Ctrl key or to press Ctrl + S and then select the items.

A Slicer pane can be customized with buttons on the Slicer Tools Options tab. Click a Slicer pane to activate this tab. Click the tab to display customization options, such as Slicer Styles. The height and width of the buttons in the Slicer pane and/or the height and width of the pane can also be changed with options on this tab.

1. Open **4-PFSales**, make PriceByProduct the active worksheet, and then display a Slicer pane for the manufacturer by completing the following steps:
   a. Make any cell active within the PivotTable.
   b. Add *Manufacturer* to the *Filters* list box and *Region* to the *Columns* list box. (If necessary, refer to Activity 3b, Steps 2e–2g for assistance.)
   c. Click the PivotTable Tools Analyze tab.
   d. Click the Insert Slicer button in the Filter group.
   e. At the Insert Slicers dialog box, click the *Manufacturer* check box to insert a check mark.
   f. Click OK. Excel inserts a Slicer pane in the worksheet with all the manufacturer names.
2. If necessary, hover the mouse pointer at the top of the Manufacturer Slicer pane until the pointer changes to a four-headed arrow and then drag the pane into an empty area below the PivotTable.
3. Click *Vision* in the Manufacturer Slicer pane to filter the PivotTable. Excel filters the PivotTable by the *Vision* manufacturer. Notice that the *Manufacturer* filter arrow in cell B1 displays *Vision*.
4. Click the Multi-Select button in the Slicer pane and then click *Cybex* to add another manufacturer to the filter.
5. Click the Clear Filter button at the top right of the Manufacturer Slicer pane to redisplay all the data, and then click the Multi-Select button to deactivate it.

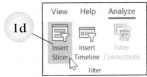

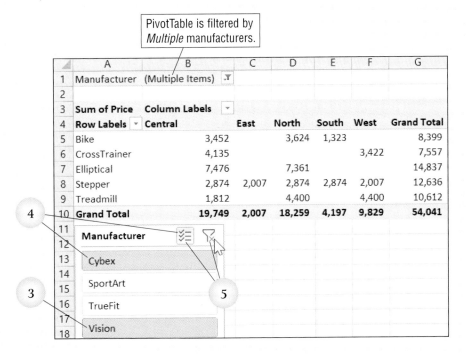

PivotTable is filtered by *Multiple* manufacturers.

	A	B	C	D	E	F	G
1	Manufacturer	(Multiple Items)					
2							
3	**Sum of Price**	**Column Labels**					
4	**Row Labels**	**Central**	**East**	**North**	**South**	**West**	**Grand Total**
5	Bike	3,452		3,624	1,323		8,399
6	CrossTrainer	4,135				3,422	7,557
7	Elliptical	7,476		7,361			14,837
8	Stepper	2,874	2,007	2,874	2,874	2,007	12,636
9	Treadmill	1,812		4,400		4,400	10,612
10	**Grand Total**	**19,749**	**2,007**	**18,259**	**4,197**	**9,829**	**54,041**

Manufacturer

Cybex

SportArt

TrueFit

Vision

6. Add a second Slicer pane and filter by two fields by completing the following steps:
   a. If necessary, make any cell active within the PivotTable.
   b. Click the PivotTable Tools Analyze tab and then click the Insert Slicer button.
   c. At the Insert Slicers dialog box, click the *Region* check box to insert a check mark and then click OK.
   d. Drag the Region Slicer pane below the PivotTable next to the Manufacturer Slicer pane.
   e. Click *West* in the Region Slicer pane to filter the PivotTable.
   f. Click *Vision* in the Manufacturer Slicer pane to filter West region sales by the Vision manufacturer.
7. Print the filtered PivotTable.
8. Redisplay all the data and remove the two Slicer panes by completing the following steps:
   a. Click the Clear Filter button at the top right of the Manufacturer Slicer pane.
   b. Click the Clear Filter button at the top right of the Region Slicer pane.
   c. Right-click the top of the Manufacturer Slicer pane and then click *Remove "Manufacturer"* at the shortcut menu.
   d. Right-click the top of the Region Slicer pane and then click *Remove "Region"* at the shortcut menu.
9. Save **4-PFSales**.

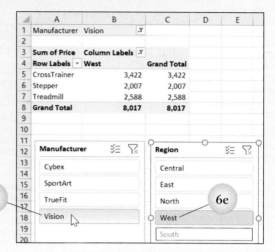

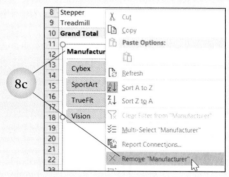

Check Your Work

Filtering a PivotTable Using a Timeline

A Timeline groups and filters a PivotTable or PivotChart based on a specific timeframe. Select a field formatted as a date and a Timeline pane containing a timeline slicer is added to the PivotTable. The timeframe can be extended or shortened to instantly filter the data by the selected date range.

To insert a Timeline, make any cell within the PivotTable active, click the PivotTable Tools Analyze tab, and then click the Insert Timeline button in the Filter group. Excel opens the Insert Timelines dialog box and displays any field that contains data formatted as a date along with a check box next to it. Click to insert a check mark in the check box of any date field to which a Timeline pane is to be added and then click OK. More than one Timeline pane can be open but the data can only be filtered using one Timeline at a time. The PivotTable will display the data for the time period that is selected. Use the Time Level indicator at the upper right of the pane to change the time period to years, quarters, months, or days.

Customize the Timeline pane with buttons on the Timeline Tools Options tab. Click a Timeline pane to activate the Timeline Tools Options tab. Click the tab to display customization options, such as Timeline styles. The height and width of the buttons in the Timeline pane and/or the height and width of the pane can also be changed.

1. With **4-PFSales** open, make the SalesByRegion worksheet active. Display one Timeline for January and then another for February and March combined by completing the following steps:
   a. Make any cell active within the PivotTable.
   b. Click the PivotTable Tools Analyze tab.
   c. Click the Insert Timeline button in the Filter group. Excel displays an Insert Timelines dialog box with all the fields that have been formatted as dates.
   d. Click the check box next to *Purchase Date* in the Insert Timelines dialog box to insert a check mark.
   e. Click OK. Excel inserts a Timeline pane in the worksheet. The selection label displays *All Periods* to indicate that the PivotTable displays all periods.
2. If necessary, hover the mouse pointer at the top of the Timeline pane until the pointer changes to a four-headed arrow and then drag the pane into an empty area below the PivotTable.
3. Click the left scroll arrow at the bottom of the Timeline pane until JAN displays under 2021 and then click *JAN*. Excel filters the PivotTable by January. Notice that the selection label displays *Jan 2021*.
4. Click immediately right of the orange box on the Timeline to filter the PivotTable to include only the sales for February 2021. The selection label displays *Feb 2021*.

Sum of Price	Column Lab				
Row Labels	Adams	Clarke	Fernandez	Kazmarek	Grand Total
Central	5,228	1,007		5,061	11,296
East	3,162	1,379	2,697		7,238
North		2,697	5,228	9,316	17,241
South		5,456	2,875		8,331
West	1,149	5,564	1,379	1,812	9,904
Grand Total	**9,539**	**16,103**	**12,179**	**16,189**	**54,010**

5. Hover the mouse pointer over the orange box representing February, click and hold down the left mouse button, drag the mouse pointer into the orange box representing March, and then release the mouse button. The February timeframe is extended to include March. The selection label displays *Feb - Mar 2021* to indicate that the PivotTable has been filtered to include data for February and March.

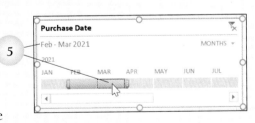

6. Change the page layout to Landscape orientation and then print the filtered PivotTable.
7. Redisplay all the data and remove the Timeline pane by completing the following steps:
   a. Click the Clear Filter button at the top right of the Timeline pane.
   b. Right-click the top of the Timeline pane and then click *Remove Timeline* at the shortcut menu.
8. Save **4-PFSales**.

Check Your Work

Creating a
PivotChart

 PivotChart

Creating a PivotChart

A *PivotChart* displays data in chart form. Like the data in a PivotTable, the data in a PivotChart can be filtered to examine various scenarios between categories. As changes are made to the PivotChart, the PivotTable associated with it also updates. Figure 4.7 displays the PivotChart you will create in Activity 3g.

In a worksheet that already contains a PivotTable, position the active cell anywhere in the PivotTable, click the PivotTable Tools Analyze tab, and then click the PivotChart button in the Tools group to create a chart from the existing summary data. The Insert Chart dialog box displays with a preview of the type of chart to create. Once the PivotChart has been generated, the PivotTable and PivotChart become connected. Making changes to the data by filtering in one causes the other to update with the same filter. For example, filtering the PivotChart by an individual salesperson name causes the PivotTable to filter by the same name.

If a PivotChart is created without a PivotTable, then Excel displays a blank chart, a PivotTable placeholder, and the PivotTable Fields task pane. Build the chart using the same techniques used to build a PivotTable. As the PivotChart is built, Excel also builds a PivotTable that is connected to the PivotChart.

Quick Steps

**Create PivotChart
from PivotTable**

1. Make cell active
   within PivotTable.
2. Click PivotTable Tools
   Analyze tab.
3. Click PivotChart
   button.
4. Select chart type.
5. Click OK.

Figure 4.7 PivotChart for Activity 3g

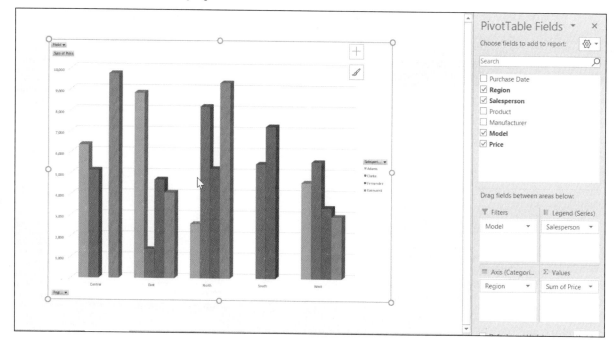

Quick Steps

Create PivotChart without Existing PivotTable
1. Select range containing data for chart.
2. Click Insert tab.
3. Click PivotChart button arrow.
4. Click *PivotChart*.
5. Click OK.
6. Add fields as needed in PivotTable Fields task pane to build chart.
7. Modify and/or format as required.

⊞ **Move Chart**

Before creating a PivotChart from scratch, examine the source data and determine the following:

- Which fields should display along the *x* (horizontal) axis? In other words, how should the data be compared when viewing the chart: by time period (such as months or years), by salesperson name, by department name, or by some other category?

- Which fields should display in the legend? In other words, how many data series (bars in a column chart) should be viewed in the chart: one for each region, product, salesperson, department, or other category?

- Which numeric field contains the values to graph in the chart?

Use the Chart Elements button and the Chart Styles button at the upper right corner of the PivotChart to add or remove titles, labels, or other chart elements and to apply a style or color scheme to the PivotChart. To move the chart to a new sheet, use the Move Chart button in the Actions group on the PivotChart Tools Analyze tab.

Activity 3g Creating a PivotChart Using a PivotTable

1. With **4-PFSales** open, make the SalesByRegion sheet active, if necessary.
2. Create a PivotChart to visually present the data in the PivotTable by completing the following steps:
   a. If necessary, click in any cell within the PivotTable to activate the PivotTable Tools contextual tabs.
   b. Click the PivotTable Tools Analyze tab.
   c. Click the PivotChart button in the Tools group.
   d. At the Insert Chart dialog box with *Column* selected in the left pane, click *3-D Clustered Column* (fourth option above the preview) and then click OK.

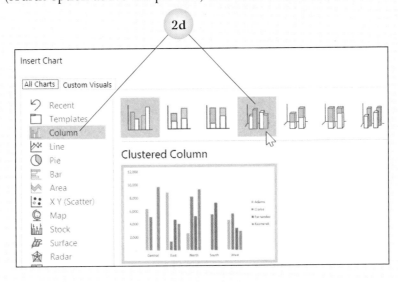

3. Filter the PivotChart to display sales for only one salesperson by completing the following steps:
   a. Click the Salesperson field button in the PivotChart. (This is the button above the salesperson names in the PivotChart legend.)
   b. Click the *(Select All)* check box to clear all the check boxes.
   c. Click the *Kazmarek* check box to insert a check mark.
   d. Click OK.
   e. Notice that the PivotTable behind the chart is also filtered to reflect the display of the chart. ***Note: If the chart is obscuring your view of the PivotTable, drag the PivotChart border to move it out of the way.***
   f. Click the Salesperson field button in the PivotChart and then click *Clear Filter From "Salesperson"*.

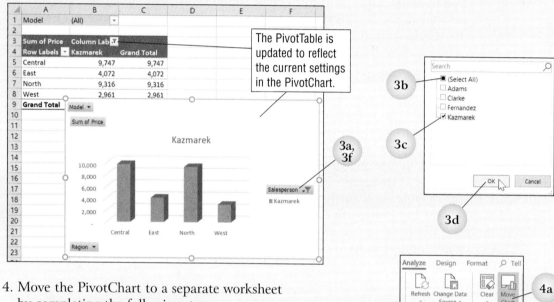

The PivotTable is updated to reflect the current settings in the PivotChart.

4. Move the PivotChart to a separate worksheet by completing the following steps:
   a. Click the Move Chart button in the Actions group on the PivotChart Tools Analyze tab.
   b. At the Move Chart dialog box, click the *New sheet* option and then type PivotChart in the *New sheet* text box.
   c. Click OK. Excel moves the PivotChart to a separate worksheet. Compare your PivotChart with the one shown in Figure 4.7 (on page 106).

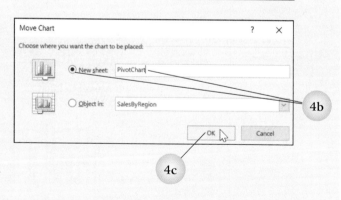

5. Print the PivotChart.
6. Save **4-PFSales**.

Check Your Work

1. With **4-PFSales** open, save the workbook with the name **4-PFChart**.
2. Create a PivotChart to display the sales by manufacturer by region by completing the following steps:
    a. Make the FirstQuarterSales worksheet active, select the named range *FirstQ,* and then click the Insert tab.
    b. Click the PivotChart button arrow in the Charts group and then click *PivotChart* at the drop-down list.

    c. At the Create PivotChart dialog box with *FirstQuarterSales!$A$4:$G$47* entered in the *Table/ Range* text box and *New Worksheet* selected in the *Choose where you want the PivotChart to be placed* section, click OK.
    d. Excel displays a blank sheet with the PivotChart Fields task pane at the right side of the window. A PivotTable placeholder and chart placeholder appear in the worksheet area. As you build the PivotChart, notice that a PivotTable is created automatically.
    e. Click the *Manufacturer* check box in the PivotChart Fields task pane. Excel adds the field to the *Axis (Categories)* list box in the layout section.
    f. Click the *Region* check box in the PivotChart Fields task pane. Excel adds the field below *Manufacturer* in the *Axis (Categories)* list box in the layout section.
    g. Click the *Region* field header in the *Axis (Categories)* list box and then click *Move to Legend Fields (Series)* at the pop-up list. Excel moves the field and updates the chart and PivotTable.

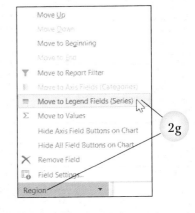

    h. Click the *Price* check box in the PivotTable Fields task pane. Excel graphs the sum of the price values in the PivotChart and updates the PivotTable.
3. Point to the border of the PivotChart and then drag the PivotChart below the PivotTable.
4. Resize the chart to the approximate height and width of the chart shown below.
5. Experiment with the Chart Elements and Chart Styles buttons at the upper right corner of the chart. (See Level 1, Chapter 7 for more information on these buttons.)
6. Rename the sheet containing the PivotTable and PivotChart as *SummaryData.*
7. Deselect the PivotChart and then print the PivotTable and PivotChart worksheet.
8. Save and then close **4-PFChart**.

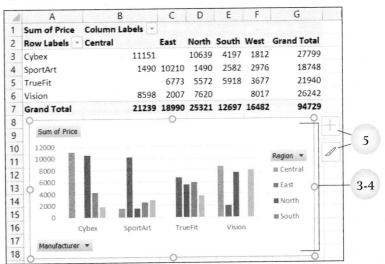

Check Your Work ➤

| Activity 4 | Add Sparklines in a Worksheet to Show Trends | 2 Parts |

You will add and format Sparklines to identify trends in fees for dental services over the first quarter.

 Tutorial

Summarizing Data with Sparklines

Quick Steps

Create Sparklines
1. Select empty range in which to insert Sparklines.
2. Click Insert tab.
3. Click Line, Column, or Win/Loss button in Sparklines group.
4. Type data range address or drag to select data range in *Data Range* text box.
5. Click OK.

Summarizing Data with Sparklines

Sparklines are miniature charts that can be embedded into the background of a cell. Entire charts exist in single cells. Since Sparklines can be placed directly next to the data set being represented, viewing them allows the quick determination of trends or patterns within the data. Consider using Sparklines to illustrate high and low values within a range, as well as trends and other patterns. Figure 4.8 illustrates the three buttons in the Sparklines group used to create Sparkline charts: Line, Column, and Win/Loss.

Creating Sparklines

To create Sparklines, select the empty cell range in which to insert the miniature charts, click the Insert tab, and then click either the Line, Column, or Win/Loss button in the Sparklines group. At the Create Sparklines dialog box, type or click the range of the cells that contain the data to graph in the *Data Range* text box and then click OK.

Figure 4.8 Line, Column, and Win/Loss Sparklines Added to a Worksheet

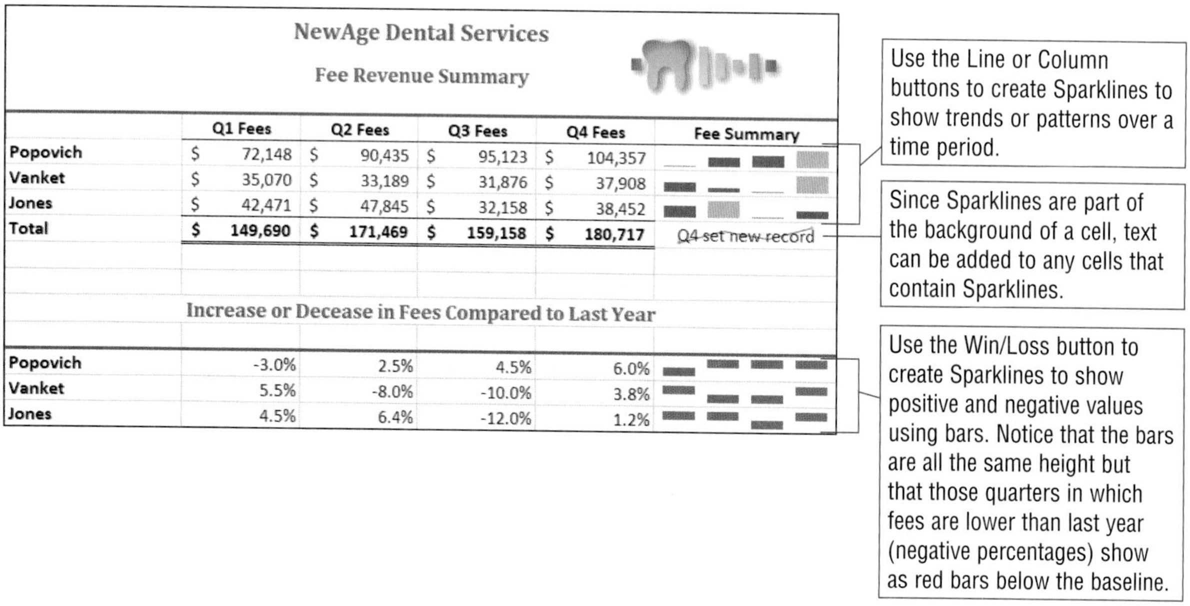

NewAge Dental Services							
Fee Revenue Summary							
	Q1 Fees	Q2 Fees	Q3 Fees	Q4 Fees	Fee Summary	
Popovich	$ 72,148	$ 90,435	$ 95,123	$ 104,357		
Vanket	$ 35,070	$ 33,189	$ 31,876	$ 37,908		
Jones	$ 42,471	$ 47,845	$ 32,158	$ 38,452		
Total	$ 149,690	$ 171,469	$ 159,158	$ 180,717	Q4 set new record	
Increase or Decease in Fees Compared to Last Year						
Popovich	-3.0%	2.5%	4.5%	6.0%		
Vanket	5.5%	-8.0%	-10.0%	3.8%		
Jones	4.5%	6.4%	-12.0%	1.2%		

Use the Line or Column buttons to create Sparklines to show trends or patterns over a time period.

Since Sparklines are part of the background of a cell, text can be added to any cells that contain Sparklines.

Use the Win/Loss button to create Sparklines to show positive and negative values using bars. Notice that the bars are all the same height but that those quarters in which fees are lower than last year (negative percentages) show as red bars below the baseline.

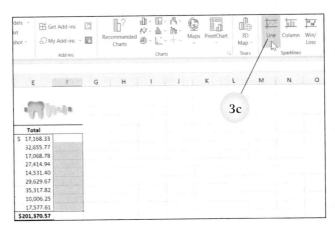

1. Open **4-NADQ1Fees**.
2. Save the workbook with the name **4-NADQ1Fees-4**.
3. Create Sparklines to illustrate the trends in categories of dental service fees during the first quarter by completing the following steps:
   a. With the FeeSummary worksheet active, select the range F5:F13.
   b. Click the Insert tab.
   c. Click the Line button in the Sparklines group.
   d. At the Create Sparklines dialog box with the insertion point positioned in the *Data Range* text box, type b5:d13.
   e. Click OK. Excel inserts miniature line charts within the cells.
   f. Click in any cell to deselect the range.
4. Spend a few moments reviewing the Sparklines to determine what the charts indicate. Notice that the lines in cell F7 (*Teeth Whitening*) and cell F10 (*Crowns and Bridges*) slope up and then downward. This shows that these dental services peaked in February and then began to decline.
5. Save **4-NADQ1Fees-4**.

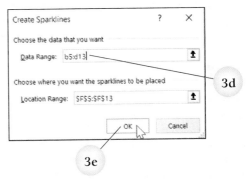

Check Your Work

Customizing Sparklines

Activate any Sparkline cell and then click the Sparkline Tools Design tab to display the contextual tab shown in Figure 4.9. Click the Edit Data button to edit the range used to generate the Sparklines or instruct Excel how to graph hidden or empty cells in the data range. Use buttons in the Type group to change the chart type from Line to Column or Win/Loss. Click the check boxes in the Show group to show or hide data points in the chart or to show markers. Use options in the Style group to change the appearance of line and/or marker. Click the Axis button in the last group to customize the horizontal or vertical axis in the charts. Sparklines can be grouped, ungrouped, or cleared using the last three buttons on the tab.

Figure 4.9 Sparkline Tools Design Tab

1. With **4-NADQ1Fees-4** open, customize the Sparklines by completing the following steps:
   a. If necessary, click in a Sparkline cell and then click the Sparkline Tools Design tab.
   b. Click the Sparkline Color button in the Style group and then click *Dark Red* (first option in the *Standard Colors* section) at the drop-down color palette.
   c. Click the *High Point* check box in the Show group to insert a check mark. Excel adds a marker at the highest point on each line graph.
   d. Click the *Markers* check box in the Show group to insert a check mark. Excel adds markers to all the other data points on each line.
   e. Click the Marker Color button in the Style group, point to *High Point*, and then click *Black, Text 1* (second column, first row in the *Theme Colors* section) at the drop-down color palette.

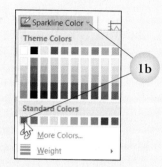

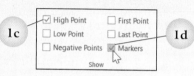

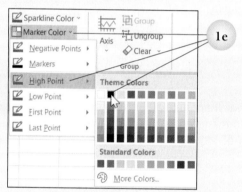

2. Widen the column and add a fill color to improve the appearance of the Sparklines by completing the following steps:
   a. Change the width of column F to 22 characters.
   b. Select the range F5:F13, click the Home tab, and then apply the Aqua, Accent 5, Lighter 80% fill color (ninth column, second row in the *Theme Colors* section) to the selected cells.
   c. Click in any cell to deselect the range.
3. Make cell F4 active, type January to March Trends, press the Enter key, and then, if necessary, format the title so it has the same formatting as the other titles in row 4.
4. Change the page layout to Landscape orientation and then print the FeeSummary worksheet.
5. Save and then close **4-NADQ1Fees-4**.

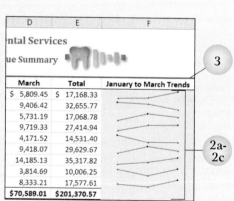

Chapter Summary

- A formula that references a cell in another worksheet within the same workbook contains a worksheet reference and a cell reference separated by an exclamation point.

- Range names can be used to simplify references to cells in other worksheets because the worksheet reference is automatically included in the definition of each range name.

- A disadvantage to using range names to reference other worksheets emerges if several worksheets are to summarized because each name has to be defined before the formula can be created.

- A 3-D reference is used to summarize the same cell in a range that extends over two or more worksheets. A 3-D reference includes the starting worksheet name and ending worksheet name separated by a colon, similar to the method used to define a range of cells.

- A formula that references another worksheet is linked to that worksheet, so that a change made in the source cell is automatically made in the other worksheet. A formula that references a cell in another workbook must include a workbook reference before the worksheet and cell references. The workbook reference is enclosed in square brackets.

- The workbook in which the external reference is added is called the *destination workbook*. The workbook containing the data that is linked to the destination workbook is called the *source workbook*.

- When a formula that links to an external reference is created, Excel includes the drive and folder names in the path to the source workbook. If the source workbook is moved or the source workbook file name is changed, the link will no longer work.

- Open the Edit Links dialog box to edit or remove a linked external reference.

- The Consolidate feature is another tool that can be used to summarize the data from multiple worksheets into a master worksheet. Open the Consolidate dialog box by clicking the Consolidate button is in the Data Tools group on the Data tab.

- At the Consolidate dialog box, the Sum function is selected by default. Add the references containing the data to summarize, specify the location of the labels to duplicate, and indicate whether to create a link to the source data.

- A PivotTable is an interactive table that organizes and summarizes data based on categories in rows or columns. Create a PivotTable using the PivotTable button in the Tables group on the Insert tab.

- Preview different PivotTable scenarios by clicking the Recommended PivotTables button.

- Add fields to a PivotTable using the field name check boxes in the PivotTable Fields task pane.

- Use buttons on the contextual PivotTable Tools Analyze and PivotTable Tools Design tabs to format the PivotTable and/or edit the features used in it.

- Once created, a PivotTable can be used to view a variety of scenarios by filtering the row, column, or report headings.

- Slicers allow filtering data in a PivotTable or PivotChart without using a filter arrow. Because the Slicer pane contains all the items in the designated field, the report can be filtered with one mouse click. Click the Insert Slicer button in the Filter group on the PivotTable Tools Analyze tab to add a Slicer pane to a PivotTable.

- Timelines group and filter data in a PivotTable or PivotChart based on specific timeframes, such as years, quarters, months, and days. With any cell within the PivotTable active, click the PivotTable Analyze tab and then click the Insert Timeline button in the Filter group.

- A PivotChart displays data in chart form. As changes are made to the PivotChart, the PivotTable associated with it also updates. Filter a PivotChart using the legend or axis field buttons on the PivotChart.

- Sparklines are miniature charts inserted into the backgrounds of cells. Add Sparklines to a worksheet to show trends or high or low values in a range of source data.

- To create Sparklines, select the empty cell range in which to insert the miniature charts, click the Insert tab, and then click the chart type in the Sparklines group. At the Create Sparklines dialog box, type or click the range of cells that contain the values to graph and then click OK. Sparklines can be customized using options in the Sparkline Tools Design tab.

Commands Review

FEATURE	RIBBON TAB, GROUP	BUTTON	KEYBOARD SHORTCUT
Consolidate	Data, Data Tools		
edit links	Data, Queries & Connections		
PivotChart	Insert, Charts OR PivotTables Tools Analyze, Tools		
PivotTable	Insert, Tables		
Slicer	PivotTable Tools Analyze, Filter		
Sparklines	Insert, Sparklines		
Timelines	PivotTable Tools Analyze, Filter		

Microsoft Excel® Level 2

Unit 2

Managing and Integrating Data and the Excel Environment

Microsoft®

Excel

Using Data Analysis Features

Performance Objectives

Upon successful completion of Chapter 5, you will be able to:

1 Transpose data arranged in columns to rows and vice versa

2 Perform a mathematical operation during a paste routine

3 Populate cells using Goal Seek

4 Save and display various worksheet models using the Scenario Manager

5 Generate a scenario summary report

6 Create one-variable and two-variable data tables

7 Use auditing tools to view relationships between cells in formulas

8 Identify Excel error message codes and troubleshoot formulas using formula auditing tools

9 Use the Circle Invalid Data feature

10 Use the Watch Window to track cells affected by key formulas

---

Excel's Paste Special dialog box includes several options for pasting copied data. Choose to paste attributes of a copied cell or alter the paste routine to perform a more complex operation. Apply a variety of What-If Analysis tools to manage data and assist with decision-making and management tasks. Use formula-auditing tools to troubleshoot formulas or view dependencies between cells. By working through the activities in this chapter, you will learn about these tools and features available in Excel to assist with accurate data analysis.

 Data Files

Before beginning chapter work, copy the EL2C5 folder to your storage medium and then make EL2C5 the active folder.

The online course includes additional training and assessment resources.

Activity 1 **Analyze Data from a Request for Proposal** **2 Parts**

You will manipulate a worksheet containing vendor quotations for an enterprise resource-planning information system by copying and pasting using Paste Special options.

Tutorial

Pasting Data
Using Paste
Special Options

  Paste

Pasting Data Using Paste Special Options

Clicking the Paste button arrow in the Clipboard group on the Home tab opens the Paste drop-down gallery. This gallery contains many options for pasting copied data and is divided into three sections: *Paste*, *Paste Values*, and *Other Paste Options*. The Paste drop-down gallery includes a live preview of how the data will be pasted to assist in choosing the correct paste option. Click *Paste Special* at the bottom of the Paste drop-down gallery to open the Paste Special dialog box, shown in Figure 5.1. Use options in this dialog box to paste specific attributes of the source data, perform a mathematical operation in the destination range based on values in the source range, or carry out a more complex paste sequence.

Several options in the Paste Special dialog box are also available by clicking a button at the Paste drop-down gallery. For example, to copy a range of cells that has border formatting applied and then paste the range without the borders, click the Paste button arrow and then click the No Borders button (first column, second row in the *Paste* section) at the drop-down gallery. This produces the same result as clicking the Paste button arrow, clicking *Paste Special* at the drop-down gallery, clicking *All except borders* in the *Paste* section of the Paste Special dialog box, and then clicking OK.

Figure 5.1 Paste Special Dialog Box

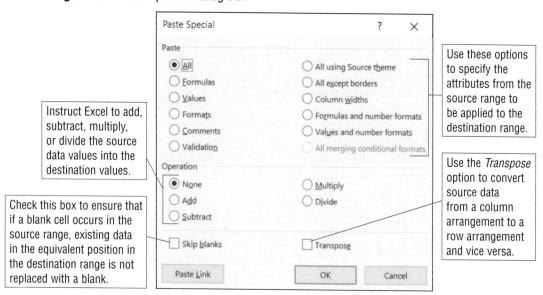

Selecting Other Paste Special Options

A variety of options can be selected at the Paste Special dialog box. Click *Formulas* or *Values* to paste only the source formulas or displayed values, click *Formats* to paste only the formatting options from the source, and click *Validation* to paste a validation rule. Click *All using Source theme* to apply the theme from the source, click *All except borders* to paste everything but the borders from the source, and click *Column widths* to adjust the destination cells to the same column widths as the source. To paste formulas or values including the number formats from the source, click the *Formulas and number formats* option or the *Values and number formats* option.

Transposing Data

Quick Steps

Transpose Range
1. Select source range.
2. Click Copy button.
3. Click starting cell in destination range.
4. Click Paste button arrow.
5. Click Transpose button.

transpose

In some cases, the data in a worksheet is arranged in a way that is not suitable for performing the required analysis. For example, examine the worksheet shown in Figure 5.2. This is the worksheet used in Activity 1. Notice that each company that submitted a proposal appears in a separate column and the criteria for analysis (such as the cost of the hardware) are arranged in rows. At first glance, this layout may seem appropriate but consider that only those vendors that offer five-year contracts are to be examined. To use the filter feature on this data, the contract term needs to be displayed in a columnar format. Rearranging the data in this worksheet manually would be time consuming and risky due to the possibility of making errors. To avoid this, convert the columns to rows and the rows to columns using the Transpose button in the Paste button drop-down gallery or the Paste Special dialog box.

Figure 5.2 Activity 1 Worksheet

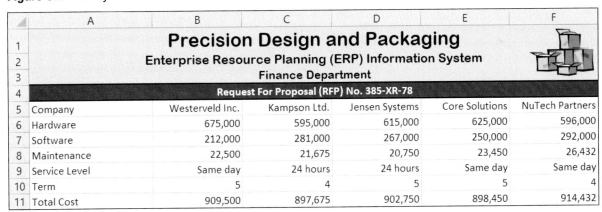

	A	B	C	D	E	F
1		**Precision Design and Packaging**				
2		Enterprise Resource Planning (ERP) Information System				
3		Finance Department				
4		Request For Proposal (RFP) No. 385-XR-78				
5	Company	Westerveld Inc.	Kampson Ltd.	Jensen Systems	Core Solutions	NuTech Partners
6	Hardware	675,000	595,000	615,000	625,000	596,000
7	Software	212,000	281,000	267,000	250,000	292,000
8	Maintenance	22,500	21,675	20,750	23,450	26,432
9	Service Level	Same day	24 hours	24 hours	Same day	Same day
10	Term	5	4	5	5	4
11	Total Cost	909,500	897,675	902,750	898,450	914,432

Activity 1a Converting Data from Rows to Columns   Part 1 of 2

1. Open **PreERP**.
2. Save the workbook with the name **5-PreERP**.
3. Convert the worksheet to arrange the company names in rows and the criteria data in columns by completing the following steps:
   a. Select the range A5:F11.
   b. Click the Copy button.

c. Click in cell A13.

d. Click the Paste button arrow and then hover the mouse pointer over the Transpose button (third column, second row in the *Paste* section) at the drop-down gallery. A live preview shows how the copied data will be pasted. Click the Transpose button.

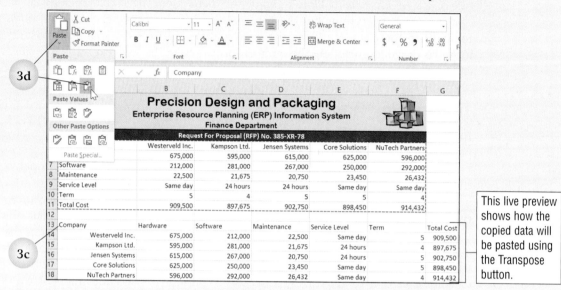

This live preview shows how the copied data will be pasted using the Transpose button.

e. Press the Esc key to remove the scrolling marquee from the source range and then click in any cell to deselect the range.

4. Delete rows 5 through 12.

5. Correct the merge and centering in rows 1 through 4 to extend the titles across columns A through G. If necessary, move or otherwise adjust the position of the picture at the right side of the worksheet after merging and centering.

6. Add a thick bottom border to cells A3 and A4 separately.

7. Apply bold formatting to and center-align the labels in the range A5:G5.

8. Select the range A5:G10, turn on the Filter feature, and then click in any cell to deselect the range.

9. Filter the worksheet to display only those vendors offering five year contracts by completing the following steps:

a. Click the filter arrow in cell F5.

b. Click the *(Select All)* check box.

c. Click the 5 check box and then click OK..

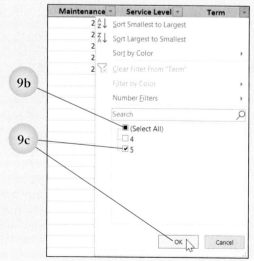

10. Click the filter arrow in cell E5 and then filter the remaining rows to display only those vendors offering same-day service using the same method utilized in Step 9.

Request For Proposal (RFP) No. 385-XR-78						
Company	Hardware	Software	Maintenance	Service Level	Term	Total Co
Westerveld Inc.	675,000	212,000	22,500	Same day	5	909,500
Core Solutions	625,000	250,000	23,450	Same day	5	898,450

10

11. Print the filtered worksheet.
12. Turn off the Filter feature and then save **5-PreERP**.

Performing a Mathematical Operation While Pasting

Quick Steps

Perform Mathematical Operation While Pasting
1. Select source range values.
2. Click Copy button.
3. Click starting cell in destination range.
4. Click Paste button arrow.
5. Click *Paste Special.*
6. Click mathematical operation.
7. Click OK.

A range of cells in a copied source range can be added to, subtracted from, multiplied by, or divided by the cells in the destination range. To do this, open the Paste Special dialog box and then select the mathematical operation to be performed. For example, in the worksheet for Activity 1a, the values in the *Maintenance* column are the annual maintenance fees charged by the various vendors. To compare the fees across all the vendors, the maintenance value for the life cycle of the contract must be known.

In Activity 1b, this calculation will be performed by copying and pasting using a multiply operation. Using this method makes it unnecessary to add a new column to the worksheet to show the maintenance fees for the entire term of the contract.

Activity 1b **Multiplying Source Cell Values by Destination Cell Values**   Part 2 of 2

1. With **5-PreERP** open, select the range F6:F10. These cells contain the terms for each company's individual contract. The data in the *Maintenance* column contains the cost of yearly maintenance while the data in the *Hardware* and *Software* columns contain data for the entire duration of the term.
2. Click the Copy button.
3. Paste the source range and instruct Excel to multiply the values in the *Maintenance* column by the values in the *Term* column when pasting by completing the following steps:
   a. Click in cell D6.
   b. Click the Paste button arrow and then click *Paste Special* at the drop-down gallery.

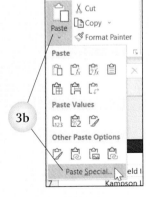

c. Click *Multiply* in the *Operation* section of the Paste Special dialog box and then click OK.

d. Press the *Esc* key to remove the scrolling marquee from the source range and then click in any cell to deselect the range.

4. Print the worksheet.

5. Save and then close **5-PreERP**.

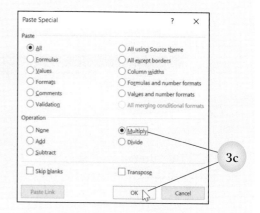

Check Your Work

Using a grades worksheet, you will determine the score a student needs to earn on a final test to achieve a specified final average grade.

Tutorial

Using Goal Seek to Populate a Cell

Quick Steps

Use Goal Seek to Return Value
1. Make cell active.
2. Click Data tab.
3. Click What-If Analysis button.
4. Click *Goal Seek*.
5. Enter cell address in *Set cell* text box.
6. Enter target value in *To value* text box.
7. Enter dependent cell address in *By changing cell* text box.
8. Click OK.
9. Click OK or Cancel.

What-If Analysis

Using Goal Seek to Populate Cells

When the result of a formula is known, use the Goal Seek feature to determine what input value should be entered in one cell to achieve the result of the formula. For example, the worksheet shown in Figure 5.3 shows Whitney's grades on the first four tutoring assessments. The value in cell B11 (average grade) is the average of the five values in the range B5:B9. Note that the final test shows a grade of 0 even though the test has not yet occurred. Once the final test grade is entered, the value in cell B11 will update to reflect the average of all five scores. Suppose Whitney wants to achieve a final average grade of 76% in her tutoring assessments. Goal Seek will determine the score she needs to earn on the final test to achieve the 76% average. In Activity 2, Goal Seek will return a value in cell B9 based on the target value of cell B11.

Goal Seek causes Excel to calculate in reverse. The ending value is specified and Excel figures out the input numbers that will achieve the result that is wanted. Note that the cell in which Excel is to calculate the target value must be referenced by a formula in the *Set cell* text box. Goal Seek is useful for any situation in which the wanted result is known but the value needed to get it is not.

Figure 5.3 Activity 2 Worksheet

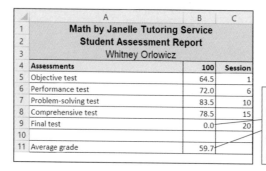

Use Goal Seek to determine the value needed in cell B9 for the final test to achieve the desired average grade in cell B11.

---

1. Open **JTutor.**
2. Save the workbook with the name **5-JTutor.**
3. Use Goal Seek to find the score Whitney needs to earn on the final test to achieve a 76% average grade by completing the following steps:
   a. Make cell B11 active.
   b. Click the Data tab.
   c. Click the What-If Analysis button in the Forecast group and then click *Goal Seek* at the drop-down list.
   d. If necessary, drag the Goal Seek dialog box so you can see all the values in column B.
   e. With *B11* already entered in the *Set cell* text box, click in the *To value* text box and then type 76.
   f. Press the Tab key and then type b9 in the *By changing cell* text box.
   g. Click OK.
   h. Click OK at the Goal Seek Status dialog box, which shows that Excel found a solution.

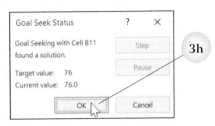

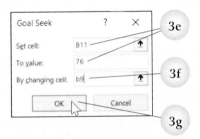

4. Notice that Excel entered the value *81.5* in cell B9. This is the score Whitney must earn to achieve a final average grade of 76%.
5. Assume that Whitney wants to achieve a final average grade of 80%. Use Goal Seek to find the score she will need to earn on the final test to accomplish the new target by completing the following steps:
   a. Click the What-If Analysis button and then click *Goal Seek* at the drop-down list.
   b. With *B11* already entered in the *Set cell* text box, click in the *To value* text box, type 80, and then press the Tab key.
   c. Type b9 in the *By changing cell* text box.
   d. Click OK.
   e. Notice that the value entered in cell B9 is *101.5*. This is the score Whitney needs on the final test to earn an 80% average grade.
   f. The final test is worth only 100, so Whitney will not be able to score 101.5. Restore the previous values in the report by clicking the Cancel button at the Goal Seek Status dialog box.

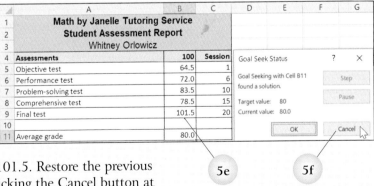

6. Save, print, and then close **5-JTutor.**

Check Your Work

Activity 3 Forecast a Budget Based on Various Inflation Rates — 3 Parts

You will determine how various rates of inflation impact a department's budget to determine the funding request to present to management to maintain service.

Tutorial
Adding Scenarios

Tutorial
Editing and Applying Scenarios

Quick Steps

Add Scenario
1. Click Data tab.
2. Click What-If Analysis button.
3. Click *Scenario Manager*.
4. Click Add button.
5. Type name in *Scenario name* text box.
6. Type or select variable cells in *Changing cells* text box.
7. Click OK.
8. Enter value for each changing cell.
9. Click OK.
10. Click Close button.

Hint Create a range name for each changing cell. This allows a descriptive reference next to the input text box, rather than a cell address, when adding a scenario.

Adding, Editing, and Applying Scenarios

The Scenario Manager allows storing multiple sets of assumptions about data and then viewing how each set of assumptions affects the worksheet. Switch between scenarios to test the various inputs on the worksheet model. Save each scenario using a descriptive name, such as *BestCase* or *WorstCase*, to indicate the type of data assumptions stored in it. Generally, the first scenario created should contain the original values in the worksheet, since Excel replaces the content of each changing cell when a scenario is shown.

Examine the worksheet shown in Figure 5.4. In it, the Computing Services Department budget for the next year has been calculated based on projected percentage increases for various expense items. Assume that the department manager has more than one projected increase for each expense item based on different inflation rates or vendor rate increases for next year. The manager can create and save various scenarios to view the impact on total costs that results from a combination of different forecasts.

Using the Scenario Manager dialog box, shown in Figure 5.5, create as many models as needed to test various what-if conditions. For example, two scenarios have been saved in the example shown in Figure 5.5: *LowInflation* and *HighInflation*. When a scenario is added, define which cells will change and then enter the data to be stored under the new scenario name.

Figure 5.4 Activity 3 Worksheet

	A	B	C	D
1	National Online Marketing Inc.			
2	Computing Services Department			
3		Current Budget	Projected Increase	New Budget
4	Wages and benefits	483,437	16,920	500,357
5	Computer supplies	195,455	2,931	198,386
6	Training and development	83,005	8,300	91,305
7	Other administrative costs	64,448	3,222	67,670
8	Total costs:	$ 826,345		$ 857,718

Figure 5.5 Scenario Manager Dialog Box and Scenario Values Dialog Box

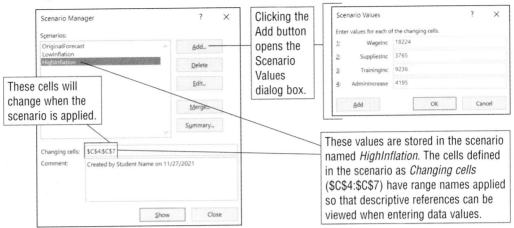

These cells will change when the scenario is applied.

Clicking the Add button opens the Scenario Values dialog box.

These values are stored in the scenario named *HighInflation*. The cells defined in the scenario as *Changing cells* ($C$4:$C$7) have range names applied so that descriptive references can be viewed when entering data values.

Activity 3a Adding Scenarios to a Worksheet Model

Part 1 of 3

1. Open **NationalBdgt.**
2. Save the workbook with the name **5-NationalBdgt.**
3. View the range names already created in the worksheet by clicking the Name box arrow and then clicking *WageInc* at the drop-down list. Cell C4 becomes active. A range name has been created for each data cell in column C, so a descriptive label displays when scenarios are added in Steps 4 and 5.
4. Add a scenario, named *OriginalForecast*, that contains the original worksheet values by completing the following steps:
   a. Click the Data tab.
   b. Click the What-If Analysis button and then click *Scenario Manager* at the drop-down list.
   c. Click the Add button at the Scenario Manager dialog box.
   d. At the Add Scenario dialog box with the insertion point positioned in the *Scenario name* text box, type OriginalForecast and then press the Tab key.
   e. Type c4:c7 in the *Changing cells* text box. (As an alternative, move the dialog box out of the way and select the cells that will change in the worksheet.)
   f. Click OK.

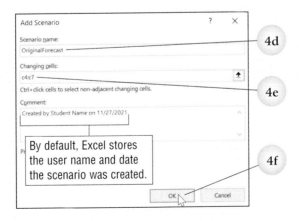

By default, Excel stores the user name and date the scenario was created.

Excel Level 2 | Unit 2

Chapter 5 | Using Data Analysis Features   **125**

g. At the Scenario Values dialog box, notice that the original value is already entered in each text box. Click OK.

5. Add another scenario to the worksheet that assumes low inflation for next year by completing the following steps:

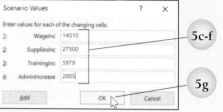

a. Click the Add button at the Scenario Manager dialog box. Notice that the *Changing cells* text box already contains the range C4:C7.

b. Type LowInflation in the *Scenario name* text box and then click OK.

c. At the Scenario Values dialog box, with the insertion point positioned in the *1: WageInc* text box, type 14010 and then press the Tab key.

d. Type 27500 and then press the Tab key.

e. Type 5979 and then press the Tab key.

f. Type 2005.

g. Click OK.

6. Add a third scenario named *HighInflation*, which assumes a high inflation rate, by completing the following steps:

a. Click the Add button at the Scenario Manager dialog box.

b. Type HighInflation in the *Scenario name* text box and then click OK.

c. At the Scenario Values dialog box, type the following values into the text boxes indicated:

1: WageInc	18224
2: SuppliesInc	3765
3: TrainingInc	9236
4: AdminIncrease	4195

d. Click OK.

7. Click the Close button to close the Scenario Manager dialog box.

8. Save **5-NationalBdgt.**

Applying a Scenario

Quick Steps

Apply Scenario
1. Click Data tab.
2. Click What-If Analysis button.
3. Click *Scenario Manager* at drop-down list.
4. Click scenario name.
5. Click Show button.
6. Click Close button.

After creating the various scenarios to save with the worksheet, apply the values stored in each scenario to the variable cells to view the effects on the worksheet model. To do this, open the Scenario Manager dialog box, click the name of the scenario that contains the values to be applied to the worksheet, and then click the Show button. Click the Close button to close the Scenario Manager dialog box.

Editing a Scenario

Change the values associated with a scenario by opening the Scenario Manager dialog box, clicking the name of the scenario that contains the values to be changed, and then clicking the Edit button. At the Edit Scenario dialog box, make any changes to the scenario name and/or changing cells and then click OK to open the Scenario Values dialog box to edit the individual value associated with each changing cell. When done, click OK and then click the Close button.

Deleting a Scenario

To delete a scenario, open the Scenario Manager dialog box, click the scenario to be removed, and then click the Delete button. Click the Close button to close the Scenario Manager dialog box.

---

1. With **5-NationalBdgt** open, apply the scenario that assumes the low inflation rate by completing the following steps:

   a. With Data the active tab, click the What-If Analysis button and then click *Scenario Manager* at the drop-down list.

   b. If necessary, drag the Scenario Manager dialog box so you can see all the values in column D.

   c. Click *LowInflation* in the *Scenarios* list box and then click the Show button. Excel changes the values in the range C4:C7 to the values stored within the scenario. Notice that based on the assumption of a low inflation rate, the total cost of the new budget shown in cell D8 is $875,839.

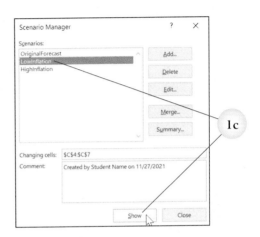

2. With the Scenario Manager dialog box still open, change the worksheet to display the scenario that assumes a high inflation rate by clicking *HighInflation* in the *Scenarios* list box and then clicking the Show button. Notice that in this high-inflation scenario, the total cost of the new budget is $861,765.

3. After the data are reviewed, it is decided that the projected increase for computer supplies should be $4,500. Edit the HighInflation scenario by completing the following steps:

   a. With *HighInflation* selected in the *Scenarios* list box, click the Edit button.

   b. Click OK at the Edit Scenario dialog box.

   c. Select *3765* in the *SuppliesInc* text box and then type 4500.

   d. Click OK and then click the Show button.

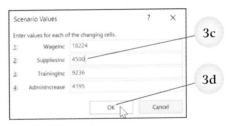

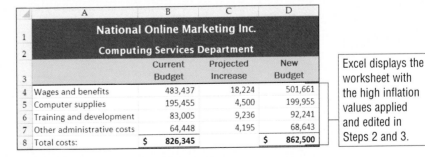

	A	B	C	D
1		National Online Marketing Inc.		
2		Computing Services Department		
3			Current Budget	Projected Increase	New Budget
4	Wages and benefits	483,437	18,224	501,661
5	Computer supplies	195,455	4,500	199,955
6	Training and development	83,005	9,236	92,241
7	Other administrative costs	64,448	4,195	68,643
8	Total costs:	$ 826,345		$ 862,500

Excel displays the worksheet with the high inflation values applied and edited in Steps 2 and 3.

4. Show the worksheet with the data values from the OriginalForecast scenario.
5. Click the Close button to close the Scenario Manager dialog box.
6. Save **5-NationalBdgt**.

Check Your Work

Tutorial

Generating
a Scenario
Summary Report

Generating a Scenario Summary Report

Create a scenario summary report to compare scenarios side by side in a worksheet or PivotTable. At the Scenario Summary dialog box, shown in Figure 5.6, enter in the *Result cells* text box the formula cell or cells that change when the data is applied in the various scenarios. Enter multiple cell addresses in this text box and use commas to separate them.

Quick Steps

**Create Scenario
Summary Report**
1. Click Data tab.
2. Click What-If
 Analysis button.
3. Click *Scenario
 Manager.*
4. Click Summary
 button.
5. If necessary, change
 cell address in
 Result cells text box.
6. Click OK.

Figure 5.6 Scenario Summary Dialog Box

Enter the address of the cell containing the total or other formula results affected by the changing cells in each scenario. Enter cell addresses for multiple results separated by commas or use a range if applicable.

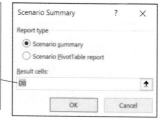

Activity 3c Generating a Scenario Summary Report

Part 3 of 3

1. With **5-NationalBdgt** open, display a scenario summary report by completing the following steps:
   a. With Data the active tab, click the What-If Analysis button and then click *Scenario Manager* at the drop-down list.
   b. Click the Summary button at the Scenario Manager dialog box.
   c. At the Scenario Summary dialog box, with the *Report type* set to *Scenario summary* and *Result cells* displaying the address D8, click OK.
2. Examine the Scenario Summary sheet added to the workbook. It displays each changing cell with the input for each scenario. Below the Changing Cells table, Excel displays the Result Cells, which provide the values that result from input from each scenario.
3. Print the Scenario Summary worksheet.
4. Save and then close **5-NationalBdgt**.

In Step 2, examine the Scenario Summary report created in Step 1.

Scenario Summary				
	Current Values:	OriginalForecast	LowInflation	HighInflation
Changing Cells:				
WageInc	16,920	16,920	14,010	18,224
SuppliesInc	2,931	2,931	27,500	4,500
TrainingInc	8,300	8,300	5,979	9,236
AdminIncrease	3,222	3,222	2,005	4,195
Result Cells:				
TotalNewCosts	$ 857,718	$ 857,718	$ 875,839	$ 862,500
Notes: Current Values column represents values of changing cells at time Scenario Summary Report was created. Changing cells for each scenario are highlighted in gray.				

Check Your Work

Activity 4 | **Compare the Effects of Various Inputs Related to Cost and Sales Pricing** | **2 Parts**

Using one-variable and two-variable data tables, you will analyze the effects on the cost per unit and the selling price per unit of a manufactured container.

Performing What-If Analysis Using Data Tables

The term *data table* refers to a range of cells that contains a series of input values. Excel calculates a formula substituting each input value in the data table range and places the result in the cell adjacent to the value. Either a one-variable or a two-variable data table can be created. A one-variable data table calculates a formula by modifying one input value in the formula. A two-variable data table calculates a formula substituting two input values. Using data tables provides a means of analyzing various outcomes in a calculation that occur as a result of changing a dependent value without creating multiple formulas.

 Tutorial

Creating a
One-Variable
Data Table

 Data Table

Quick Steps

Create One-Variable Data Table
1. Create variable data in column at right of worksheet.
2. Enter formula one row above and one cell right of variable data.
3. Select data range, including formula cell.
4. Click Data tab.
5. Click What-If Analysis button.
6. Click *Data Table.*
7. Type cell address for variable data in source formula in *Column input cell* text box.
8. Click OK.

Creating a One-Variable Data Table

Design a one-variable data table with the variable input data values in a series down a column or across a row. Examine the worksheet shown in Figure 5.7. Assume that management wants to calculate the effects on the cost per unit for a variety of production volumes given a standard set of costs per factory shift. The worksheet includes the total costs for direct materials, direct labor, and overhead.

The formula in cell B8 sums the three cost categories. Based on a standard production volume of 500,000 units, the cost per unit is $3.21, calculated by dividing the total cost by the production volume (cell B8 divided by cell B10). In the range E6:E12, the factory manager has input varying levels of production. The manager would like to see the change in the cost per unit for each level of production volume, assuming the costs remain the same. In Activity 4a, a data table is used to show the various costs. This data table will manipulate one input value—production volume—so it is a one-variable data table.

Figure 5.7 Activity 4a One-Variable Data Table

	A	B	C	D	E	F	G	H
1			**Precision Design and Packaging**					
2			**Cost Price Analysis**					
3			"E" Container Bulk Cargo Box					
4	Factory costs per shift				Variable unit production impact on cost			
5	Direct materials	$ 580,000						
6	Direct labor	880,552			425,000			
7	Overhead	145,350			450,000			
8	Total cost	$ 1,605,902			475,000			
9					500,000			
10	Standard production	500,000 units			525,000			
11					550,000			
12	Cost per unit	$ 3.21			575,000			

In this area of the worksheet, calculate the change in cost per unit based on varying the production volume using a data table.

1. Open **PreEBoxCost**.
2. Save the workbook with the name **5-PreEBoxCost**.
3. Calculate the cost per unit for seven different production levels using a one-variable data table by completing the following steps:
   a. In a data table, the formula for calculating the various outcomes must be placed in the cell in the first row above and one column right of the table values. The data table values have been entered in the range E6:E12; therefore, make cell F5 active.
   b. The formula that calculates the cost per unit is *=B8/B10*. This formula has already been entered in cell B12. Link to the source formula by typing =b12 and then pressing the Enter key.

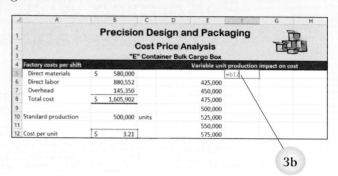

3b

   c. Select the range E5:F12.
   d. Click the Data tab.
   e. Click the What-If Analysis button in the Forecast group and then click *Data Table* at the drop-down list.

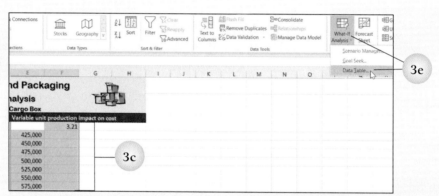

3e

3c

   f. At the Data Table dialog box, click in the *Column input cell* text box and then type b10. At the Data Table dialog box, Excel needs to know which reference in the source formula is the address where the variable data is to be inserted. (The production volume is cell B10 in the source formula.)
   g. Click OK.
   h. Click in any cell to deselect the range.
4. Print the worksheet.
5. Save and then close **5-PreEBoxCost**.

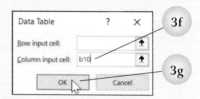

3f

3g

Variable unit production	
	3.21
425,000	3.78
450,000	3.57
475,000	3.38
500,000	3.21
525,000	3.06
550,000	2.92
575,000	2.79

The data table calculates costs at all the production volumes. Notice that the costs are higher at lower volumes and decrease as the production volume increases.

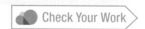

Check Your Work

Tutorial

Creating Two-
Variable Data
Table

Creating a Two-Variable Data Table

A data table can substitute two variables in a source formula. To modify two input cells, design the data table with a column along the left containing one set of variable input values and a row along the top containing a second set of variable input values. In a two-variable data table, the source formula is placed at the top left cell in the table. In the worksheet shown in Figure 5.8, the source formula will be inserted in cell E5, which is the top left cell in the data table.

Quick Steps

Create Two-Variable Data Table

1. Create variable data at right of worksheet with one input series in column and another in row across top of table.
2. Enter formula in top left cell of table.
3. Select data table range.
4. Click Data tab.
5. Click What-If Analysis button.
6. Click *Data Table*.
7. Type cell address for variable data in source formula in *Row input cell* text box.
8. Press Tab key.
9. Type cell address for variable data in source formula in *Column input cell* text box.
10. Click OK.

Figure 5.8 Activity 4b Two-Variable Data Table

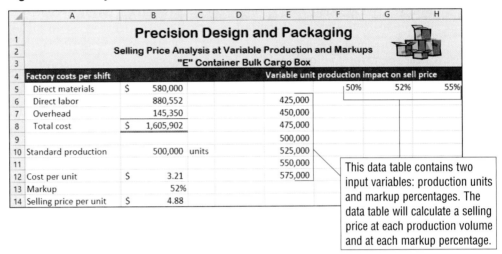

This data table contains two input variables: production units and markup percentages. The data table will calculate a selling price at each production volume and at each markup percentage.

Activity 4b Creating a Two-Variable Data Table

Part 2 of 2

1. Open **PreEBoxSell**.
2. Save the workbook with the name **5-PreEBoxSell**.
3. Calculate the selling price per unit for seven different production levels and three different markups using a two-variable data table by completing the following steps:
   a. In a two-variable data table, the source formula must be placed in the top left cell in the data table; therefore, make cell E5 active.
   b. Type **=b14** and then press the Enter key. The formula that Excel is to use to create the data table is in cell B14. The selling price per unit, found in cell B14, is calculated by adding the cost per unit (cell B12) to the result of multiplying the cost per unit (cell B12) by the markup (cell B13).
   c. Select the range E5:H12.
   d. Click the Data tab.
   e. Click the What-If Analysis button and then click *Data Table* at the drop-down list.

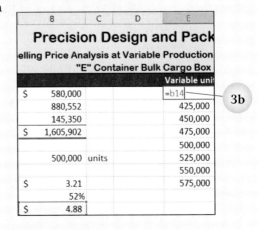

f. At the Data Table dialog box with the insertion point positioned in the *Row input cell* text box, type b13 and then press the Tab key. Excel needs to know which reference in the source formula is the address relating to the variable data in the first row of the data table. (The markup value is in cell B13 in the source formula.)

g. Type b10 in the *Column input cell* text box. As in Activity 4a, Excel needs to know which reference relates to the production volume in the source formula.

h. Click OK.

i. Click in any cell to deselect the range.

4. Print the worksheet.

5. Save and then close **5-PreEBoxSell**.

Data Table	? ×		3f
Row input cell:	b13	⬆	
Column input cell:	b10	⬆	3g
OK	Cancel		
			3h

Variable unit production impact on sell price			
$ 4.88	50%	52%	55%
425,000	5.67	5.74	5.86
450,000	5.35	5.42	5.53
475,000	5.07	5.14	5.24
500,000	4.82	4.88	4.98
525,000	4.59	4.65	4.74
550,000	4.38	4.44	4.53
575,000	4.19	4.25	4.33

The selling price is calculated by the data table at each production volume and each percentage markup.

Check Your Work

Activity 5 **Audit a Worksheet to View and Troubleshoot Formulas** **3 Parts**

You will use buttons in the Formula Auditing group to view relationships between cells that comprise a formula, identify error codes in a worksheet, and troubleshoot errors using error checking tools.

Using Auditing Tools

Using Auditing Tools

The Formula Auditing group on the Formulas tab, shown in Figure 5.9, contains options that are useful for viewing relationships between cells in formulas. Checking a formula for accuracy can be difficult when it is part of a complex sequence of operations. Opening a worksheet created by someone else can also present a challenge in understanding the relationships between sets of data. When Excel displays an error message in a cell, finding the source of the error can be made easier by viewing the relationships between the dependencies of cells.

Trace Precedent Cells
1. Open worksheet.
2. Make cell active.
3. Click Formulas tab.
4. Click Trace Precedents button.
5. Continue clicking until all relationships are visible.

Trace Dependent Cells
1. Open worksheet.
2. Make cell active.
3. Click Formulas tab.
4. Click Trace Dependents button.
5. Continue clicking until all relationships are visible.

Figure 5.9 Formula Auditing Group on the Formulas Tab

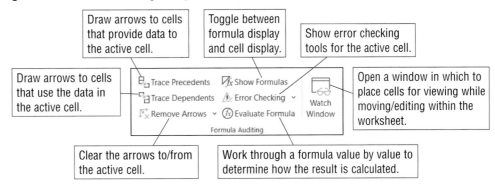

Draw arrows to cells that provide data to the active cell.

Toggle between formula display and cell display.

Show error checking tools for the active cell.

Draw arrows to cells that use the data in the active cell.

Open a window in which to place cells for viewing while moving/editing within the worksheet.

Clear the arrows to/from the active cell.

Work through a formula value by value to determine how the result is calculated.

Tracing Precedent and Dependent Cells

Precedent cells provide data to formula cells. For example, if cell B3 contains the formula $=B1+B2$, then cell B1 and cell B2 are precedent cells. Dependent cells contain formulas that refer to other cells. In the previous example, cell B3 is the dependent cell to cells B1 and B2, since cell B3 relies on the data from cells B1 and B2.

 Trace Precedents

Click in a cell and then click the Trace Precedents button to draw tracer arrows that show direct relationships to a cell or cells that provide data to the active cell. Click the button a second time to show indirect relationships to a cell or cells that provide data to the active cell at the next level. Continue clicking the button until no further arrows are drawn. Excel will sound a beep if the button is clicked and no more relationships exist.

 Trace Dependents

Click in a cell and then click the Trace Dependents button to draw tracer arrows that show direct relationships to other cells in the worksheet that use the contents of the active cell. As with the Trace Precedents button, click a second time to show the next level of indirect relationships and continue clicking the button until no further tracer arrows are drawn.

 Remove Arrows

 Show Formulas

Excel draws blue tracer arrows if no error is detected in the active cell and red tracer arrows if an error is detected within the active cell.

Activity 5a Viewing Relationships between Cells and Formulas

Part 1 of 3

1. Open **5-PreEBoxSell**.
2. Display tracer arrows between cells to view the relationships between cells and formulas by completing the following steps:
   a. Make cell B8 active.
   b. Click the Formulas tab.
   c. Click the Trace Precedents button in the Formula Auditing group. Excel draws a blue tracer arrow that shows the cells that provide data to cell B8.
   d. Click the Remove Arrows button in the Formula Auditing group. The blue tracer arrow leading to cell B8 is cleared.
   e. Make cell B14 active.

This blue precedent arrow is drawn to cell B8 in Step 2c.

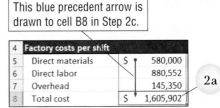

f. Click the Trace Precedents button.

g. Click the Trace Precedents button a second time to show the next level of cells that provide data to cell B14.

h. Click the Trace Dependents button to view the cell dependent on cell B14.

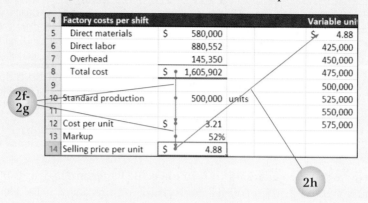

3. Click the Remove Arrows button in the Formula Auditing group to clear all the arrows.

4. Click the Show Formulas button in the Formula Auditing group to display the cell formulas. Click the Show Formulas button again to turn off the display of formulas.

5. Close **5-PreEBoxSell**. Click the Don't Save button when prompted to save changes.

Troubleshooting Formulas

Formulas in Excel can contain various types of errors. Some errors are obvious because Excel displays an error message, such as *#VALUE!* Other errors occur without the display of an error message but are incorrect because the logic is flawed. For example, a formula could be entered in a cell that Excel does not flag as an error because the syntax is correct; however, the calculation could be incorrect for the data and the situation. Logic errors are difficult to find and require checking a worksheet by entering proof formulas or by manually checking the accuracy of each formula.

A proof formula is a formula entered outside the main worksheet area that checks key figures within the worksheet. For example, in a payroll worksheet, a proof formula to check the total net pay column could add the total net pay to the totals of all the deduction columns. The total displayed should be equal to the total gross pay amount in the worksheet.

Excel displays an error message code in a cell that is detected to have an error. Two types of error flags can occur. A green diagonal triangle in the upper left corner of a cell indicates an error condition. Activate the cell and an error checking button displays that can be used to access error checking tools. Errors can also be indicated with text entries, such as *#NAME?* Figure 5.10 displays a portion of the worksheet used in Activity 5b to troubleshoot errors. Table 5.1 describes the three types of error codes displayed in Figure 5.10.

Error Checking

Evaluate Formula

The Error Checking button in the Formula Auditing group can be used to help find the source of an error condition in a cell by displaying the Error Checking dialog box or drawing a red tracer arrow to locate the source cell that is contributing to the error. The Evaluate Formula button can be used to work through a formula value by value to determine where within the formula an error exists.

Figure 5.10 Activity 5b Partial Worksheet

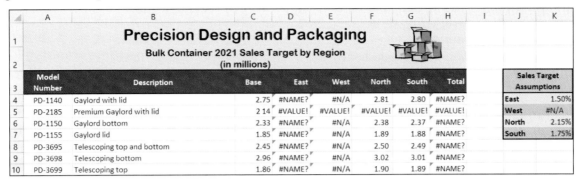

Table 5.1 Types of Error Codes in Figure 5.10

Error Code	Description of Error Condition
#N/A	A required value for the formula is not available.
#NAME?	The formula contains an unrecognized entry.
#VALUE!	A value within the formula is of the wrong type or otherwise invalid.

Activity 5b Troubleshooting Formulas

Part 2 of 3

1. Open **PreSalesTrgt**.
2. Save the workbook with the name **5-PreSalesTrgt**.
3. Solve the #N/A error by completing the following steps:
   a. Make cell E4 active.
   b. Point to the Trace Error button next to the cell and read the ScreenTip below the button.
   c. Look in the Formula bar at the formula that has been entered into the cell. Notice that the formula includes a reference to a named cell. Tracer arrows will be used in the next step to locate the source of the named cell.

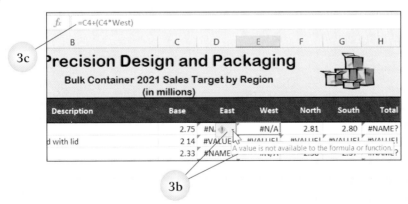

d. Click the Error Checking button arrow in the Formula Auditing group on the Formulas tab and then click *Trace Error* at the drop-down list.

e. Excel moves the active cell to cell K5 and draws a red tracer arrow from cell K5 to cell E4. Look in the Formula bar and notice that *#N/A* displays as the entry in cell K5. Also notice that the cell name *West* displays in the Name box. Since there is no value in the cell named *West*, which is cell K5, the dependent cell E4 is not able to calculate its formula.

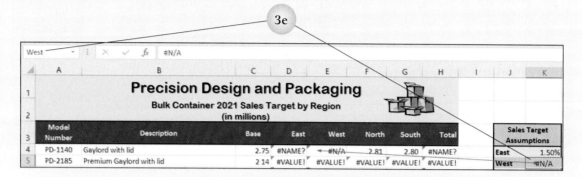

f. With cell K5 active, type 1.25% and then press the Enter key. The red tracer arrow changes to blue because the error is corrected and the #N/A error messages no longer display.

g. Click the Remove Arrows button to clear the blue tracer arrow and then right-align the entry in cell K5.

4. Solve the #NAME? error by completing the following steps:

a. Make cell D4 active, point to the Trace Error button that appears, and then read the ScreenTip that appears. The message indicates that the formula contains unrecognized text.

b. Look at the entry in the Formula bar: *=C4+(C4*East)*. Notice that the formula is the same as the one reviewed in Step 3c except that the named range is *East* instead of *West*. The formula appears to be valid.

c. Click the Name box arrow and view the range names in the drop-down list. Notice that the range name *East* is not in the list.

d. Click *North* at the Name box drop-down list. Cell K6 becomes the active cell. You know from this step and Step 3d that the named ranges should reference the percentage values within column K.

e. Make cell K4 active, type *East* in the Name box, and then press the Enter key. The #NAME? error is resolved.

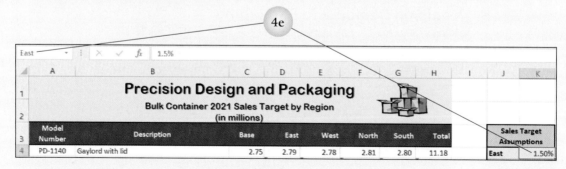

5. Solve the #VALUE! error by completing the following steps:

a. Make cell D5 active, point to the Trace Error button that appears, and then read the ScreenTip that appears. The message indicates that a value within the formula is of the wrong data type.

b. Click the Trace Precedents button to display tracer arrows that show the source cells that provide data to cell D5. Two blue arrows appear, indicating that two cells provide the source values: cells K4 and C5.

c. Make cell K4 active and look at the entry in the Formula bar: *1.5%*. This value is valid.

d. Make cell C5 active and look at the entry in the Formula bar: *2 14*. Notice that there is a space instead of a decimal point between *2* and *1*.

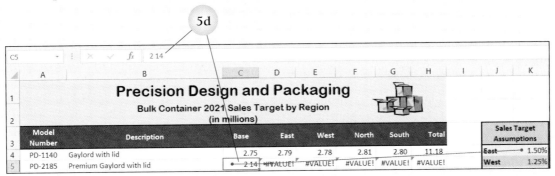

e. Click in the Formula bar and then edit the formula to delete the space between *2* and *1* and type a period (inserting a decimal point). Press the Enter key. The #VALUE! error is resolved.

f. Click the Remove Arrows button to clear the blue tracer arrows.

6. Save **5-PreSalesTrgt**.

Check Your Work

Circling Invalid Data

Circling Invalid Data and Watching a Formula Cell

Data Validation

Recall from Chapter 3 that the data validation feature is used to restrict cell entries. If data validation rules are set up after data has been entered, existing values will not be tested against the new rules. In this situation, use the Circle Invalid Data feature, which draws red circles around the cells that do not conform to the new rule. To circle invalid data, click the Data Validation button arrow in the Data Tools group on the Data tab, and then click the *Circle Invalid Data* option.

Quick Steps

Circle Invalid Data
1. Open worksheet containing validation rules.
2. Click Data tab.
3. Click Data Validation button arrow.
4. Click *Circle Invalid Data*.

 Watch Window

Quick Steps

Watch Formula Cell
1. Click Formulas tab.
2. Click Watch Window button.
3. Click Add Watch button.
4. Click in cell.
5. Click Add button.

Watching a Formula Cell

In a large worksheet, a dependent cell may not always be visible while changes are being made to other cells that affect a formula. Open a Watch Window and add a dependent cell to it to view changes made to the cell as the worksheet is modified. Multiple cells can be added to the Watch Window to create a single window where cells affected by key formulas within a large worksheet can be tracked. To watch a cell, click the Watch Window button in the Formula Auditing group on the Formulas tab, click the Add Watch button, click to select the cell you want to watch, and then click the Add button.

Consider assigning a name to a cell to be tracked using the Watch Window. At the Watch Window, the cell name will appear in the *Name* column and provide a descriptive reference to the entry being watched. Expand the width of the *Name* column if a range name is not entirely visible.

The Watch Window can be docked at the top, left, bottom, or right edge of the worksheet area by clicking the top edge of the window and dragging it to the edge of the screen. When the Watch Window is docked, Excel changes it to a Watch Window task pane.

1. With **5-PreSalesTrgt** open, view the data
   validation rule in effect for column C by
   completing the following steps:
   a. If necessary, make active any cell
      containing a value in column C.
   b. Click the Data tab.
   c. Click the top of the Data Validation
      button in the Data Tools group. (Do not
      click the arrow on the button.) The Data
      Validation dialog box opens.
   d. Review the parameters for data entry
      on the Settings tab. Notice that the
      restriction is that values should be greater
      than or equal to 1.57.
   e. Click OK.

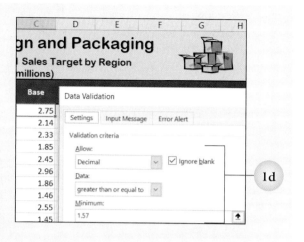

2. Click the Data Validation button arrow and then click
   Circle Invalid Data at the drop-down list. Three cells are
   circled in the worksheet: C11, C13, and C16.

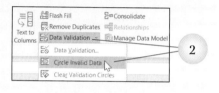

3. Watch the total in cell H22 update as the invalid data
   is corrected by completing the following steps:
   a. Make cell H22 active and then click the Formulas tab.
   b. Click the Watch Window button in the Formula Auditing group. A Watch Window opens.
   c. Click the Add Watch button in the Watch Window.
   d. At the Add Watch dialog box, move the dialog box out of the way, if necessary, to view
      cell H22. Notice that cell H22 is entered by default as the watch cell. Click the Add button.

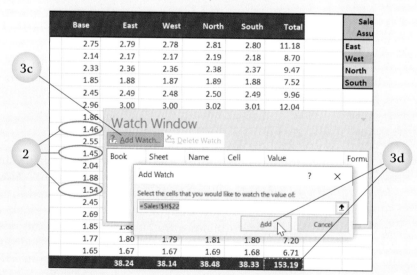

   e. Scroll up the worksheet, if necessary, until you can view cell C11. If necessary, drag
      the Watch Window out of the way so the cells being watched and the cells used in the
      formula are visible.
   f. Make cell C11 active, type 1.58, and then press the Enter key. Notice that the red circle
      disappears because a value has been entered that conforms to the validation rule. Look
      at the value for cell H22 in the Watch Window. The new value is *153.67*.

g. Make cell C13 the active cell, type 1.61, and then press the Enter key. Look at the updated value for cell H22 in the Watch Window.

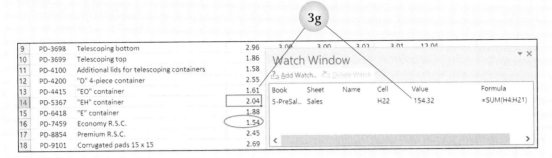

h. Make cell C16 active, type 1.57, and then press the Enter key.
i. Click the Watch Window button to close the Watch Window.
4. Print the worksheet.
5. Save and then close **5-PreSalesTrgt**.

Check Your Work

Chapter Summary

- Click the Paste button arrow to open the Paste drop-down gallery, which contains many options for pasting copied data. Open the Paste Special dialog box to paste attributes of the source cell(s) or perform a mathematical operation during the paste.

- Transposing data during a paste routine means that data arranged in columns is converted to rows and data arranged in rows is converted to columns. Transpose data using the Transpose button in the Paste button drop-down gallery or the Paste Special dialog box.

- The Goal Seek feature returns a value in a cell based on a target value specified for another cell. The two cells must have a dependent relationship for Excel to calculate a value.

- Click the What-If Analysis button in the Forecast group on the Data tab to use the Goal Seek, Scenario Manager, or Data Table feature.

- The Scenario Manager allows storing multiple sets of assumptions about data and then viewing how each set affects the worksheet. Switch between scenarios to test the various inputs on the worksheet model.

- Create a scenario summary report to compare scenarios side by side in a worksheet or PivotTable. Enter the formula cell or cells that change when the data is applied in various scenarios at the Scenario Summary dialog box.

- A data table is a range of cells that contains a series of input values; a calculated formula result is placed adjacent to each input value. A one-variable data table calculates a formula by modifying one input value in the formula. A two-variable data table calculates a formula substituting two input values.

- Design a one-variable data table with the variable input data values in a series down a column or across a row. Enter the formula one row above and one column right of the variable data.

- Design a two-variable data table with a column along the left containing one set of variable input values and a row along the top containing a second set of variable input values. Enter the formula in the top left cell of the table.

- Options in the Formula Auditing group on the Formulas tab are useful for viewing relationships between cells and finding and resolving errors.

- Use the Trace Precedents button to draw tracer arrows that show direct relationships to the cell or cells that provide data to the active cell. Use the Trace Dependents button to draw tracer arrows that show direct relationships to another cell or other cells that use data from the active cell.

- Click the Trace Precedents or Trace Dependents button a second time to display an indirect set of relationship arrows at the next level.

- A logic error occurs when the formula is not correct for the data or situation. A reference error occurs when a formula refers to the wrong data.

- Use a proof formula to test the accuracy of key figures in a worksheet. A proof formula is entered outside the main worksheet area and double-checks key figures within the worksheet.

- Excel displays two types of error messages in a cell in which an error has been detected. A green diagonal triangle in the upper left corner of the cell indicates an error condition. Errors can also be indicated with text entries. For example, *#NAME?* means that the formula contains text that Excel cannot recognize.

- Other error codes include *#VALUE!*, which means a value within the formula is not valid, and *#N/A*, which means a value needed by the formula is not available.

- Use the Error Checking button in the Formula Auditing group to help find the source of an error in a cell. Display the Error Checking dialog box or draw a red tracer arrow to locate the source cell that is contributing to the error.

- If data validation rules are set up after data has been entered, existing values will not be tested against the new rules. Use the Circle Invalid Data feature from the Data Validation button to draw red circles around the cells that do not conform to the new rule.

- Open a Watch Window and add a dependent cell to it to view changes made to the cell as the worksheet is modified. Multiple cells can be added to create a single window where cells can be tracked.

- After completing a worksheet, take time to examine the data carefully for data entry errors, values that do not appear realistic, and other indications of potential errors that should be fixed.

Commands Review

FEATURE	RIBBON TAB, GROUP	BUTTON	KEYBOARD SHORTCUT
circle invalid data	Data, Data Tools		
data table	Data, Forecast		
display formulas	Formulas, Formula Auditing		Ctrl + `
Goal Seek dialog box	Data, Forecast		
Paste Special dialog box	Home, Clipboard		Ctrl + Alt + V
remove tracer arrow	Formulas, Formula Auditing		
Scenario Manager	Data, Forecast		
trace dependent cell	Formulas, Formula Auditing		Ctrl +]
trace error	Formulas, Formula Auditing		
trace precedent cell	Formulas, Formula Auditing		Ctrl + [
transpose data	Home, Clipboard		
Watch Window	Formulas, Formula Auditing		

Microsoft®
Excel®

Exporting, Importing, and Transforming Data

Performance Objectives

Upon successful completion of Chapter 6, you will be able to:

1. Copy, embed, link, and unlink Excel data in a Word document
2. Copy, paste, and embed Excel data in a PowerPoint presentation
3. Copy and paste Excel data in an Access table
4. Export an Excel worksheet as a text file
5. Import data from an Access database
6. Modify imported data with the Query Editor
7. Import data from a text file
8. Refresh, modify, and delete queries
9. Use Flash Fill to transform data
10. Modify text using the text functions PROPER, UPPER, LOWER, SUBSTITUTE, RIGHT, LEFT, MID, TEXTJOIN, and CONCAT

Exchanging data between programs by exporting or importing eliminates duplication of effort and reduces the likelihood of data errors or missed entries, which could occur if the data was retyped. One of the advantages of working with a suite of programs such as Microsoft Word, Excel, Access, and PowerPoint is being able to easily integrate data from one program to another. In this chapter, you will learn how to export data in a worksheet to other programs and how to bring data into an Excel worksheet from external sources.

 Data Files

Before beginning chapter work, copy the EL2C6 folder to your storage medium and then make EL2C6 the active folder.

The online course includes additional training and assessment resources.

You will copy and paste data related to car inventory from an Excel worksheet to integrate with an Word report, a PowerPoint presentation, and an Access database. You will also save a worksheet as a comma-separated text file for use in a non-Microsoft program.

Exporting Data from Excel

Applications in Office 365 are designed for integration so that an object can easily be created in one application and copied to another application. For example, use Excel data in other Microsoft programs by copying cells to the Clipboard and then pasting them in the destination files. Integration is possible because the applications have a common interface that allows each application to understand another application's file format.

To use Excel data in Word, PowerPoint, or Access, use the copy and paste, copy and embed, or copy and link method. During an export or import, the file containing the original data is called the *source file*, and the file to which the original data is being copied, embedded, or linked is called the *destination file*.

To export Excel data for use in another program, open the Save As dialog box and then change the *Save as type* option to the desired file format. If the file format for the destination program does not appear in the *Save as type* list, try copying and pasting the data or go to the Microsoft Office Online website and search for a file format converter that can be downloaded and installed.

Exporting Data into Word

Quick Steps

Embed or Link Excel Data in Word Document

1. Select cells.
2. Click Copy button.
3. Open Word.
4. Position insertion point in document.
5. Click Paste button arrow.
6. Click Paste Special.
7. Click *Microsoft Excel Worksheet Object*.
8. Click OK to embed, or click *Paste link* and then OK to link.

Copying and Pasting Data into Word

Data from Excel can be copied and pasted directly into Word, or it can be copied and then pasted as an embedded or linked object. Use the simple copy and paste method if the data being brought into the Word document is not likely to be updated or edited later. Copy and embed the data to be able to edit it in Word using Excel. Copy and link the data to allow it to be updated whenever edits are made to the source file.

Embedding Excel Data in a Word Document To embed copied Excel data in a Word document, open the document, move the insertion point to where the copied Excel data should be inserted, and then open the Paste Special dialog box. At the Paste Special dialog box, click the option to paste as a *Microsoft Excel Worksheet Object* and then click OK.

To edit an embedded Excel object in Word, double-click the embedded object to open it for editing. The worksheet object opens in Excel. Click the Excel Close button to close Excel and make Word the active application. Any changes made to the Excel object in the Word document are not reflected in the Excel file containing the original data and vice versa.

Linking Excel Data to a Word Document When Excel data is linked to a Word document, the source data exists only in Excel. Word places a shortcut to the source data file name and range in the document. When a Word document is opened that contains one or more links, Word prompts the user to update the links. Since the data resides only in the Excel workbook, the original workbook that contains the original data should not be moved or renamed. If either happens, the link in the Word document will no longer work.

To paste copied Excel data as a link in a Word document, open the document, move the insertion point to where the cells should be linked, open the Paste Special dialog box, click *Microsoft Excel Worksheet Object*, click *Paste link*, and then click OK.

Activity 1a **Embedding Excel Data in a Word Document**

1. Open **CRInventory**.
2. Copy and embed the data in the CarCosts worksheet in a Word document by completing the following steps:
   a. Make CarCosts the active worksheet, if necessary.
   b. Select the range A4:F9.
   c. Click the Copy button in the Clipboard group on the Home tab.
   d. Start Microsoft Word 365.
   e. Open **CRCarRptW** from the EL2C6 folder on your storage medium. If a security warning displays stating that the document is in Protected View, click the Enable Editing button.

   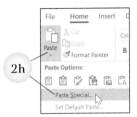

   f. Save the document with the name **6-CRCarRptW**.
   g. Press Ctrl + End to move the insertion point to the end of the document.
   h. Click the Paste button arrow and then click *Paste Special* at the drop-down list.
   i. At the Paste Special dialog box, click *Microsoft Excel Worksheet Object* in the *As* list box and then click OK.
3. Save **6-CRCarRptW**.
4. When Paste Special is used, the copied cells are embedded as an object in the Word document. Edit the embedded object using Excel by completing the following steps:
   a. Double-click in a cell in the embedded worksheet object. The object opens in Excel. *Note: Depending on your version of Office, an Excel ribbon may open within Word and your steps will vary slightly as you will need to click within the Word document to close the Excel ribbon.*
   b. Select the range B4:F4 and then click the Center button.
   c. Click the Excel Close button. If necessary, make Word the active application.

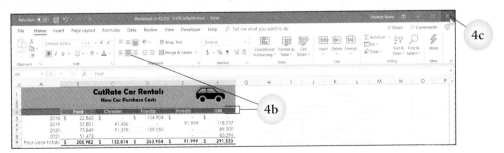

5. Save and then print **6-CRCarRptW**.
6. Close Word.
7. Click in any cell to deselect the range in the CarCosts worksheet and leave the **CRInventory** workbook open for the next activity.

1. With **CRInventory** open, copy and link the data in the CarCosts worksheet to a Word document by completing the following steps:
   a. With CarCosts the active worksheet, select the range A4:F9 and then click the Copy button.
   b. Start Microsoft Word 365.
   c. Open **CRCarRptW**.
   d. Save the document with the name **6-CRCarRptW-Linked**.
   e. Press Ctrl + End to move the insertion point to the end of the document.
   f. Click the Paste button arrow and then click *Paste Special* at the drop-down list.
   g. At the Paste Special dialog box, click *Microsoft Excel Worksheet Object* in the *As* list box and then click the *Paste link* radio button.
   h. Click OK.

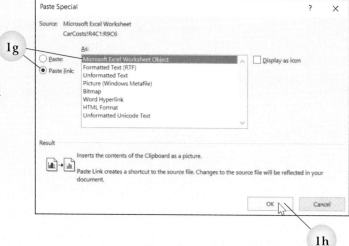

2. Save and then close **6-CRCarRptW-Linked**. When data is linked, it exists only in the source file. In the destination document, Word inserts a shortcut to the specified range in the source file. Edit the source range and view the update to the Word document by completing the following steps:
   a. Click the button on the taskbar representing the Excel workbook **CRInventory**.
   b. With CarCosts the active worksheet, press the Esc key to remove the scrolling marquee, if necessary, and then click in any cell to deselect the copied range.
   c. Make cell E5 active, type 85000, and then press the Enter key.
   d. Click the button on the taskbar representing Word.
   e. Open **6-CRCarRptW-Linked**.
   f. At the Microsoft Word message box asking whether to update the document with data from the linked files, click Yes.

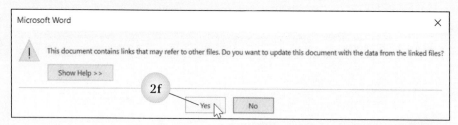

3. Notice that the data inserted in the Excel worksheet is also shown in the linked Word document.
4. Save and then print **6-CRCarRptW-Linked**.
5. Exit Word.
6. With CarCosts the active worksheet in **CRInventory**, delete the content of cell E5 and leave the workbook open for a later activity.

Breaking a Link to an Excel Object

Quick Steps

Break Link to Excel Object
1. Open Word document.
2. Right-click linked object.
3. Point to *Linked Worksheet Object.*
4. Click *Links.*
5. Click Break Link button.
6. Click Yes.
7. Save document.

If the Excel data in a Word document no longer needs to be linked, the connection between the source and destination files can be broken. Breaking the link means that the data in the Word document will no longer be connected to the data in the Excel workbook. If a change is made to the original data in Excel, the Word document will not reflect the update. Once the link to the document is broken, the prompt to update the object each time the Word document is opened will no longer appear.

To break a link, open the Word document, right-click the linked object, point to *Linked Worksheet Object,* and then click *Links* at the shortcut menu. This opens the Links dialog box. If more than one linked object exists in the document, click the source object for the link to be broken and then click the Break Link button. At the message box that appears, click Yes to confirm that the link is to be broken.

Activity 1c Breaking a Link   Part 3 of 6

1. Start Word and open **6-CRCarRpt-Linked.**
2. At the message asking whether to update the links, click No.
3. Break the link between the Excel workbook and the linked object by completing the following steps:
   a. Right-click the linked Excel worksheet object.
   b. Point to *Linked Worksheet Object* and then click *Links* at the shortcut menu.
   c. At the Links dialog box with the linked object file name selected in the *Source file* list box, click the Break Link button.

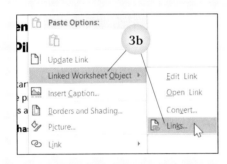
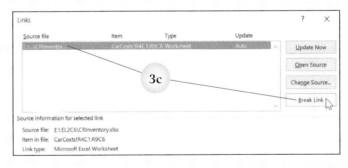

   d. At the Microsoft Word dialog box asking for confirmation to break the selected link, click Yes.
4. Save **6-CRCarRptW-Linked** and then exit Word.

Check Your Work

Tutorial

Copying and Pasting Data into PowerPoint

Copying and Pasting Data into PowerPoint

As they can with Word, users can copy and paste, copy and embed, or copy and link Excel data to slides in a PowerPoint presentation. Charts are often incorporated to presentations to visually depict numerical data in a graph format that is easy to understand. Although tables and charts can be created in PowerPoint slides, users may prefer to use Excel to create these items and then copy and paste them into PowerPoint. Depending on the version of Office 365 you are using, copy and paste is the best method to use if the chart will need to be formatted.

Since the chart feature is fully integrated within Word, Excel, and PowerPoint, a chart that has been pasted in a PowerPoint presentation can be edited using the same techniques for editing a chart in Excel. Clicking a chart in a PowerPoint slide causes the contextual Chart Tools Design and Chart Tools Format tabs to become active with the same groups and buttons available as in Excel. Three buttons—Chart Elements, Chart Styles, and Chart Filter—are also available for editing.

Activity 1d Pasting and Embedding Excel Data into a PowerPoint Presentation

Part 4 of 6

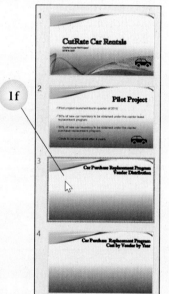

1. With **CRInventory** open, copy and embed the chart from the CarCostsChart worksheet in a PowerPoint slide by completing the following steps:
   a. Make CarCostsChart the active worksheet.
   b. Click the Home tab and then click the Copy button.
   c. Start Microsoft PowerPoint 365.
   d. Open **CRCarPres.**
   e. Save the presentation with the name **6-CRCarPres.**
   f. Click Slide 3 in the slide thumbnails pane.
   g. Click in the *Click to add text* placeholder and then click the Paste button in the Clipboard group. Since all charts are embedded by default, it is not necessary to use Paste Special.

2. Make the following changes to the chart:
   a. With the object placeholder selected, click the font color option box arrow and then click *Black, Background 1* (first column, first row) in the *Theme Colors* section.
   b. Change the chart colors by clicking the Chart Styles button and then clicking the Color tab. Click the *Colorful Palette 2* option (second option in the *Colorful* section of the color palette).

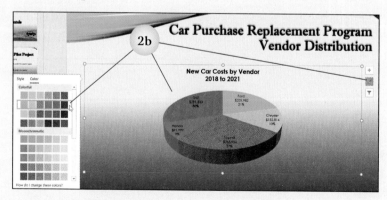

   c. Click outside the chart.

3. Copy the table used to generate the chart in the CarCosts worksheet and embed it in the next slide by completing the following steps:
   a. Click Slide 4 in the slide thumbnails pane.
   b. Click the button on the taskbar representing the Excel workbook **CRInventory**.
   c. Make CarCosts the active worksheet, select the range A1:F9, and then click the Copy button.

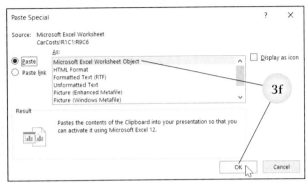

   d. Click the button on the taskbar representing the PowerPoint presentation **6-CRCarPres**.
   e. Click the Paste button arrow and then click *Paste Special* at the drop-down list.
   f. With *Microsoft Excel Worksheet Object* selected in the *As* list box, click OK.

4. Resize and position the embedded table to the approximate height, width, and position shown at the right.

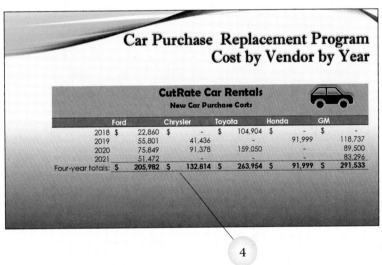

5. Click the File tab and then click the *Print* option. At the Print backstage area, click the button in the *Settings* category that reads *Full Page Slides* and then click *4 Slides Horizontal* at the drop-down list. Click the Print button.

6. Save **6-CRCarPres** and then exit PowerPoint.

7. Press the Esc key to remove the scrolling marquee and then click in any cell to deselect the range in the CarCosts worksheet. Leave the **CRInventory** workbook open for the next activity.

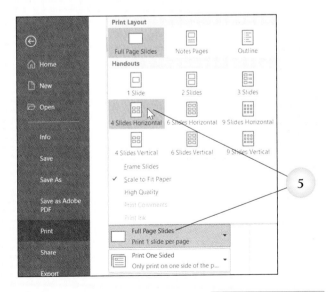

Check Your Work

Tutorial

Copying and
Pasting Data
into Access

Copying and Pasting Data into Access

Data in an Excel worksheet can be copied and pasted into an Access table datasheet, query, or form using the Clipboard task pane. Before pasting data into a table datasheet, make sure that the column structures in the two programs match. If the Access datasheet already contains records, choose to replace the existing records or append the Excel data to the end of the table. To export Excel data to an Access database that does not have an existing table in which to receive the data, perform an import routine from Access. To do this, start Access, open the database, click the External Data tab, and then click the Import Excel spreadsheet button.

Activity 1e Copying and Pasting Excel Data into an Access Datasheet

1. With **CRInventory** open, copy and paste the rows in the Inventory worksheet to the bottom of an Access table by completing the following steps:
   a. Make Inventory the active worksheet.
   b. Select the range A5:G33 and then click the Copy button.
   c. Start Microsoft Access 365.
   d. At the Access 365 opening screen, click the *Open Other Files* option.
   e. At the Open backstage area, click the *Browse* option. At the Open dialog box, navigate to the EL2C6 folder on your storage medium and then double-click **CRInventoryData**. If a security warning message displays below the ribbon stating that some active content has been disabled, click the Enable Content button.
   f. Double-click *CarInventory* in the Tables group in the Navigation pane at the left side of the Access window. This opens the CarInventory table in Datasheet view. Notice that the structure of the columns in the datasheet is the same as in the source worksheet in Excel.
   g. With the table open in Datasheet view, click the Paste button arrow in the Clipboard group and then click *Paste Append* at the drop-down list.

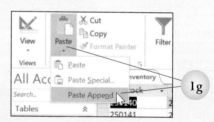

   h. At the Microsoft Access message box stating that you are about to paste 29 records and asking if you are sure, click Yes.

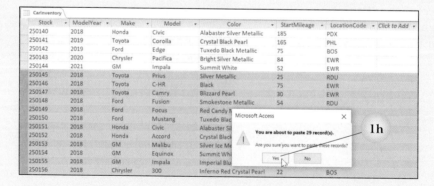

   i. Click in any cell within the datasheet to deselect the pasted records.

2. Print the Access datasheet in landscape orientation by completing the following steps:
   a. Click the File tab, click the *Print* option, and then click the *Print Preview* option.
   b. Click the Landscape button in the Page Layout group on the Print Preview tab.
   c. Click the Page Setup button in the Page Layout group.

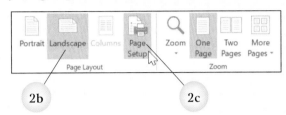

   d. At the Page Setup dialog box with the Print Options tab selected, change the top and bottom margins to 0.5 inch. The left and right margins should already be set to 1 inch. Click OK.
   e. Click the Print button in the Print group and then click OK at the Print dialog box.
   f. Click the Close Print Preview button in the Close Preview group.

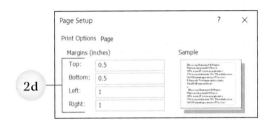

3. Click the Close button in the upper right corner to close Access.
4. Click in any cell to deselect the range in the Inventory worksheet and then press the Esc key to remove the scrolling marquee.
5. Leave the **CRInventory** workbook open for the next activity.

 Check Your Work

 Tutorial

Exporting a Worksheet as a Text File

Exporting a Worksheet as a Text File

To exchange Excel data with someone who cannot import a Microsoft Excel worksheet or cannot copy and paste using the Clipboard task pane, save the data as a text file. Excel provides several text file options, including file formats suitable for computers that use the Apple operating system (Macintosh computers), as shown in Table 6.1. To save a worksheet as a text file, open the Save As dialog box and then change the file type to the correct option. Type a file name for the text file and then click the Save button. Click OK at the message box stating that only the active worksheet will be saved and then click Yes at the next message box to confirm saving the data as a text file.

 Quick Steps

Export Worksheet as Text File
1. Make sheet active.
2. Click File tab.
3. Click *Export* option.
4. Click *Change File Type.*
5. Click text file type in *Other File Types* section.
6. Click Save As button.
7. If necessary, navigate to drive and/or folder.
8. Type file name.
9. Click Save button.
10. Click OK.
11. Click Yes.

Table 6.1 Supported Text File Formats for Exporting

Text File Format	File Extension
text (tab delimited)	.txt
unicode text	.txt
CSV (comma delimited)	.csv
formatted text (space delimited)	.prn
text (Apple)	.txt
text (MS-DOS)	.txt
CSV (Apple)	.csv
CSV (MS-DOS)	.csv

Another way to save the current worksheet in a text file format is to click the File tab and then click the *Export* option. At the Export backstage area, click *Change File Type*. In the *Change File Type* section at the right, click *Text (Tab delimited)*, *CSV (Comma delimited)*, or *Formatted Text (Space delimited)* in the *Other File Types* section and then click the Save As button. If necessary, navigate to the appropriate drive and/or folder in the Save As dialog box. Type the file name and then click the Save button. Click OK at the message box stating that the selected file type does not support workbooks that contain multiple sheets.

Activity 1f Exporting a Worksheet as a Text File

1. With **CRInventory** open, export the Inventory worksheet data as a text file by completing the following steps:
   a. With Inventory the active worksheet, click the File tab and then click the *Export* option.
   b. Click the *Change File Type* option at the Export backstage area.
   c. Click the *CSV (Comma delimited)* option in the *Other File Types* section.
   d. Click the Save As button.

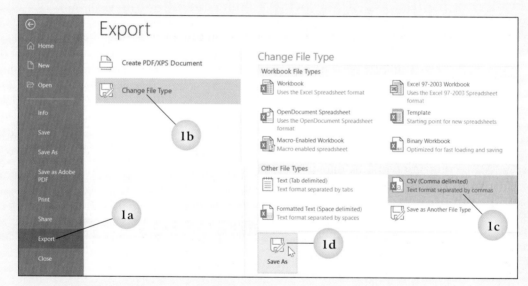

   e. Type 6-CRInventoryTxt in the *File name* text box.
   f. Click the Save button.

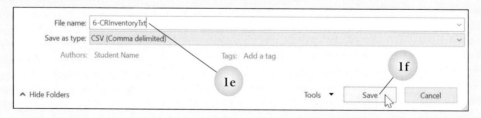

g. Click OK to save only the active sheet at the Microsoft Excel message box stating that the selected file type does not support workbooks that contain multiple sheets.

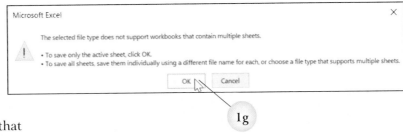

1g

h. A message displays above the Formula bar stating that there is some possible data loss. Click the Message Close button.

1h

POSSIBLE DATA LOSS Some features might be lost if you save this workbook in the comma-delimited (.csv) format. To preserve these features, save it in an Excel file format.   Don't show again   Save As...

2. Close **6-CRInventoryTxt**. Click Don't Save when prompted to save changes. (The file does not need to be saved because no changes have been made since the file type was changed.)

3. Open Notepad and view the text file created in Step 1 by completing the following steps:
   a. Click the Start button. At the Start screen, start typing notepad. When *Notepad* appears in the *Best match* area, press the Enter key. (Depending on your operating system, these steps may vary. If Notepad is not available, use another text editor.)

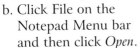

3d

   b. Click File on the Notepad Menu bar and then click *Open*.
   c. Navigate to the EL2C6 folder on your storage medium.
   d. Click the *File type* option box arrow (which displays *Text Documents (*.txt)*) and then click *All Files* at the drop-down list.
   e. Double-click **6-CRInventoryTxt**.
   f. If necessary, scroll down to view all the data in the text file. Notice that commas have been inserted between the items of data previously arranged in columns.

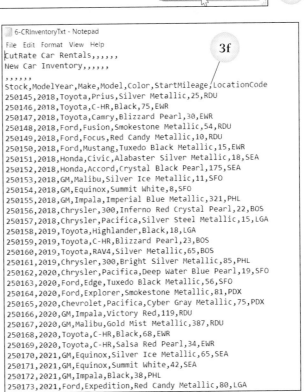

3f

```
6-CRInventoryTxt - Notepad
File  Edit  Format  View  Help
CutRate Car Rentals,,,,,,
New Car Inventory,,,,,,
,,,,,,
Stock,ModelYear,Make,Model,Color,StartMileage,LocationCode
250145,2018,Toyota,Prius,Silver Metallic,25,RDU
250146,2018,Toyota,C-HR,Black,75,EWR
250147,2018,Toyota,Camry,Blizzard Pearl,30,EWR
250148,2018,Ford,Fusion,Smokestone Metallic,54,RDU
250149,2018,Ford,Focus,Red Candy Metallic,10,RDU
250150,2018,Ford,Mustang,Tuxedo Black Metallic,15,EWR
250151,2018,Honda,Civic,Alabaster Silver Metallic,18,SEA
250152,2018,Honda,Accord,Crystal Black Pearl,175,SEA
250153,2018,GM,Malibu,Silver Ice Metallic,11,SFO
250154,2018,GM,Equinox,Summit White,8,SFO
250155,2018,GM,Impala,Imperial Blue Metallic,321,PHL
250156,2018,Chrysler,300,Inferno Red Crystal Pearl,22,BOS
250157,2018,Chrysler,Pacifica,Silver Steel Metallic,15,LGA
250158,2019,Toyota,Highlander,Black,18,LGA
250159,2019,Toyota,C-HR,Blizzard Pearl,23,BOS
250160,2019,Toyota,RAV4,Silver Metallic,65,BOS
250161,2019,Chrysler,300,Bright Silver Metallic,85,PHL
250162,2020,Chrysler,Pacifica,Deep Water Blue Pearl,19,SFO
250163,2020,Ford,Edge,Tuxedo Black Metallic,56,SFO
250164,2020,Ford,Explorer,Smokestone Metallic,81,PDX
250165,2020,Chevrolet,Pacifica,Cyber Gray Metallic,75,PDX
250166,2020,GM,Impala,Victory Red,119,RDU
250167,2020,GM,Malibu,Gold Mist Metallic,387,RDU
250168,2020,Toyota,C-HR,Black,68,EWR
250169,2020,Toyota,C-HR,Salsa Red Pearl,34,EWR
250170,2021,GM,Equinox,Silver Ice Metallic,65,SEA
250171,2021,GM,Equinox,Summit White,42,SEA
250172,2021,GM,Impala,Black,38,PHL
250173,2021,Ford,Expedition,Red Candy Metallic,80,LGA
```

4. Click File on the Notepad Menu bar and then click *Print*. Click the Print button at the Print dialog box.
5. Exit Notepad.
6. Close **CRInventory**.

Check Your Work

<table>
<tr>
<td>

Activity 2 **Import Data from an Access Database
and from Text Files**

5 Parts

You will import site manager and tenant data from an Access database and then append the data from a text file to the previously imported tenant data. The data will be modified during the import. Rental listings data will also be imported from a text file.

</td>
</tr>
</table>

Tutorial

Importing Data
into Excel

Importing Data into Excel

Importing data from other applications allows for the manipulation, organization, and analyzing of data in Excel in a variety of ways. Time and money are saved by not having to enter the information manually. Importing data also reduces errors that may be introduced during data entry.

The Get & Transform Data group on the Data tab contains buttons for importing data from external sources into an Excel worksheet using Power Query technology. To import data, make active the cell in which the imported data is to start and then click the button representing the source application or point to the Get Data button and then select the source from a drop-down list. Previously, Excel used wizards to import data. Those wizards are now called *legacy wizards* and can be added to a new group in an existing or new tab. Adding buttons is discussed in Chapter 7.

 Get Data

Importing Data from Access

Quick Steps

Import Access Table
1. Click Data tab.
2. Click Get Data button.
3. Point to *From Database*.
4. Click *From Microsoft Access Database*.
5. Navigate to drive and/or folder.
6. Double-click source database file name.
7. If necessary, click table name and then *Load*.

Exchanging data between Access and Excel is a seamless process, since the data in an Access datasheet is structured in the same row and column format as the data in an Excel worksheet. The imported data can be appended to an existing worksheet or placed in a new worksheet.

To import an Access table, click the Data tab, click the Get Data button, point to the *From Database* option at the drop-down list, and then click the *From Microsoft Access Database* option at the second drop-down list. Navigate to the drive and/or folder in which the source database resides and then double-click the Access database file name in the file list. At the Navigator dialog box, click the table containing the data to be imported. A preview of the data appears in the

Figure 6.1 Import Data Dialog Box

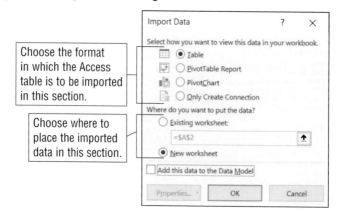

right panel. Click the Load button to import the data in a new worksheet, click the Load button arrow, and then click the *Load To* option at the drop-down list to open the Import Data dialog box, shown in Figure 6.1 (on page 154), to import the data in a different location, or click the Edit button to modify and then import the data.

When data is imported into Excel, the data is imported in a table format and a query is created. The query specifies the import steps and any modifications made to the data. The Queries & Connections task pane displays with the Queries tab active and the new query selected.

💡 **Hint** Only one table can be imported at a time. To import all the tables in the source database, repeat the import process for each table.

Activity 2a Importing Data from an Access Database

Part 1 of 5

1. Open **PropMgt**.
2. Save the workbook with the name **6-PropMgt**.
3. Import the SiteManagers table stored in an Access database and place the information in the Site Managers worksheet by completing the following steps:
   a. If necessary, make cell A2 active.
   b. Click the Data tab.
   c. Click the Get Data button in the Get & Transform Data group. Point to the *From Database* option and then click the *From Microsoft Access Database* option at the second drop-down list.

   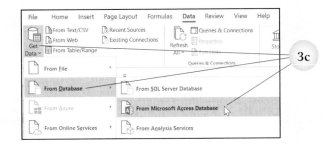

   d. If necessary, navigate to the EL2C6 folder on your storage medium and then double-click **PropMgtData**.
   e. Click *SiteManagers* in the left panel. A preview of the table displays in the right panel.
   f. Click the Load button arrow and then click the *Load To* option.

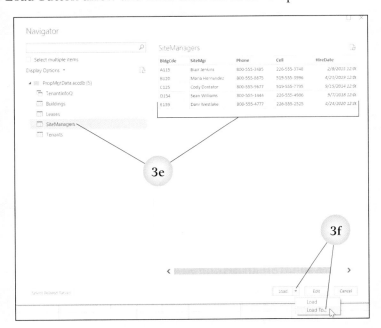

g. At the Import Data dialog box, click the Existing worksheet radio button.

h. With *=$A$2* in the *Existing worksheet* text box, click OK.

4. Look at the imported table data. Notice that the data is formatted as a table with filter arrows. The Queries & Connections panel displays the query with details of the new import.

5. With the Table Tools Design tab active, make the following changes to the worksheet:

a. Remove the filter arrows.

b. Change the table style to Blue, Table Style Light 9 (third column, second row in the *Light* section).

c. Make the Home tab active and apply the Short Date format to the range E3:E7.

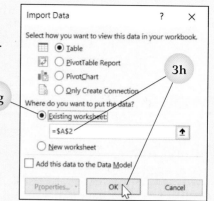

d. Click in any cell to deselect the range.

6. Save **6-PropMgt**.

Tutorial

Modifying Data with the Power Query Editor

Modifying Data with the Power Query Editor

Use the Power Query Editor to transform data before it is imported into Excel. To display the Query Editor window before the data is imported, click the Edit button at the Navigator dialog box. Depending on the version of Excel, the Edit button may display as the Transform Data button. To transform data, use tools on the Home tab of the Power Query Editor window shown in Figure 6.2. For example, if a field contains both the first names and the last names of tenants, separate the field into two fields: one containing first names and the other containing last names. The steps used to transform the data are saved as part of the query in the APPLIED STEPS section at the Query Settings task pane in the Power Query Editor window. The steps in the APPLIED STEPS section will be reapplied to the data every time the data is refreshed.

Figure 6.2 Power Query Editor Window

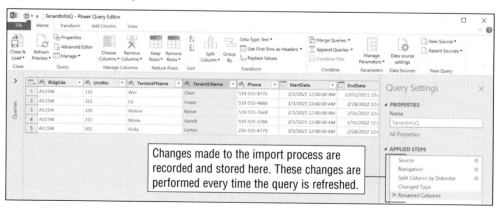

Changes made to the import process are recorded and stored here. These changes are performed every time the query is refreshed.

1. With **6-PropMgt** open, import the *TentantInfoQ* query from the PropMgtData database into a new worksheet by completing the following steps:
   a. With any cell active, click the Data tab.
   b. Click the Get Data button.
   c. Point to the *From Database* option and then click the *From Microsoft Access Database* option at the second drop-down list.
   d. If necessary, navigate to the EL2C6 folder on your storage medium and then double-click *PropMgtData*.
   e. Click *TenantInfoQ* in the left panel. A preview of the query displays in the right panel.
   f. Click the Edit button in the right panel. ***Note: Depending on the version of Excel, the Edit button may display as the Transform Data button***.
   g. Click in any cell in the *TenantName* column, click the Split Column button in the Transform group on the Home tab, and then click the *By Delimiter* option at the drop-down list.

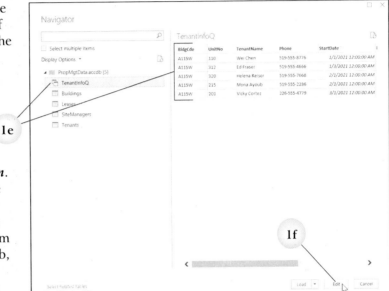

   h. With the *Space* option appearing in the *Select or enter delimiter* option box and a bullet appearing in the *Each occurrence of the delimiter* radio button, click OK.

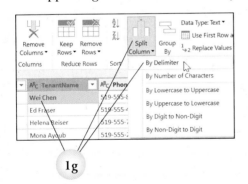
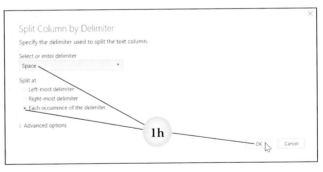

   i. Right-click the *TenantName.1* column header, click the *Rename* option, type TenantFName, and then press the Enter key.
   j. Right-click the *TenantName.2* column header, click the *Rename* option, type TenantLName, and then press the Enter key.
   k. Click the Close & Load button in the Close group.
2. Rename the worksheet **Tenants**.
3. Save **6-PropMgt**.

Importing Data from a Text File

 From Text/CSV

As noted when exporting, a text file is often used to exchange data between different programs because the file format is recognized by nearly all applications. Text files contain no formatting and consist only of letters, numbers, punctuation symbols, and a few control characters. Two commonly used text file formats separate fields with tabs (delimited file format) or commas (comma-separated file format). One of the text files used in Activity 2c is shown in a Notepad window in Figure 6.3. If necessary, view and edit a text file in Notepad before importing it.

To import a text file into Excel, use the From Text/CSV button in the Get & Transform Data group on the Data tab and then select the source file at the Import Data dialog box. Excel displays in the file list any file in the active folder that ends with the file extension *.prn, .txt,* or *.csv.* Once the source file is selected, Excel displays a preview of the file. Click the Load button to import the data in a new worksheet, click the Load button arrow, and then click the *Load To* option at the drop-down list to import the data in a different location, or click the Edit button to edit and then import the data.

Non-native files—including but not limited to web pages, extensible markup language (XML) files, text files, and data sources—can also be opened directly in Excel. To open a non-native file directly in Excel, click the File tab and then click the *Open* option. Click the file location and then click the *Browse* option to display the Open dialog box. Navigate to the specific folder and then click the *File Type* option box to display a drop-down list of all the different file types that can be opened in Excel. Click the specific file type and then double-click the file name. If the exact file type is not known, select *All Files* to display all the available files. Save the file as an Excel workbook, or if changes were made, resave it as a text file (but note that some features might be lost).

Figure 6.3 Activity 2c Text File Content

A text file contains no formatting codes. In this delimited file format tabs separate the fields. During the import, Excel begins a new column at each tab.

BldgCde	UnitNo	TenantName	Phone	StartDate	EndDate	Rent	SecDeposit
A115W	112	Pat McCann	519-555-3485	3/1/2021	2/28/2022	1490	1490
A115W	113	Craig Degroot	226-555-6485	3/1/2021	2/28/2022	1490	1490
A115W	114	Diane Bower	519-555-6748	3/1/2021	2/28/2022	1684	1684
A115W	116	Norman Kilborn	226-569-3652	4/1/2021	3/31/2022	1490	1490
A115W	117	Bruce Hanley	226-555-7486	4/1/2021	3/31/2022	1684	1684
A115W	121	Chase Caughlin	519-555-6348	4/1/2021	3/31/2022	1684	1684
A115W	125	Marc Bernardi	226-555-6485	4/1/2021	3/31/2022	1490	1490
A115W	102	Chantal Alder	519-555-9647	5/1/2021	4/30/2022	1116	1116
A115W	104	Gerri Schell	226-555-7469	5/1/2021	4/30/2022	1116	1116
A115W	105	Karl Walters	519-555-1258	5/1/2021	4/30/2022	991	991
A115W	106	John Ridley	226-555-6345	5/1/2021	4/30/2022	1231	1231
A115W	107	Erin Micks	519-555-4589	5/1/2021	4/30/2022	1116	1116
B120F	108	Toni Hwang	519-555-6348	5/1/2021	4/30/2022	991	991
B120F	109	Felix Kirkton	519-555-7486	5/1/2021	4/30/2022	991	991
B120F	110	Miranda Ley	226-555-3615	6/1/2021	5/31/2022	1404	1404
B120F	120	Fatima Mancini	226-555-6441	6/1/2021	5/31/2022	1404	1404
C125L	122	Perri Paulson	519-555-3452	6/1/2021	5/31/2022	1404	1404
C125L	201	Dawson Riccardi	226-555-1223	7/1/2021	6/30/2022	1620	1620
C125L	205	Cyril Gallagher	519-555-4523	7/1/2021	6/30/2022	1620	1620
C125L	203	Brian Forsyth	226-555-7466	7/1/2021	6/30/2022	1404	1404
C125L	201	Ken Haskell	519-555-6663	7/1/2021	6/30/2022	1231	1231
D154L	402	Angela Labelle	519-555-9967	8/1/2021	7/31/2022	1800	1800
D154L	410	Ron Millette	519-555-8823	9/1/2021	8/31/2022	1900	1900
D154L	411	Dave Pristas	226-555-7774	9/1/2021	8/31/2022	1850	1850
E139P	230	Heather Schwab	226-555-5662	9/1/2021	8/31/2022	2300	2300
E139P	228	Winnie Tilson	226-555-3446	9/1/2021	8/31/2022	2100	2100
E139P	224	Anna Weston	226-555-4555	9/1/2021	8/31/2022	2000	2000

1. With **6-PropMgt** open, import, edit, and then append the data to the Tenants list previously imported. Choose the data source and edit the data by completing the following steps:
   a. With any cell active in the Tenants worksheet, click the Data tab, if necessary.
   b. Click the From Text/CSV button in the Get & Transform Data group.
   c. At the Import Data dialog box, navigate to the EL2C6 folder on your storage medium, if necessary, and then double-click *TenantsTxt* in the file list.
   d. At the **TenantsTxt.txt** preview, click the Edit button.
   e. Click in any cell in the *TenantName* column, click the Split Column button, and then click the *By Delimiter* option at the drop-down list.
   f. With the *Space* option appearing in the *Select or enter delimiter* option box and a bullet appearing in the *Each occurrence of the delimiter* radio button, click OK.
   g. Right-click the *TenantName.1* column header, click the *Rename* option, type TenantFName, and then press the Enter key.
   h. Right-click the *TenantName.2* column header, click the *Rename* option, type TenantLName, and then press the Enter key.

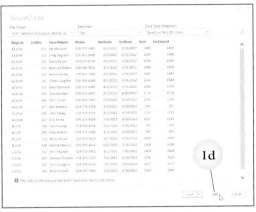

2. Append the data from the text file to the previously imported Access query by completing the following steps:
   a. Click the Append Queries button in the Combine group.
   b. Click the *Table to append* option box arrow, click the *TenantInfoQ* option, and then click OK.
   c. Click the Close & Load button.

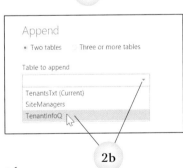

3. Make the following changes to the data:
   a. Select the range B29:B33 and right-align the numbers.
   b. Select the range F2:G33 and apply the Short Date format.
   c. Select the range H2:I33 and apply Currency formatting with no digits past the decimal point.
   d. Sort the table in ascending order by the *BldgCde* field.
   e. Remove the filter arrows.
   f. Change the table style to Blue, Table Style Light 9 (third column, second row in the *Light* section).
   g. Rename the worksheet **All Tenants**.
4. Import the RentalListingsCSV CSV file into a new worksheet by completing the following steps:
   a. Click the Data tab and then click the From Text/CSV button.
   b. At the Import Data dialog box, navigate to the EL2C6 folder on your storage medium, if necessary, and then double-click *RentalListingsCSV* in the file list.
   d. At the **RentalListingsCSV.csv** preview, click the Load button.
   e. Rename the worksheet **Rental Listings**.
5. Save **6-PropMgt**.

Refreshing, Modifying, and Deleting Queries

When data is imported into Excel, a connection is established between the source file and the destination file. If the file is imported using Power Query technology, the connection is created using a query. Refreshing, modifying, and removing queries helps maintain the data needed to make sound business decisions by ensuring the most current data is in the destination file. Editing a query allows further changes to be made to the data. Removing a connection allows for the data to be captured at a specific time.

 Refresh All

To refresh a query, click the Refresh All button in the Queries & Connections group on the Data tab as shown in Figure 6.4. To refresh just the selected query, click the Refresh All button arrow and then click the *Refresh* option at the drop-down list. To modify the data to refresh at a specific time period or when the workbook is opened, click the Refresh All button arrow on the Data tab, click the *Connections Properties* option at the drop-down list, and then choose options at the Query Properties dialog box, shown in Figure 6.5.

Figure 6.4 Queries & Connections Group on the Data Tab

Click the Refresh All button to refresh all the queries and connections in the workbook or click the Refresh All button arrow to view a list of refresh options.

Click here to display the Queries & Connections task pane.

Figure 6.5 Query Properties Dialog Box

Click here to insert a check mark and then adjust the number of minutes in the measurement box if you want Excel to refresh the query at a specific time period.

Click here to insert a check mark if you want Excel to refresh the data when you open the file.

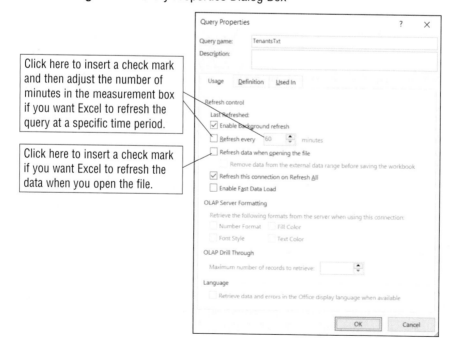

Queries & Connections

To redisplay the Query & Connections task pane, click the Queries & Connections button in the Queries & Connections group on the Data tab, as shown in Figure 6.4 (on page 160). Edit a query if further changes need to be made to the data on a query that will be refreshed. To edit a query, double-click the query item at the Queries & Connections task pane, make the necessary changes in the Query Editor window, and then click the Close & Load button in the Close group on the Home tab in the Power Query Editor window. The features on the Query Tools Query tab are also found at the pop-up menu when you right-click a query item at the Queries & Connections task pane.

To display the Query dialog box, as shown in Figure 6.6, point to the query at the task pane. The Query dialog box provides options for previewing, editing, and deleting a query.

To delete a query, right-click the query at the Queries & Connections task pane and then click the *Delete* option at the pop-up menu or click the Delete button in the Edit group on the Query Tools Query tab. If you convert the table to a range, a message box displays asking if you want to permanently remove the query definition.

Figure 6.6 Query Dialog Box

Point to the query item in the Queries & Connections task pane to display a dialog box with options for previewing, editing, and deleting the data.

SiteManagers

BldgCde	SiteMgr	Phone	Cell	HireDate
A115	Blair Jenkins	800-555-3485	226-555-3748	2/8/2015 12:00:00 AM
B120	Maria Hernandez	800-555-8675	519-555-3996	4/23/2019 12:00:00 A
C125	Cody Doxtator	800-555-9677	519-555-7795	9/15/2014 12:00:00 A
D154	Sean Williams	800-555-1444	226-555-4906	9/7/2018 12:00:00 AM
E139	Dani Westlake	800-555-4777	226-555-2525	4/24/2020 12:00:00 A

Columns [5]

BldgCde, SiteMgr, Phone, Cell, HireDate

Last refreshed

8:41 AM

Load status

Loaded to worksheet

Data Sources [1]

e:\el2c2\propmgtdata.accdb

VIEW IN WORKSHEET   EDIT   •••   DELETE

Queries & Connections

Queries | Connections

4 queries

SiteManagers
5 rows loaded.

TenantInfoQ
5 rows loaded.

TenantsTxt
32 rows loaded.

RentalListingsCSV
15 rows loaded.

Click here to delete the query.

Click here to select the imported data in the worksheet.

Click here to display the Power Query Editor.

Click here to display a drop-down list of options, including *Load To*, *Duplicate*, and *Append*.

1. With **6-PropMgt** open, edit the SiteManagers query by completing the following steps:
   a. Make the Site Managers worksheet active.
   b. If the Queries & Connections panel is not open, click the Queries & Connections button in the Queries & Connections group on the Data tab.
   c. Double-click the *SiteManagers* query in the Queries & Connections task pane.
   d. Click in any cell in the *SiteMgr* column and then click the Sort Ascending button in the Sort group.
   e. Click in any cell in the *HireDate* column, click the *Data Type* option arrow in the Transform group, and then click the *Date* option.

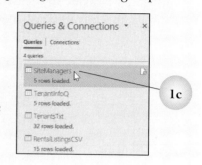

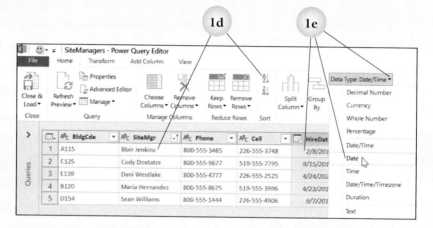

   f. Click the Close & Load button.
   g. Click in any cell to deselect the range.
2. Save and then close **6-PropMgt**.
3. Start Access 365 and then open the data file **PropMgtData** from the EL2C6 folder on your storage medium. Click the Enable Content button if a security warning displays stating that some active content has been disabled. Click the Yes button if a message displays asking if you want to make this a trusted document.
4. Double-click *SiteManagers* in the Tables group in the Navigation pane.
5. In row 1, change the contact name *Blair Jenkins* to *Sherri Blythe*.
6. Close the **6-PropMgtData** database.
7. Open **6-PropMgt** and notice the name *Blair Jenkins* in cell B3.
8. Click the Data tab and then click the Refresh All button in the Queries & Connections group. *Blair Jenkins* has been replaced by *Sherri Blythe* in cell B7.
9. Save **6-PropMgt**.

1. With **6-PropMgt** open, delete the *TenantsTxt*, *TenantInfoQ*, and *RentalListingsCSV* queries by completing the following steps:
   a. If the Queries & Connections task pane is not open, click the Data tab and then click the Queries & Connections button.
   b. Right-click the *TenantsTxt* query item at the task pane.
   c. Click the *Delete* option.
   d. Click the Delete button at the Delete Query message box that asks if you are sure you want to delete the TenantsTxt query.

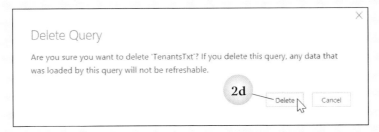

   e. Follow Steps 1b through 1d to delete the *TenantInfoQ* and the *RentalListingsCSV* queries.
2. Delete the Tenants worksheet.
3. Save **6-PropMgt**.

Editing or Removing the Source for a Query

If you move or rename a source, Excel will not know where to locate the file and a yellow triangle with an exclamation mark will appear beside the query item at the Queries & Connections task pane, as shown in Figure 6.7.

To edit the source, double-click the query item at the Queries & Connections task pane. Click the Data source settings button in the Data sources group on the Home tab in the Power Query Editor window. Click the Change Source button at the Data source settings dialog box, as shown in Figure 6.8. Click the File Path Browse button at the source information dialog box. Navigate to the folder containing the source file, click the source file in the file list box, and then click the OK button. Click the Close button at the Data source settings dialog box. Click the Close & Load button in the Close group on the Home tab at the Power Query Editor window to import the data from the new source file.

Figure 6.7 Source File Moved or Renamed

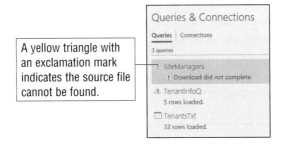

Figure 6.8 Data Source Settings Dialog Box

The sources for the queries in the current workbook are listed in the list box.

To change the source, select the query in the list box and then click the Change Source button.

Activity 3 **Transform Data Using Flash Fill and Text Functions**   **4 Parts**

You will continue working with a property management spreadsheet, using Flash Fill and text functions to split site managers' names into two fields and creating tenant IDs as well as new email addresses for site managers.

 Tutorial

Populating Data Using Flash Fill

Quick Steps

Extract Data Using Flash Fill

1. Insert blank column(s) next to source data.
2. Type first record.
3. Press Enter key.
4. Start typing second record.
5. When grayed-out text appears, press Enter key.

Transforming Data Using Flash Fill

The Flash Fill feature extracts, joins, and inserts text, numbers, dates, and times. It is useful for organizing data that has been pasted or imported from another source. Join all or extract parts of the contents of cells. Flash Fill analyzes adjacent columns while entering data, detects any patterns, and suggests how the rest of the column should be completed.

Flash Fill can split columns, like the Text to Columns button in the Data Tools group on the Data tab or the Split Column feature in the Transform group on the Home tab of the Power Query Editor. To split a column using Flash Fill, insert two new columns. Type the first name *Cody* in column C, as shown in Figure 6.9. Press the Enter key and then type *D* to start the second name, *Dani*. Excel recognizes that the first word of the adjacent column B is to be extracted and suggests doing the same for the remaining cells in column C. Notice that the rest of the names are grayed out. Press the Enter key to accept the suggestion or continue typing to reject the suggestion. Repeat the process for the last name.

A few rows of data may need to be entered before Excel recognizes the pattern. Once the pattern is established, press the Enter key. Other methods for using Flash

Figure 6.9 Flash Fill

	A	B	C	D
1			Riverside Property Manag	
2	**BldgCde**	**SiteMgr**	**MgrFName**	**MgrLName**
3	C125	Cody Doxtator	Cody	
4	E139	Dani Westlake	Dani	
5	B120	Maria Hernandez	Maria	
6	D154	Sean Williams	Sean	
7	A115	Sherri Blythe	Sherri	

Start typing a cell entry. Once Excel recognizes the pattern, press the Enter key.

Flash Fill

Fill are to click the Fill button in the Editing group on the Home tab and then choose *Flash Fill* from the drop-down menu, to click the Flash Fill button in the Data Tools group on the Data tab, or to use the keyboard shortcut Ctrl + E.

Activity 3a Separating Site Manager Names into Two Columns Using Flash Fill   Part 1 of 4

1. With **6-PropMgt** open, split the site managers' names in column B into two columns by completing the following steps:
   a. If necessary, make the Site Managers worksheet active.
   b. Insert two columns between the *SiteMgr* and *Phone* columns in the table. Type MgrFName in cell C2 and MgrLName in cell D2.
   c. In cell C3, type Cody and then press the Enter key.
   d. In cell C4, type D. Flash Fill recognizes the sequence and suggests how to fill the rest of the column.
   e. Press the Enter key to accept the suggestions. If Excel does not recognize the pattern right away, continue to type the first names or click the Flash Fill button in the Data Tools group on the Data tab.
   f. In cell D3, type Doxtator and then press the Enter key.
   g. In cell D4, type W. Flash Fill recognizes the sequence and suggests how to fill the rest of the column.
   h. Press the Enter key to accept the suggestions. If Excel does not recognize the pattern right away, continue to type the last names or click the Flash Fill button in the Data Tools group on the Data tab.
2. Delete column B.
3. Save **6-PropMgt**.

 Check Your Work

 Tutorial
Using Text
Functions

 Text

Using Text Functions

Text can be formatted or modified using text functions. Insert a text function by typing it or by clicking the Text button in the Function Library group on the Formulas tab and then selecting a function from the drop-down list. For example, use the LOWER and UPPER functions to convert text from uppercase to lowercase and vice versa. Text that has incorrect capitalization can be changed to title case using the PROPER function. New text can be substituted for existing text using the SUBSTITUTE function.

Use text functions to extract the data when only some of the characters in a cell need to be copied. Text can be extracted from the rightmost, leftmost, or middle of a string of characters using the RIGHT, LEFT, or MID function, respectively. These three functions—along with the TRIM function, which removes extra spaces between characters—also can be used on data that has been imported or copied from another source. Table 6.2 provides more information about each text function.

 Tutorial
Using the
CONCAT Function

The CONCAT function was introduction in Excel 2016 and replaces the CONCATENATE function. The CONCATENATE function is still available for compatibility with earlier version of Excel. Use the CONCAT function to join the content of two or more cells, including text, numbers, or cell references. Additional information, including spaces and characters, can also be added to the combined data. After extracting data, you can use these functions to combine the data in different ways to make unique customer numbers, employee IDs, email addresses, and other useful strings of text. Spaces or characters (text, numbers, or symbols) added directly to the function are enclosed in quotation marks. Numbers do not need quotation marks. The TEXTJOIN function is similar to the CONCAT function in that it joins the contents of two or more cells. With the TEXTJOIN function a constant delimiter, such as a hyphen, is specified and is placed between the contents of each cell.

The formula used in Activity 3b, =TEXTJOIN("-",TRUE,K2,L2,M2), joins the middle three characters of *BldgCde*, a hyphen, the first three letters of the tenant's last name, a hyphen, and the last four digits of the tenant's phone number to create a new TenantID. TRUE instructs Excel to ignore any empty cells. If this parameter is left out of the formula, Excel assumes TRUE. In a TEXTJOIN or a CONCAT formula, cell references are separated by commas and any spaces or characters (text or symbols) added directly to the formula are enclosed in quotation marks.

Table 6.2 Examples of Text Functions

Text Function	Description	Example
=PROPER(text)	Capitalizes first letter of each word	=PROPER("annual budget") returns *Annual Budget* in formula cell OR A3 holds text *annual budget*; =PROPER(a3) entered in C3 causes C3 to display *Annual Budget*
=UPPER(text)	Converts text to uppercase	=UPPER("annual budget") returns *ANNUAL BUDGET* in formula cell OR A3 holds text *annual budget*; =UPPER(a3) entered in C3 causes C3 to display *ANNUAL BUDGET*
=LOWER(text)	Converts text to lowercase	=LOWER("ANNUAL BUDGET") returns *annual budget* in formula cell OR A3 holds text *ANNUAL BUDGET*; =LOWER(a3) entered in C3 causes C3 to display *annual budget*
=SUBSTITUTE(text)	Inserts new text in place of old text	A3 holds text *Annual Budget*; =SUBSTITUTE(a3,"Annual","2021") entered in C3 causes C3 to display *2021 Budget*
=RIGHT(text,num_chars)	Extracts requested number of characters, starting at rightmost character	=RIGHT("2021 Annual Budget",13) returns *Annual Budget* in formula cell OR A3 holds text *2021 Annual Budget*; =RIGHT(a3,13) entered in C3 causes C3 to display *Annual Budget*
=LEFT(text,num_chars)	Extracts requested number of characters, starting at leftmost character	=LEFT("2021 Annual Budget",4) returns *2021* in formula cell OR A3 holds text *2021 Annual Budget*; =LEFT(a3,4) entered in C3 causes C3 to display *2021*

Table 6.2 Examples of Text Functions—*Continued*

Text Function	Description	Example
=MID(text,start-num, num-chars)	Extracts requested number of characters, starting at given position	=MID("2021 Annual Budget",6,13) returns *Annual Budget* in formula cell OR A3 holds text *2021 Annual Budget*; =MID(a3,6,13) entered in C3 causes C3 to display *Annual Budget*
=CONCAT(text1, text2,text3...)	Joins contents of two of more cells plus additional information	=CONCAT("Sara","Jones","@ppi-edu.net") returns *SaraJones@ppi-edu.net* in formula cell OR A3 holds text *Sara*; A4 holds *Jones* =CONCAT(a3,a4,"@ppi-edu.net") entered in C5 causes C5 to display *SaraJones@ppi-edu.net*
=TEXTJOIN(delimeter, ignore_empty,text1,text2, text3...)	Joins contents of two or more cells and places a constant delimiter between each cell content	A3 holds text *115*, B3 holds text *112* and C3 holds text *McC* =TEXTJOIN("-",true,a3,b3,c3) returns *115-112-McC*
=LEN(text)	Returns the number of characters	A3 holds text *Annual Budget* =LEN(a3) entered in C3 causes C3 to display *13*

Activity 3b **Extracting and Combining Text Using the RIGHT, LEFT, MID, and TEXTJOIN Functions**

Part 2 of 4

1. With **6-PropMgt** open, make the All Tenants worksheet active.
2. Extract data and then combine it to create a TenantID number using the middle three letters or digits of *BldgCde*, followed by a hyphen, the first three letters of the tenant's last name, a hyphen, and the last four digits of the tenant's phone number (for example: *115-McC-3485*). To extract the middle three characters of *BldgCde*, complete the following steps:
   a. Click in cell K1, type BldgCde, and then press the Enter key.
   b. Click the Formulas tab and then click the Text button in the Function Library group.
   c. Click *MID* at the drop-down list.
   d. If necessary, drag the Function Arguments dialog box out of the way so that the first few rows of the worksheet can be seen.
   e. With the insertion point positioned in the *Text* text box, type a2 and then press the Tab key.
   f. Type 2 in the *Start-num* text box and then press the Tab key.
   g. Type 3 in the *Num_chars* text box and then click OK.

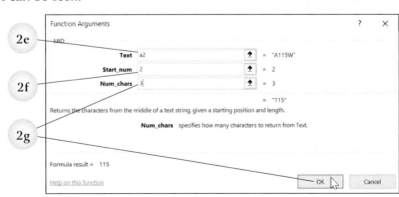

3. To extract the first three letters of the tenant's last name, complete the following steps:
   a. Click in cell L1, type TenantLName, and then press the Enter key.
   b. AutoFit the width of column L.
   c. With cell L2 active, click the Text button.
   d. Click *LEFT* at the drop-down list.
   e. If necessary, drag the Function Arguments dialog box out of the way so that the first few rows of the worksheet can be seen.
   f. With the insertion point positioned in the *Text* text box, type d2 and then press the Tab key.
   g. Type 3 in the *Num_chars* text box and then click OK.

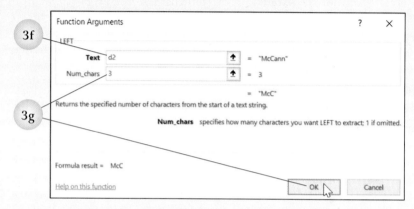

4. To extract the last four numbers of the tenant's phone number, complete the following steps:
   a. Click in cell M1, type Phone, and then press the Enter key.
   b. With cell M2 active, click the Text button.
   c. Click *RIGHT* at the drop-down list.
   d. If necessary, drag the Function Arguments dialog box out of the way so that the first few rows of the worksheet can be seen.
   e. With the insertion point positioned in the *Text* text box, type e2 and then press the Tab key.
   f. Type 4 in the *Num_chars* text box and then click OK.

5. Use the TEXTJOIN function to combine the extracted data to create the new TenantID using the middle three characters of *BldgCde*, the first three letters of the tenant's last name, the last four digits of the tenant's phone number, and a hyphen as the delimiter—for example, *115-McC-3485*—by completing the following steps:
   a. Click in cell N1, type TenantID, and then press the Enter key.
   b. With cell N2 active, click the Text button.
   c. Scroll down the drop down-list and then click *TEXTJOIN*.
   d. If necessary, drag the Function Arguments dialog box out of the way.

e. With the insertion
point positioned in
the *Delimiter* text
box, type - (a hyphen
character) and then
press the Tab key.

f. Type true in the
Ignore_empty text box
and then press the tab
key.

g. Type k2 in the *Text1*
text box and then
press the Tab key.

h. Type l2 in the *Text2*
text box and then
press the Tab key.

i. Type m2 in the *Text3* text box and then click OK.

6. AutoFit the width of column N.

7. Copy the range K2:N2 to row 33 and then deselect the range.

8. Save **6-PropMgt**.

Activity 3c Converting Text Using the UPPER Function

Part 3 of 4

1. With **6-PropMgt** open, place the new TenantID within the table and convert all
the letters in the *TenantID* column in a new column to uppercase by completing the
following steps:

a. Click in cell A1, right click, point to the *Insert* option, and then click *Table Columns to the Left* option.

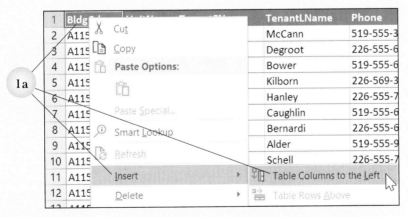

b. With cell A1 active, type TenantID and then press the Enter key.

c. With cell A2 active, type =upper(o2) and then press the Enter key. Excel fills the
column with the formula.

2. AutoFit the width of columns A through O.

3. Save **6-PropMgt**.

1. With **6-PropMgt** open, create new email addresses for the site managers by completing the following steps:
   a. Make the Site Managers worksheet active.
   b. Click in cell G2, type Email, and then press the Enter key.
   c. Click the Formulas tab and then click the Text button.
   d. Click *CONCAT* at the drop-down list.
   e. If necessary, drag the Function Arguments dialog box out of the way so that the first few rows of the worksheet can be seen.
   f. With the insertion point positioned in the *Text1* text box, type b3 and then press the Tab key.
   g. Type . (a period) in the *Text2* text box and then press the Tab key. Excel will enter quotes around the period.
   h. Type c3 in the *Text3* text box and then press the Tab key.
   i. Type @ppi-edu.net in the *Text4* text box and then click OK.
   j. AutoFit the width of column G.
2. With cell G3 active, click in the Formula bar, click between the equal sign and the function CONCAT, and then type lower(. Press the End key, type), and then press the Enter key. The formula in the range G3:G7 is *=LOWER(CONCAT(B3,".",C3,"@ppi-edu.net"))*.

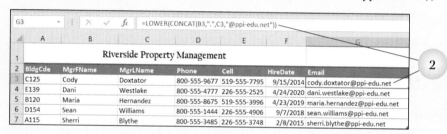

3. Count the number of characters in the email address by completing the following steps:
   a. Click in cell H2 and type Length and then press the Enter key.
   b. Click the Text button.
   c. Click *LEN* at the drop-down list.
   d. With the insertion point in the *Text* text box, type g3 and then click OK. The formula in the range H3:H4 is *=LEN(G3)*.
4. Change the Tenants worksheet to Landscape orientation and then print the workbook.
5. Save, print, and then close **6-PropMgt**.

Check Your Work

Chapter Summary

- Excel data can be embedded in or linked to a Word document. Embedding inserts a copy of the source data in the Word document and allows the object to be edited using Excel's tools within the Word environment. Linking the object inserts a shortcut in Word to the Excel workbook from which the source data is retrieved.

- To embed copied Excel data in a Word document, open the document, move the insertion point where the copied Excel data should be inserted, and then open the Paste Special dialog box. At the Paste Special dialog box, click *Microsoft Excel Worksheet Object* in the *As* list box and then click OK. To link data, follow the same steps for embedding, but click the *Paste link* radio button.

- Breaking a link involves removing the connection between the source file and destination file. This means that the data will no longer be updated in the destination file when the original data changes.

- To break a link in a Word document, right-click the linked object, point to *Linked Worksheet Object*, and then click *Links* at the shortcut menu. Click the source object for the link to be broken and then click the Break Link button. At the message box that appears, click Yes to confirm that the link is to be broken.

- Copy and paste, copy and embed, or copy and link Excel data into slides in a PowerPoint presentation using the same techniques used to embed cells in or link cells to a Word document.

- In Office 365, the charting tools are fully integrated. A chart copied and pasted from Excel to a PowerPoint presentation or Word document is embedded by default.

- Data in an Excel worksheet can be copied and pasted into an Access table datasheet, query, or form using the Clipboard task pane. Before pasting data into a table datasheet, make sure that the column structures in the two programs match.

- To exchange Excel data with someone who cannot import an Excel worksheet or cannot copy and paste using the Clipboard task pane, save the data as a text file.

- To save a worksheet as a text file, open the Save As dialog box and then change the file type to the correct option. Type a file name for the text file and then click the Save button. Click OK at the message box stating that only the active worksheet will be saved and then click Yes at the next message box to confirm saving the data as a text file.

- Excel provides several text file formats to accommodate differences across operating systems, which configure text files using various end-of-line character codes.

- The Get & Transform Data group on the Data tab contains buttons for importing data from external sources into an Excel worksheet using Power Query technology. To import data, make active the cell in which the imported data is to start and then click the button representing the source application or point to the Get Data button and select the source from a drop-down list.

- Exchanging data between Access and Excel is a seamless process, since the data in an Access datasheet is structured in the same row and column format as the data in an Excel worksheet. The imported data can be appended to an existing worksheet or placed in a new worksheet.

- When data is imported into Excel, the data is imported in a table format a query is created. The Queries & Connections task pane displays with the Queries tab active and the new query selected.

- Text files are often used to exchange data between different programs because the file format is recognized by nearly all applications. In a text file, the data between fields is generally separated with a tab character or a comma.

- If you move or rename a source, Excel will not know where to locate the file and a yellow triangle with an exclamation mark will appear beside the query item at the Queries & Connections task pane.

- Refreshing, modifying, and removing queries helps ensure that the most current data is in a destination file. Removing a connection allows the user to capture data at a specific time.

- Convert text from lowercase to uppercase or from uppercase to lowercase using the UPPER and LOWER text functions.
- Text that has incorrect capitalization can be changed to title case using the PROPER function. New text can be substituted for existing text using the SUBSTITUTE function.
- Extract data from a cell based on its position in a cell using the RIGHT, LEFT, or MID text functions.
- Combine the content of two or more cells using the TEXTJOIN or CONCAT function.
- Count the number of characters in a cell using the LEN function.
- Use the Flash Fill feature to extract, join, and insert text, numbers, dates, and times.

Commands Review

FEATURE	RIBBON TAB, GROUP/OPTION	BUTTON, OPTION	KEYBOARD SHORTCUT
copy	Home, Clipboard		Ctrl + C
embed Excel data in PowerPoint presentation or Word document	Home, Clipboard	, *Paste Special*	
export as a text file	File, *Export*		
Flash Fill	Home, Editing OR Data, Data Tools		Ctrl + E
import Access table	Data, Get & Transform Data		
import from text file	Data, Get & Transform Data		
insert text function (CONCAT, LEFT, LEN, LOWER, MID, PROPER, RIGHT, SUBSTITUTE, TEXTJOIN, UPPER)	Formulas, Function Library		
link Excel data to PowerPoint presentation or Word document	Home, Clipboard	, *Paste Special*	

Microsoft®

Excel®

Automating Repetitive Tasks and Customizing Excel

CHAPTER

7

Performance Objectives

Upon successful completion of Chapter 7, you will be able to:

1. Customize the display options for Excel
2. Minimize the ribbon
3. Customize the ribbon by creating a custom tab and adding buttons
4. Customize the Quick Access Toolbar by adding and removing buttons for frequently used commands
5. Create and apply custom views
6. Record, run, and edit a macro
7. Save a workbook containing macros as a macro-enabled workbook
8. Assign a macro to a shortcut key
9. Insert and configure form controls
10. Create and use templates
11. Customize save options to AutoRecover files
12. View Trust Center settings

Automating and customizing the Excel environment to accommodate preferences can increase efficiency. For example, create a macro if the same task is being frequently repeated to save time and ensure consistency. Add a button for a frequently used command to the Quick Access Toolbar to provide single-click access to it. Other ways to customize Excel include creating a custom template, ribbon tab, or view and modifying display and save options. By completing the activities in this chapter, you will learn how to effectively automate and customize the Excel environment.

 Data Files

Before beginning chapter work, copy the EL2C7 folder to your storage medium and then make EL2C7 the active folder.

The online course includes additional training and assessment resources.

You will customize the Excel environment by minimizing the ribbon, changing display options, importing and exporting custom settings for the Quick Access Toolbar and ribbon, creating a custom ribbon tab, adding buttons to the Quick Access Toolbar to make features more accessible, and then creating custom views.

Tutorial

Changing Display Options

Quick Steps

Change Display Options
1. Click File tab.
2. Click *Options*.
3. Click *Advanced* in left pane.
4. Change display options as required.
5. Click OK.

Minimize Ribbon
Press Ctrl + F1.
OR
1. Click Ribbon Display Options button.
2. Click *Show Tabs*.
OR
Click Collapse the Ribbon button.

Changing Display Options

The Excel Options dialog box contains many options for customizing the environment to suit the user's needs. As shown in Figure 7.1, Excel groups options that affect the display by those that are global settings, those that affect the entire workbook, and those that affect only the active worksheet. Changes to workbook and/or worksheet display options are saved with the workbook.

Figure 7.1 Excel Options Dialog Box with the Display Options Shown

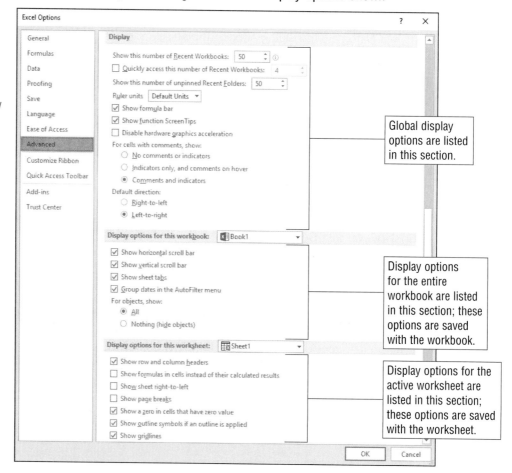

Minimizing the Ribbon

When working with a large worksheet, it may be easier to work with the ribbon minimized, which creates more space within the work area. Figure 7.2 shows the worksheet for Activity 1a with the customized display options and minimized ribbon.

 Collapse the Ribbon

One way to minimize the ribbon is to click the Collapse the Ribbon button located at the right edge of the ribbon. With the ribbon minimized, clicking a tab temporarily redisplays it to allow selecting a feature. After the feature has been selected, the ribbon returns to the minimized state. Press Ctrl + F1 or double-click the ribbon to toggle it on or off.

 Ribbon Display Options

Another way to minimize the ribbon is to click the Ribbon Display Options button, which remains in the upper right corner of the screen. Options under this button allow for quickly auto-hiding the ribbon (including tabs and commands), showing only the ribbon tabs (commands are hidden), or redisplaying the ribbon tabs and commands.

Activity 1a Changing Display Options and Minimizing the Ribbon   Part 1 of 7

1. Open **NWinterSch.**
2. Save the workbook with the name **7-NWinterSch.**
3. Turn off the display of the Formula bar (since there are no formulas in the workbook), turn off the display of sheet tabs (since there is only one sheet in the workbook), and turn off the display of row and column headers and gridlines by completing the following steps:
   a. Click the File tab.
   b. Click *Options*.
   c. Click *Advanced* in the left pane.
   d. Scroll down the Excel Options dialog box to the *Display* section and then click the *Show formula bar* check box to remove the check mark.
   e. Scroll down to the *Display options for this workbook* section and then click the *Show sheet tabs* check box to remove the check mark.
   f. Scroll down to the *Display options for this worksheet* section and then click the *Show row and column headers* check box to remove the check mark.
   g. Click the *Show gridlines* check box to remove the check mark.
   h. Click OK.
4. Press Ctrl + F1 to hide the ribbon.
5. Compare your screen with the one shown in Figure 7.2.
6. Save and then close **7-NWinterSch.**

3d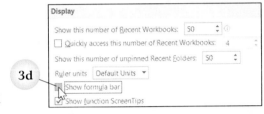

3e

3f
3g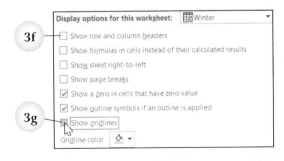

Figure 7.2 Activity 1a Worksheet with Customized Display Options and Minimized Ribbon

Double-click a tab to show or hide the ribbon.

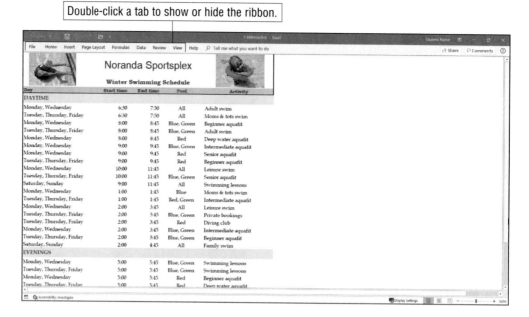

Activity 1b Restoring Default Display Options

1. Press Ctrl + N to open a new blank workbook.
2. Notice that the workbook and worksheet display options that were changed in Activity 1a are restored to the default options. The Formula bar remains hidden (since this is a global display option) and the ribbon remains minimized (since the display of the ribbon is a toggle on/off option).
3. Open **7-NWinterSch**.
4. Notice that the sheet tabs, row and column headers, and gridlines are hidden (since these display option settings are saved with the workbook).
5. Close **7-NWinterSch** without saving it.
6. With the blank workbook active, click the Ribbon Display Options button next to the Minimize button in the upper right corner of the screen and then click *Show Tabs and Commands* at the drop-down list.
7. Redisplay the Formula bar by completing the following steps:
   a. Click the File tab and then click *Options*.
   b. Click *Advanced* in the left pane.
   c. Scroll down the Excel Options dialog box to the *Display* section, click the *Show formula bar* check box to insert a check mark, and then click OK.
8. Close the workbook without saving it.

Customizing Ribbons and the Quick Access Toolbar

When working with Excel, a user may prefer to access frequently used features from the Quick Access Toolbar or in a new group within an existing or new ribbon. Activities 1d and 1e demonstrate how to customize both the ribbon and the Quick Access Toolbar.

Tutorial

Exporting and
Importing
Customizations

Exporting and Importing Customizations

The ribbon or the Quick Access Toolbar may already have been customized on the computers in your institution's computer lab. To be able to restore these customizations after making changes in the upcoming activities, Activity 1c will demonstrate how to save (export) them and Activity 1f will demonstrate how to reinstall (import) them.

To save the current ribbon and Quick Access Toolbar settings, click the File tab and then click *Options*. At the Excel Options dialog box, click *Customize Ribbon* in the left pane. The dialog box will display as shown in Figure 7.3. Click the Import/Export button in the lower right corner of the Excel Options dialog box. Click *Export all customizations* to save the file with the custom settings. Use this file to reinstall the saved settings in Activity 2f or to install customized settings on a different computer. Click the Import/Export button and then click *Import customization file*. Locate the file and reinstall the customized settings.

Activity 1c Exporting Customizations

Part 3 of 7

1. Press Ctrl + N to open a new blank workbook.
2. Save the current ribbon and Quick Access Toolbar settings to the desktop by completing the following steps:
   a. Click the File tab and then click *Options*.
   b. Click *Customize Ribbon* in the left pane of the Excel Options dialog box.
   c. Click the Import/Export button at the bottom right of the Excel Options dialog box.
   d. Click *Export all customizations* at the drop-down list.
   e. Click *Desktop* in the *This PC* list in the left panel of the File Save dialog box.
   f. Change the file name to **7-ExcelCustomizations** and then click the Save button. The file is saved as an Exported Office UI file with the name **7-ExcelCustomizations**.
   g. Click OK.
   h. Close the workbook. Click Don't Save if prompted to save changes.

Tutorial

Customizing the
Ribbon

💡 **Hint** To save the mouse clicks used when switching tabs and choosing options from drop-down lists, create a custom tab with buttons used on a regular basis.

Customizing the Ribbon

To customize the ribbon by adding a new tab, group, or button, click the File tab and then click *Options*. At the Excel Options dialog box, click *Customize Ribbon* in the left pane. The dialog box will display as shown in Figure 7.3. The dialog box can also be accessed by right-clicking anywhere in the ribbon or Quick Access Toolbar and then choosing the *Customizing the Ribbon* option.

The commands shown in the left list box are dependent on the current option in the *Choose commands from* option box. Click the *Choose commands from* option box arrow (displays *Popular Commands*) to select from a variety of options, such as *Commands Not in the Ribbon* and *All Commands*. The tabs shown in the right list box are dependent on the current option in the *Customize the Ribbon* option box. Click the *Customize the Ribbon* option box arrow (displays *Main Tabs*) to select *All Tabs*, *Main Tabs*, or *Tool Tabs*.

Figure 7.3 Excel Options Dialog Box with *Customize Ribbon* Selected

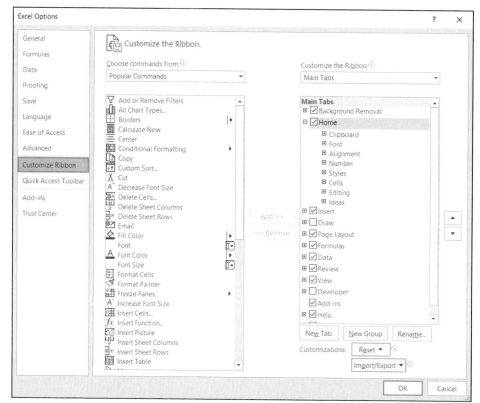

Quick Steps

**Create New Tab
and Group**

1. Click File tab.
2. Click *Options*.
3. Click *Customize Ribbon* in left pane.
4. Click tab name to precede new tab.
5. Click New Tab button.

Add New Group to Existing Tab

1. Click File tab.
2. Click *Options*.
3. Click *Customize Ribbon* in left pane.
4. Click tab name on which to add new group.
5. Click New Group button.

Add Button to Group

1. Click File tab.
2. Click *Options*.
3. Click *Customize Ribbon* in left pane.
4. Click group name in which to insert new button.
5. Select *All Commands* in the drop-down list.
6. Click command.
7. Click Add button.

Rename Tab or Group

1. Click File tab.
2. Click *Options*.
3. Click *Customize Ribbon* in left pane.
4. Click tab or group to be renamed.
5. Click Rename button.
6. Type new name.
7. Click OK.

Create a new group in an existing tab and add buttons within the new group or create a new tab, create a new group within the tab, and then add buttons to the new group.

Creating a New Tab To create a new tab, click any tab in the list box and then click the New Tab button. The newly created tab will appear with the name *New Tab (Custom)* as shown in Figure 7.4. It will also include a new group, called *New Group (Custom)*. Rename the tab and group by clicking the Rename button and entering a new name (see below). Move the tab up or down in order by clicking on it and then clicking the Move Up or Move Down arrow buttons at the right side of the dialog box.

Adding Buttons to a Group Click the group name within the tab, click the desired command in the list box at the left, and then click the Add button that displays between the two list boxes. Remove commands in a similar manner: Click the command to be removed from the tab group and then click the Remove button between the two list boxes.

Renaming a Tab, Group, or Command Click the tab name in the *Main Tabs* list box and then click the Rename button below the *Main Tabs* list box. At the Rename dialog box, type the name for the tab and then press the Enter key or click OK. Display the Rename dialog box by right-clicking the tab name and then clicking *Rename* at the shortcut menu.

Complete similar steps to rename a group or command. The Rename dialog box for a group or command name contains the *Symbol* list box and the *Display name* text box. Type the new name for the group in the *Display name* text box and then press the Enter key or click OK. Using symbols helps to identify new buttons.

Figure 7.4 New Tab and Group Created in the Customize the Ribbon Pane at the Excel Options Dialog Box

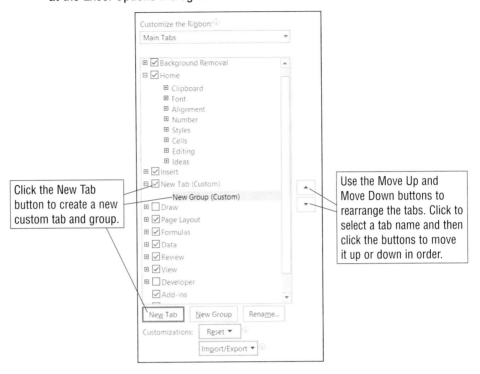

Click the New Tab button to create a new custom tab and group.

Use the Move Up and Move Down buttons to rearrange the tabs. Click to select a tab name and then click the buttons to move it up or down in order.

Activity 1d Customizing the Ribbon

Part 4 of 7

1. Open **NationalJE**.
2. Save the workbook with the name **7-NationalJE**.
3. Customize the ribbon by adding a new tab and a new group within the tab by completing the following steps. *Note: The ribbon will be reset to its original settings in Activity 1f.*
   a. Click the File tab and then click *Options*.
   b. Click *Customize Ribbon* in the left pane of the Excel Options dialog box.
   c. Click *Insert* in the *Main Tabs* list box at the right of the dialog box.
   d. Click the New Tab button below the list box. (This inserts a new tab below the Insert tab and a new group below the new tab.)

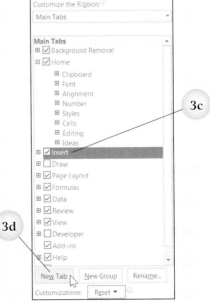

4. Rename the tab and the group by completing the following steps:
   a. Click to select *New Tab (Custom)* in the *Main Tabs* list box.
   b. Click the Rename button below the list box.
   c. At the Rename dialog box, type your first and last names and then click OK.
   d. Click to select the *New Group (Custom)* group name below the new tab.
   e. Click the Rename button.
   f. At the Rename dialog box, type Borders in the *Display name* text box and then click OK. (The Rename dialog box for a group or button displays symbols in addition to the *Display name* text box. You will apply a symbol to a button in a later step.)

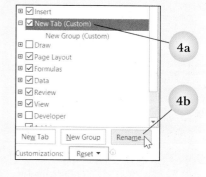

5. Add buttons to the *Borders (Custom)* group by completing the following steps:
   a. With *Borders (Custom)* selected, click the *Choose commands from* option box arrow (displays *Popular Commands*) and then click *All Commands* at the drop-down list.
   b. Scroll down the *All Commands* list box (the commands display alphabetically), click *Thick Bottom Border*, and then click the Add button between the two list boxes. (This inserts the command below the *Borders (Custom)* group name.)

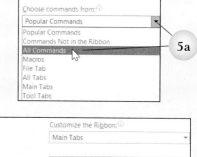

   c. With the *Thick Outside Borders* option selected, click the Add button.
   d. Scroll down the *All Commands* list box, click *Top and Double Bottom Border*, and then click the Add button.

6. Rename the Thick Outside Borders button by completing the following steps:
   a. Right-click *Thick Outside Borders* below *Thick Bottom Border* in the *Main Tabs* list box and then click *Rename* at the shortcut menu.
   b. At the Rename dialog box, click the white square with a black outline symbol in the *Symbol* list box (seventh row, second column) and then click OK. *Note: The position of the symbol may vary on your computer.*

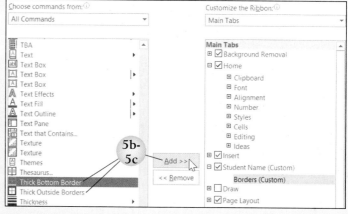

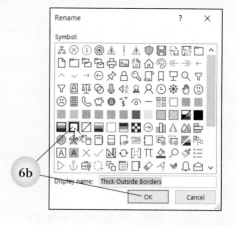

7. Click OK to close the Excel Options dialog box.
8. Use buttons on the custom tab to format and add formulas to the worksheet by completing the following steps:
   a. Select the range A1:A3, click the custom tab labeled with your name, and then click the Thick Outside Borders button in the Borders group.

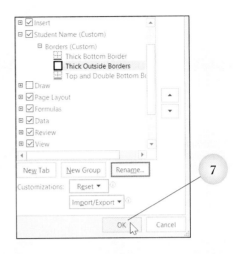

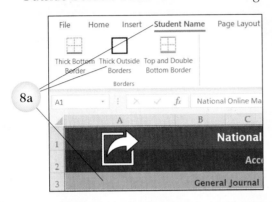

   b. Select the range B6:H6 and then click the Thick Bottom Border button in the Borders group.
   c. Make cell D18 the active cell and then click the Top and Double Bottom Border button in the Borders group.
9. Save **7-NationalJE**.
10. In a new Excel document, insert a screenshot of the worksheet showing the custom tab by using either the Screenshot feature (Insert tab, Screenshot button in Illustrations group) or the Windows key + Shift + S with Paste. Type your name a few lines below the screenshot.
11. Save the workbook with the name **7-NationalScreenshot**.
12. Print the first page of **7-NationalScreenshot** and then close the workbook.
13. Print and then close 7-**NationalJE**.

Check Your Work

Customizing the Quick Access Toolbar

Click the Customize Quick Access Toolbar button at the right side of the Quick Access Toolbar to open the Customize Quick Access Toolbar drop-down list, as shown in Figure 7.5. Click *More Commands* at the drop-down list to open the Excel Options dialog box with *Quick Access Toolbar* selected in the left pane, as shown in Figure 7.6. Change the list of commands shown in the left list box by clicking the *Choose commands from* option box arrow and then clicking the appropriate category. Scroll down the list box to locate the command and then double-click the command name to add it to the Quick Access Toolbar.

A few of Excel's less popular features are available only by adding buttons to the Quick Access Toolbar. If a feature is not available in any tab on the ribbon, search for it in the *All Commands* list box.

Delete a button from the Quick Access Toolbar by clicking the Customize Quick Access Toolbar button and then clicking the command at the drop-down list. If the command is not in the drop-down list, click the *More Commands* option. At the Excel Options dialog box, double-click the command in the right list box.

Add Button to Quick Access Toolbar

1. Click Customize Quick Access Toolbar button.
2. Click button.

OR

1. Click Customize Quick Access Toolbar button.
2. Click *More Commands*.
3. Click *Choose commands from* option box arrow.
4. Click category.
5. Double-click command in commands list box.
6. Click OK.

Remove Button from Quick Access Toolbar

1. Click Customize Quick Access Toolbar button.
2. Click command.

OR

1. Click Customize Quick Access Toolbar button.
2. Click *More Commands*.
3. Click command in right list box.
4. Click Remove button.
5. Click OK.

Figure 7.5 Customize Quick Access Toolbar Drop-Down List

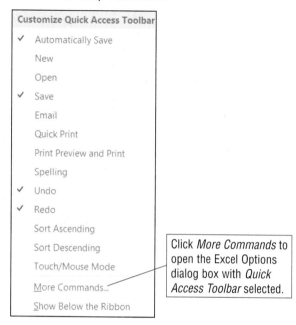

Click *More Commands* to open the Excel Options dialog box with *Quick Access Toolbar* selected.

Figure 7.6 Excel Options Dialog Box with *Quick Access Toolbar* Selected

Begin by selecting the category from which to choose commands.

In this list box, double-click the command to be added.

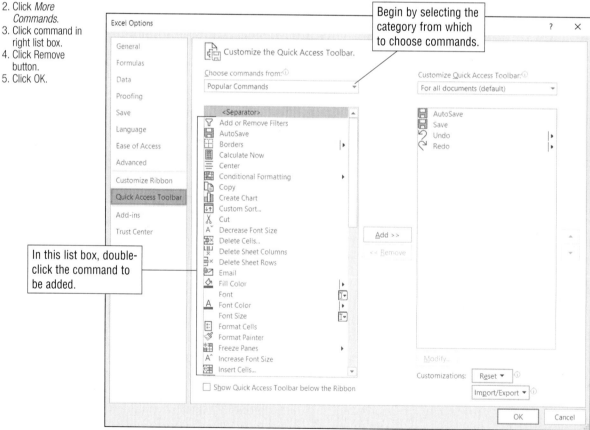

1. Press Ctrl + N to open a new blank workbook and then add the Print Preview and Print and Sort commands to the Quick Access Toolbar by completing the following steps. *Note: You will reset the Quick Access Toolbar to the original settings in Activity 1f.*
   a. Click the Customize Quick Access Toolbar button at the right side of the Quick Access Toolbar.
   b. Click *Print Preview and Print* at the drop-down list. The Print Preview and Print button is added to the end of the Quick Access Toolbar. *Note: Skip to Step 1d if the Print Preview and Print button already appears on your Quick Access Toolbar*.
   c. Click the Customize Quick Access Toolbar button.
   d. Click *More Commands* at the drop-down list.
   e. At the Excel Options dialog box with *Quick Access Toolbar* selected in the left pane, click the *Choose commands from* option box arrow and then click *All Commands*.

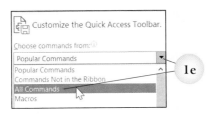

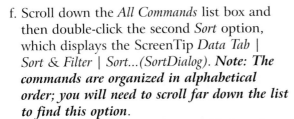
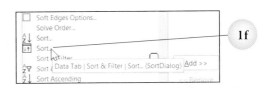

   f. Scroll down the *All Commands* list box and then double-click the second *Sort* option, which displays the ScreenTip *Data Tab | Sort & Filter | Sort...(SortDialog)*. *Note: The commands are organized in alphabetical order; you will need to scroll far down the list to find this option*.
   g. Click OK. The Sort button is added to the end of the Quick Access Toolbar.
2. Type your name in cell A1, press the Enter key, and then click the Print Preview and Print button on the Quick Access Toolbar to display the Print backstage area.
3. Press Esc to close the Print backstage area.
4. Click the Sort button on the Quick Access Toolbar to open the Sort dialog box.
5. Click the Cancel button at the Sort dialog box.
6. Close the workbook. Click the Don't Save button when prompted to save changes.

Resetting the Ribbons and the Quick Access Toolbar

Restore the ribbons and Quick Access Toolbar to the original settings that came with Excel 365 by clicking the Reset button below the *Main Tabs* list box in the Excel Options dialog box with *Customize Ribbon* selected. Clicking the Reset button displays two options: *Reset only selected Ribbon tab* and *Reset all customizations*. Click *Reset all customizations* to restore the ribbons and Quick Access Toolbar to their original settings and then click Yes at the message box that displays the question *Delete all Ribbon and Quick Access Toolbar customizations for this program?* To remove a tab that was created previously, right-click the tab and then click *Customize the Ribbon*. Right-click the tab in the *Main Tabs* list box and then click *Remove*.

To restore the ribbons and Quick Access Toolbar to your institution's original settings, import the settings exported in Activity 1c. Click the Import/Export button in the lower right corner of the Excel Options dialog box and then click *Import customization file*. Locate the file and reinstall the customized settings.

Activity 1f Importing Ribbon and Quick Access Toolbar Customizations   Part 6 of 7

1. Import the ribbon and Quick Access Toolbar customizations you saved in Activity 1c to reset your institution's original settings by completing the following steps:
   a. Press Ctrl + N to open a new blank workbook.
   b. Click the File tab and then click *Options*.
   c. Click *Customize Ribbon* in the left pane of the Excel Options dialog box.
   d. Click the Import/Export button at the bottom right of the Excel Options dialog box.
   e. Click *Import customization file* at the drop-down list.
   f. Click *Desktop* in the *This PC* list in the left panel of the File Open dialog box.
   g. Click **7-ExcelCustomizations**.
   h. Click Open.
   i. Click Yes at the message asking if you want to replace all the existing ribbon and Quick Access Toolbar customizations for this program.
   j. Click OK.
2. Close the workbook. Click Don't Save if prompted to save changes.

Tutorial

Creating and Applying a Custom View

Quick Steps

Create Custom View
1. Change display and print settings as desired.
2. Click View tab.
3. Click Custom Views.
4. Click Add button.
5. Type name for view.
6. Choose *Include in view* options.
7. Click OK.

 Custom Views

Quick Steps

Apply Custom View
1. Click View tab.
2. Click Custom Views button.
3. Click view name.
4. Click Show button.

Hint A custom view cannot be used in a worksheet with a table.

Creating and Applying a Custom View

A custom view saves display and print settings for the active worksheet. These settings can involve column widths, row heights, hidden rows and/or columns, filter settings, cell selections, windows settings, page layout options, and print areas. Create multiple custom views for the same worksheet and access stored views using the Custom Views dialog box. In Activity 1g, three custom views are created that store display settings, hidden rows, and a row height for a swimming schedule. Switch between views to show different portions of the worksheet, such as only the daytime swimming activities.

Begin creating a custom view by applying the required settings to the active worksheet, clicking the cell to be active, and displaying the rows and columns to be shown on the screen. When finished, click the View tab, click the Custom Views button in the Workbook Views group, click the Add button, type a name for the custom view, and then click OK.

Change a worksheet to display the settings for a custom view by opening the Custom Views dialog box, selecting the view name in the *Views* list box, and then clicking the Show button. Another method for displaying the settings is to double-click the view name. If a different worksheet is active, Excel will switch to the worksheet to which the view applies. A custom view can be applied only to the worksheet in which it was created.

If a custom view is no longer required, delete it by opening the Custom Views dialog box, selecting the custom view name in the *Views* list box, and then clicking the Delete button.

1. Open **7-NWinterSch**.
2. Save the workbook with the name **7-NWinterSch-CV** and then redisplay the row and column headers in the worksheet. Refer to Activity 1b for assistance with this step.
3. Create a custom view with display settings for all the swimming sessions by completing the following steps:
   a. Select rows 4 through 37, click the Format button in the Cells group on the Home tab, click *Row Height* at the drop-down list, type 20 in the *Row height* text box at the Row Height dialog box, and then click OK.
   b. Press Ctrl + Home.
   c. Click the View tab.
   d. Click the Custom Views button in the Workbook Views group.

   e. Click the Add button at the Custom Views dialog box.
   f. With the insertion point positioned in the *Name* text box at the Add View dialog box, type AllSessions.

   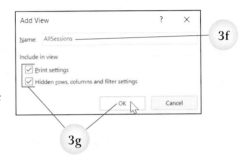

   g. Make sure that the *Print settings* and *Hidden rows, columns and filter settings* check boxes contain check marks and then click OK.
4. Create a second custom view to display the daytime swimming activities and hide the evening activities by completing the following steps:
   a. Select rows 24 through 37 and then press Ctrl + 9 to hide the rows.
   b. Press Ctrl + Home.
   c. Click the Custom Views button.
   d. At the Custom Views dialog box, click the Add button.
   e. At the Add View dialog box, type DaytimeSessions in the *Name* text box.

   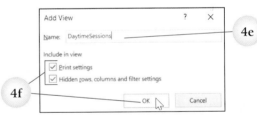

   f. Make sure that the *Print settings* and *Hidden rows, columns and filter settings* check boxes contain check marks and then click OK.
5. Click the Custom Views button in the Workbook Views group.
6. With *AllSessions* selected in the *Views* list box, click the Show button to apply the custom view.

   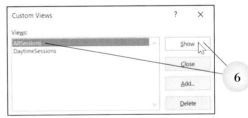

7. Create a third custom view to show only the evening swimming sessions by completing the following steps:
   a. Select rows 4 through 23 and hide the rows by completing a step similar to Step 4a.
   b. Create a custom view named *EveningSessions* by completing steps similar to Steps 4b–4f.
8. Click the Custom Views button and then double-click *DaytimeSessions* in the *Views* list box at the Custom Views dialog box.
9. Show the *EveningSessions* custom view.
10. Show the *AllSessions* custom view.
11. Save and then close **7-NWinterSch-CV**.

Activity 2 **Create Macros in a New Workbook** | **4 Parts**

You will create, run, edit, and delete macros to automate tasks; assign a macro to a shortcut key; and then store frequently used macros in a macro workbook.

Automating Tasks Using Macros

A macro is a series of instructions stored in sequence that can be recalled and carried out whenever the need arises. Consider creating a macro to perform the same task repeatedly without variation. Saving the instructions for a task in a macro not only saves time, but it also ensures that the steps are performed consistently every time. This can prevent errors in data entry, formatting, or other worksheet tasks.

Creating a Macro

Quick Steps

Create Macro
1. Click View tab.
2. Click Macros button arrow.
3. Click *Record Macro*.
4. Type macro name.
5. Click in *Description* text box and type description text.
6. Click OK.
7. Perform required actions.
8. Click Stop Recording button.

Creating a Macro

Before recording a new macro, take a few moments to plan the steps. Also consider if it is necessary to specify which cell must be active when the macro is run. For example, will the first step in the macro involve making a specific cell active? If so, designate the active cell using a shortcut key or Go To command during the recording.

To create a macro, begin by turning on the macro recorder by clicking the Macros button arrow in the macros group on the View tab and then clicking *Record Macro* at the drop-down list. This opens the Record Macro dialog box, as shown in Figure 7.7. Identify the macro by assigning a unique name to the steps that will be saved. A macro name must begin with a letter and can be a combination of letters, numbers, and underscore characters. A macro name cannot include spaces; use the underscore character to separate the words in a macro name. Also use the Record Macro dialog box to choose the location in which the macro is saved. By default, Excel saves the macro within the current workbook.

A macro can be assigned to a shortcut key combination. Doing so allows the user to run the macro more quickly by pressing the Ctrl key plus the chosen lowercase or uppercase letter. Enter a description of the purpose of a macro to provide information to other users who might use or edit it. In a macro workbook

Figure 7.7 Record Macro Dialog Box

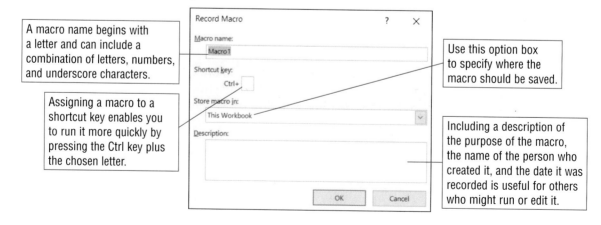

Hint When a macro is being recorded, the mouse clicks for select tabs within the ribbon are not saved.

Stop Recording

that will be shared, also consider entering the creator's name and the creation date into the description box for reference purposes. Click OK when finished identifying the macro and the recorder will begin saving the text and/or steps that are performed. Do not be concerned with making typing mistakes or canceling a dialog box while recording a macro. Correct mistakes as they happen, since only the result is saved. After completing the tasks to be saved, click the Stop Recording button on the Status bar to end the recording.

Saving Workbooks Containing Macros

Quick Steps

Save Macro-Enabled Workbook
1. Click File tab.
2. Click *Save As.*
3. Click *Browse.*
4. Navigate to appropriate folder.
5. Type file name in *File name* text box.
6. Click *Save as type* list arrow.
7. Click *Excel Macro-Enabled Workbook.*
8. Click Save.

When a macro is created in Excel, the commands are written and saved in a language called Microsoft Visual Basic for Applications (VBA). A workbook that contains a macro should be saved using the macro-enabled file format (.xlsm). The default XML-based file format (.xlsx) cannot store the macro code. The macro recorder used when creating a macro converts the actions to VBA statements behind the scenes. View and edit the VBA code or create macros from scratch by using the VBA Editor in Microsoft Visual Basic for Applications, which can be opened through the Macros dialog box. Activity 2d looks at the VBA statements created for the PrintInv macro and edits an instruction.

To save a new or existing workbook as a macro-enabled workbook, perform one of the following actions:

- *New workbook.* Click the Save button on the Quick Access Toolbar or click the File tab and then click the *Save As* option. At the Save As backstage area, click the *Browse* option to display the Save As dialog box and then navigate to the appropriate folder. Type the file name and then change the *Save as type* option to *Excel Macro-Enabled Workbook.* Click the Save button.

- *Existing workbook.* Click the File tab and then click the *Save As* option. At the Save As backstage area, click the *Browse* option to display the Save As dialog box and then navigate to the appropriate folder. Type the file name and then change the *Save as type* option to *Excel Macro-Enabled Workbook.* Click the Save button.

Activity 2a **Creating a Macro and Saving a Workbook as a Macro-Enabled Workbook**   Part 1 of 4

1. You work in the Accounting Department at a large company. The company has a documentation standard for all Excel workbooks that requires each worksheet to show the department name, author's name, creation date, and revision history. To standardize the documentation, you decide to create a macro that will insert row labels for this data. Begin by opening a new blank workbook.
2. Create the documentation macro by completing the following steps:
   a. Make cell C4 the active cell and then click the View tab. (Make a cell other than A1 active so you can move the active cell to the top left cell in the worksheet during the macro.)
   b. Click the Macros button arrow in the Macros group.
   c. Click *Record Macro* at the drop-down list.

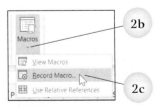

d. At the Record Macro dialog box with the insertion point positioned in the *Macro name* text box, type AcctgDocumentation.

e. Click in the *Description* text box and then type Accounting Department documentation macro. Created by [Student Name] on [Date]. Substitute your name for *[Student Name]* and the current date for *[Date]*.

f. Click OK. The macro recorder is now turned on, as indicated by the appearance of the Stop Recording button in the Status bar (which displays as a gray square next to *Ready*).

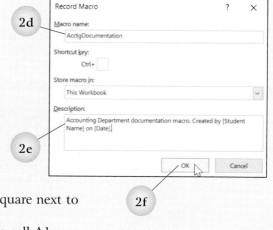

g. Press Ctrl + Home to move the active cell to cell A1. Including this command in the macro ensures that the documentation will begin at cell A1 in every workbook.

h. Type Accounting Department and then press the Enter key.

i. With cell A2 active, type Author and then press the Enter key.

j. With cell A3 active, type Date created and then press the Enter key.

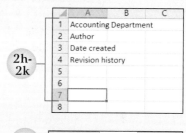

k. With cell A4 active, type Revision history and then press the Enter key three times to leave two blank rows before the start of the worksheet.

l. Click the Stop Recording button at the left side of the Status bar, next to *Ready*.

3. Save the workbook as a macro-enabled workbook by completing the following steps:

a. Click the Save button on the Quick Access Toolbar.

b. At the Save As backstage area, click the *Browse* option.

c. At the Save As dialog box, navigate to the EL2C7 folder in the Navigation pane and then double-click the *EL2C7* folder in the Content pane.

d. Click in the *File name* text box and then type 7-Macros.

e. Click the *Save as type* option box, scroll up or down the pop-up list, and then click *Excel Macro-Enabled Workbook*.

f. Click the Save button.

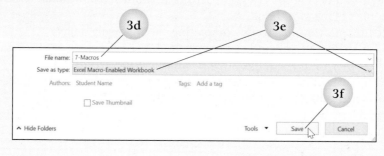

Tutorial

Running a Macro

Running a Macro

Running a Macro

Running a macro is sometimes referred to as *playing a macro*. Since a macro is a series of recorded tasks, running a macro involves instructing Excel to *play back* the recorded tasks. Think of a macro as a video. When the video is played, the same thing happens every time.

Quick Steps

Run Macro
1. Click View tab.
2. Click Macros button.
3. Double-click macro name.

To run (play) a macro, view the list of macros by clicking the Macros button in the Macros group on the View tab. This opens the Macro dialog box, shown in Figure 7.8. Click the name of the macro to run and then click the Run button or double-click the name of the macro in the *Macro name* list box.

Figure 7.8 Macro Dialog Box

By default, all the macros in all the open workbooks are displayed in this list box. Double-click the name of a macro to run it.

If the currently selected macro contains a description, the text displays here.

Click this button to run the currently selected macro.

Change the list of macros to view using this option box. View the macros in all the open workbooks, in only the current workbook, or in another open workbook.

Activity 2b Running a Macro   Part 2 of 4

1. With **7-Macros** open, run the AcctgDocumentation macro to test that it works correctly by completing the following steps:
   a. Select the range A1:A4 and then press the Delete key to erase the cell contents.
   b. To test the Ctrl + Home command in the macro, make sure cell that A1 is not active when the macro begins playing. Click in any cell other than cell A1 to deselect the range.
   c. Click the Macros button in the Macros group on the View tab. Make sure to click the button and not the button arrow.

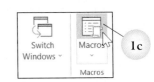

   d. At the Macro dialog box with *AcctgDocumentation* already selected in the *Macro name* list box, click the Run button.

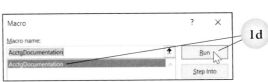

2. Save and then close **7-Macros**.

Assigning a Macro to a Shortcut Key

Quick Steps

Assign Macro to Shortcut Key
1. Click View tab.
2. Click Macros button arrow.
3. Click *Record Macro.*
4. Type macro name.
5. Click in *Shortcut key* text box.
6. Type a letter.
7. Click in *Description* text box.
8. Type description text.
9. Click OK.
10. Perform actions.
11. Click Stop Recording button.

When a macro is being recorded, it can be assigned to a Ctrl key combination. A macro assigned to a keyboard shortcut can be run without displaying the Macro dialog box. To create a keyboard shortcut, choose any lowercase or uppercase letter. Excel distinguishes the case of the letter when typing it in the *Shortcut key* text box at the Record Macro dialog box. For example, if an uppercase O is typed, Excel defines the shortcut key as *Ctrl + Shift + O*, as shown in Figure 7.9.

If an Excel feature is already assigned to the chosen key combination, the macro will override the feature. For example, pressing Ctrl + p in Excel causes the Print backstage area to display. If a macro is assigned to Ctrl + p, using this keyboard shortcut will run the new macro instead of displaying the Print backstage area. View a list of Excel-assigned keyboard shortcuts in Help by typing *keyboard shortcuts* in the *Search* text box. Point to *Get Help on "keyboard shortcuts"*. Choose *Keyboard shortcuts in Excel for Windows* in the results list.

Figure 7.9 Record Macro Dialog Box with a Shortcut Key Assigned

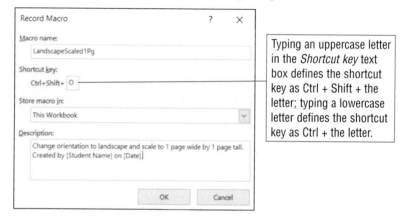

Typing an uppercase letter in the *Shortcut key* text box defines the shortcut key as Ctrl + Shift + the letter; typing a lowercase letter defines the shortcut key as Ctrl + the letter.

Activity 2c **Creating and Running a Macro Using a Shortcut Key**   Part 3 of 4

1. Open **7-Macros**.
2. When a workbook that contains a macro is opened, the default security setting is *Disable all macros with notification*. This causes a security warning to appear in the message bar (between the ribbon and the formula bar) stating that macros have been disabled. Enable the macros in the workbook by clicking the Enable Content button.

3. Create a macro that changes the print options for a worksheet and assign it to a shortcut key by completing the following steps:

a. Once the recording of a macro has stopped in an Excel session, the Stop Recording button in the Status bar changes to the Record New Macro button. Click the Record New Macro button at the left side of the Status bar next to *Ready*. (If you exited Excel before starting this activity, start a new macro by clicking the View tab, clicking the Macros button arrow, and then clicking *Record Macro*.)

Your taskbar may vary depending on your operating system.

b. Type LandscapeScaled1Pg in the *Macro name* text box.

c. Click in the *Shortcut key* text box, press and hold down the Shift key, type the letter O, and then release the Shift key.

d. Click in the *Description* text box and then type Change orientation to landscape and scale to 1 page wide by 1 page tall. Created by [Student Name] on [Date]. Substitute your name for *[Student Name]* and the current date for *[Date]*.

e. Click OK.

f. Click the Page Layout tab.

g. Click the Page Setup dialog box launcher at the bottom right of the Page Setup group.

h. At the Page Setup dialog box with the Page tab selected, click *Landscape* in the *Orientation* section.

i. Click *Fit to* in the *Scaling* section to scale the printout to 1 page wide by 1 page tall.

j. Click OK.

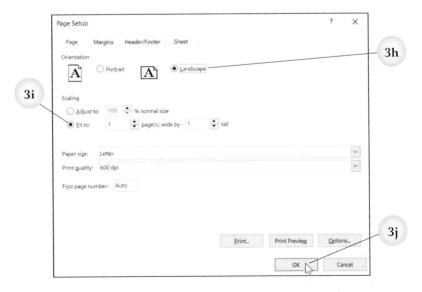

k. Click the Stop Recording button.

4. Press Ctrl + N to open a new blank workbook.
5. Press Ctrl + Shift + O to run the LandscapeScaled1Pg macro.
6. Type your name in cell A1, press the Enter key, and then press Ctrl + F2 to display the worksheet in the Print backstage area. Notice in Print Preview that the page orientation is landscape. Review the options in the Settings category. Notice that *Landscape Orientation* and *Fit Sheet on One Page* have been selected by the macro.
7. Click the Back button to return to the worksheet and then close the workbook. Click Don't Save when prompted to save changes.
8. Save and then close **7-Macros**.

Tutorial

Editing a Macro

Editing a Macro

The actions performed while a macro is being recorded are stored in VBA code. Each macro is saved as a separate module within a VBAProject for the workbook. A module can be described as a receptacle for the macro instructions. Figure 7.10 displays the window containing the VBA code module for the macro created in Activity 2a.

Use the module to edit a macro if the change needed is easy to decipher within the VBA statements. If several changes to a macro are required or if you do not feel comfortable with the VBA code, re-record the macro. When a new macro has been recorded and is being saved with the same name as an existing macro, Excel prompts the user to replace the existing macro. Save the re-recorded macro by overwriting the original macro.

Quick Steps

Edit Macro
1. Open workbook containing macro.
2. Click View tab.
3. Click Macros button.
4. Click macro name.
5. Click Edit button.
6. Make changes in VBA code window.
7. Click Save button.
8. Click File.
9. Click *Close and Return to Microsoft Excel.*

Figure 7.10 Microsoft Visual Basic for Applications Window for Activity 2a AcctgDocumentation Macro

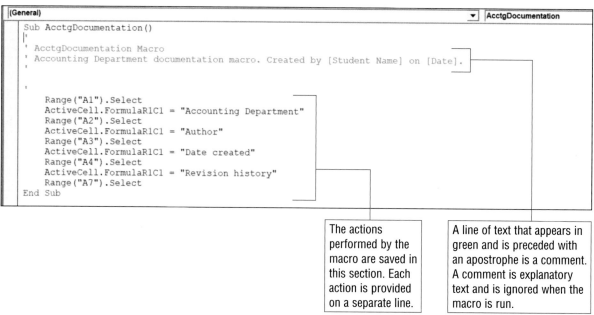

1. Open **NationalInv** and enable the content, if necessary.
2. Save the workbook with the name **7-NationalInv**.
3. The workbook contains a macro called *PrintInv* that automatically prints the invoice. Modify the macro to have the invoice display in print preview when the macro is run by completing the following steps:
   a. If necessary, click the View tab.
   b. Click the Macros button.
   c. At the Macro dialog box with *PrintInv* already selected in the *Macro name* list box, click the Edit button. A Microsoft Visual Basic for Applications window opens with the program code displayed for 7-NationalInv.xlsm - [Module1 (Code)].

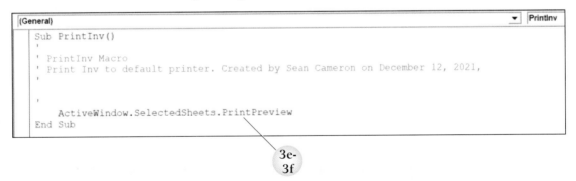

   d. Read the statements between the *Sub* and *End Sub* statements. *Sub* indicates the beginning of the procedure and *End Sub* indicates the end of the procedure. A procedure is a set of VBA statements that perform actions. The name of the procedure appears after the opening *Sub* statement and is the macro name. Each line beginning with a single apostrophe (') is a comment. A comment is used in programming to insert explanatory text that describes the logic or purpose of a statement. A statement that begins with an apostrophe is ignored when the macro is run. The commands that are executed when the macro is run display as indented lines of text below the comments.
   e. Remove the command that has Excel print one copy of the selected worksheet by selecting the text after the second period in the commands, starting with the word *Printout* and ending with the world *False*, and then press the Delete key.
   f. Type PrintPreview. The new command now reads *ActiveWindow.SelectedSheets.PrintPreview*. **Note: Do not include the period after PrintPreview**.

```
(General)                                                                          PrintInv

Sub PrintInv()
'
' PrintInv Macro
' Print Inv to default printer. Created by Sean Cameron on December 12, 2021,
'

'
    ActiveWindow.SelectedSheets.PrintPreview
End Sub
```

3e-
3f

   g. Click the Save button on the toolbar.

3g

4. Click File and then click *Close and Return to Microsoft Excel*.
5. Test the edited macro to make sure that the invoice displays in print preview by completing the following steps:
   a. Click the Macros button.
   b. At the Macro dialog box, double-click *PrintInv* in the *Macro name* list box.
   c. Click the Close Print Preview button.
6. Save **7-NationaInv**.

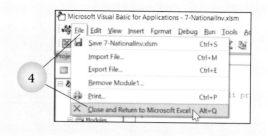

Managing and Deleting Macros

Quick Steps

Delete Macro
1. Open Macro dialog box.
2. Click macro name.
3. Click Delete button.
4. Click Yes.

By default, a macro is stored within the workbook that is active when it is recorded. When the workbook is closed, the macros within it are no longer available. For example, if the file 7-Macros is closed, the AcctgDocumentation macro will not be available in a new workbook. To continue using the macros, leave the workbook that contains them open, since by default, the Macro dialog box displays the macros for all the open workbooks in the *Macro name* list box.

Consider creating a macros workbook with a set of standard macros, similar to the macros workbook created or modified in Activities 2a through 2d. Open this workbook when working in Excel and the macros stored within it will be available for all the files that are created or edited during the Excel session. Create one macros workbook and copy it to other computers so a set of standard macros can be distributed to others for use.

If a macro is no longer needed, delete it in the Macro dialog box. Open the Macro dialog box, select the macro name in the *Macro name* list box, and then click the Delete button.

Activity 3 Insert and Configure Form Controls in an Invoice Workbook   **3 Parts**

You will insert a combo box form control, a check box form control, and a macro button form control into an invoice workbook.

Inserting and Configuring Form Controls

Insert a form control to allow users to enter information in a worksheet. For example, insert a combo box form control or a list box form control to allow users to select an option from a list, or insert a check box form control to allow users to select an option by inserting a check mark in a check box. After inserting a form control in a worksheet, configure the control to define how it will be used; also size the control and align multiple controls.

Inserting Form Controls

Quick Steps

Insert Form Control
1. Click Developer tab.
2. Click Insert button.
3. Click control.
4. Draw control.

To insert a form control in an active worksheet, click the Insert button in the Controls group on the Developer tab, click an option in the *Form Controls* section at the drop-down list, and then draw a box in the worksheet. The size of the form control box depends on the control options. For example, a form control that allows users to select from a drop-down list of two-letter state abbreviations (AL, AK, etc.) will be narrower than a form control that offers a drop-down list of city names (eg., Abbeville, Aberdeen, etc.). Table 7.1 describes selected types of form controls.

Configuring Form Controls

To configure and add options to a form control, right-click the control, click the *Format Control* option at the pop-up menu, and then enter information on the Control tab at the Format Control dialog box. The information entered at the Format Control dialog box depends on the type of form control. Figure 7.11 shows the Format Control dialog box for a combo box form control.

Table 7.1 Selected Types of Form Controls

Type of Form Control	Display	How to Use	Example
combo box form control	an option box with an arrow	Click the option box arrow to see a drop-down list of available options and then click an option.	Method of Payment: e-Transfer, Check, Visa, MC
list box form control	a box containing all the available options—with scroll bars, if necessary	Click an option in the list box to select it. The control can be configured to allow the user to select more than one option.	Method of Payment: e-Transfer, Check, Visa, MC
check box form control	a check box with a text label	Click the check box to insert or remove a check mark.	Ship to: ☐ Same as billing address
button form control	a button with a label and with a macro assigned to it	Click the button to run the macro.	Print Preview
option button form control	a radio button with a label	Click the radio button to insert or remove a bullet.	⦿ Option Button 3

Figure 7.11 Control Tab at the Format Control Dialog Box for a Combo Box Form Control

Format Control   ?   ✕

Size   Protection   Properties   Alt Text   Control

Input range: MOP ———————————— ⬆

Cell link: C11 ——   ⬆

Drop down lines: 4

☐ 3-D shading

> Enter the defined name, or range reference for the worksheet cells that contain the options to be displayed.

> Enter the cell reference that will store the value chosen.

> Enter the number of options to display. If the number entered is less than the number of items in the Input range, a scroll bar will appear at the drop-down list for the form control.

MOP   ▾   ⋮   ✕   ✓   *f*

	A	B
1	Method of Payment	
2	e-Transfer	1
3	Check	2
4	Visa	3
5	MC	4

OK   Cancel

Activity 3a Inserting a Combo Box Form Control

Part 1 of 3

1. With **7-NationalInv** open, add the Developer tab to the toolbar by completing the following steps:
   a. Right-click on any part of the ribbon.
   b. Click the *Customize the Ribbon* option.
   c. Click the *Developer* check box in the *Main Tabs* list box to insert a check mark and then click OK.
2. Add a combo box form control to include the different methods of payment by completing the following steps:
   a. Click the Developer tab and then click the Insert button in the Controls group.
   b. Click the *Combo Box (Form Control)* option (second column, first row in the *Form Controls* section).
   c. Draw a box in cell A11 that is the same width and height as the cell.

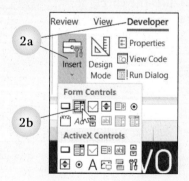

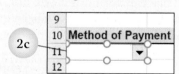

d. Right-click the border of the combo box and then click the *Format Control* option at the pop-up menu.
e. Click in the *Input range* text box, type MOP, and then press the Tab key.
f. Type al l in the *Cell link* text box and then press the Tab key.
g. Type 4 in the *Drop down lines* text box and then click OK.
h. Click in any worksheet cell outside the form control.
3. Save **7-NationalInv**.

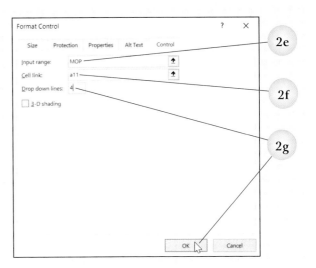

Activity 3b Inserting a Check Box Form Control

Part 2 of 3

1. With **7-NationalInv** open, insert a check box form control to have customers indicate that the shipping address is the same as the billing address by completing the following steps:
   a. Click the Insert button in the Controls group.
   b. Click the *Check Box (Form Control)* option (third column, first row in the *Form Controls* section).
   c. Draw a box in cell B8 that is the same width and height as the cell.

2. Change the text of the check box form control by clicking in the check box form control, selecting the text, and then typing Same as billing address.
3. Click in any worksheet cell outside the form control.
4. Save **7-NationalInv**.

Creating a Macro Button Form Control

A macro can be assigned to a button form control that allows the user to quickly run the macro without having to remember the shortcut key combination or ribbon commands.

To create a button form control with a macro assigned to it, click the Insert button in the Controls group on the Developer tab, click the *Button (Form Control)* option, draw the button, click the macro name in the *Macro name* list box at the Assign Macro dialog box, and then click OK. Macro button form controls do not display in Print Preview and do not print.

1. With **7-NationalInv** open, insert a macro form control to have customers indicate that the shipping address is the same as the billing address by completing the following steps:
   a. Click the Insert button in the Controls group on the Developer tab.
   b. Click the *Button (Form Control)* option (first column, first row in the *Form Controls* section).
   c. Draw a box in cell A30 that is the same width and height as the cell.
   d. Click the *PrintInv* option in the *Macro name* list box and then click OK.
   e. Type Print Preview and then click in any worksheet cell outside the form control.

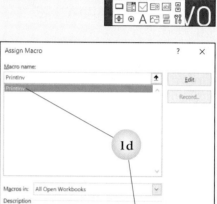

2. Format the control object by completing the following steps:
   a. Right-click the Print Preview button form control and then click the *Format Control* option at the pop-up menu.
   b. Click the Font tab, if necessary; click the *Color* option box arrow; click the *Dark Red* option (first column, second row) at the drop-down gallery; and then click OK.
   c. Click in any worksheet cell outside the Print Preview button form control.
3. Save **7-NationalInv**.

Activity 4 **Save a Workbook as a Template**   **2 Parts**

You will save a workbook as a template and then use the template to create a new invoice.

Saving a Workbook as a Template

Quick Steps

Save Workbook as Template
1. Open workbook.
2. Make changes.
3. Click File tab.
4. Click *Save As*.
5. Click *Browse*.
6. Change *Save as type* to *Excel Template*.
7. Type file name.
8. Click Save button.

Saving a Workbook as a Template

A template is a workbook that contains standard text, formulas, and formatting. Cell entries are created and formatted for all the data that does not change. Cells that will contain variable information have formatting applied but are left empty, since they will be filled in when the template is used to generate a worksheet. Examples of worksheets that are well suited to templates include invoices, purchase orders, time cards, and expense forms. These types of worksheets are usually filled in with the same kinds of data but the data itself varies.

Several templates have already been created and are installed with Excel or can be installed after they are downloaded. To use a template to create a worksheet, first check the New backstage area to see if the template already exists. Another option is to search online for templates using categories such as *Budget, Invoice, Calendars,* and *Expenses.* Once a topic has been selected in the *Suggested Searches* section of the New backstage area, either download one of the templates shown or choose another topic from the Category task pane.

If none of the existing templates meets your needs, create a custom template. To do this, create a workbook that contains all the standard data, formulas, and formatting. Leave the cells empty for any information that is variable but format those cells as required. Save the workbook as a template at the Save As dialog box by changing the *Save as type* option to *Excel Template (*.xltx)* or *Excel Macro-Enabled Template (*.xltm)* if the workbook contains macros. Before saving the worksheet as a template, consider protecting it by locking all the cells except those that will hold variable data.

Activity 4a **Saving a Workbook as a Template**   Part 1 of 2

1. With **7-NationalInv** open, save the workbook as a template containing macros by completing the following steps:
   a. Click the File tab.
   b. Click *Save As*.
   c. Select the current text in the *File name* text box and then type NationalTemplate-StudentName, substituting your name for *StudentName*.
   d. Click the *Save as type* option box arrow and then click *Excel Macro-Enabled Template (*.xltm)* at the pop-up list.
   e. Click the Save button.
2. Close **NationalTemplate-StudentName**.

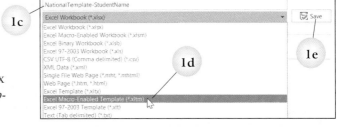

Check Your Work

Using a Custom Template

Quick Steps

Use Custom Template
1. Click File tab.
2. Click *New*.
3. Click *Personal*.
4. Double-click template.

Delete Custom Template
1. Click File tab.
2. Click *Open*.
3. Click *Computer*.
4. Click Browse button.
5. Navigate to [c:]\ Users*username*\ Documents\\Custom Office Templates.
6. Right-click template name.
7. Click *Delete*.
8. Click Cancel.

To use a template that you created, click the File tab and then click *New*. At the New backstage area, click *Personal*. This opens the Personal template section, as shown in Figure 7.12. Double-click the name of the template to open it. A workbook opens with the name of the template followed by a *1*. Save the document with a more descriptive name.

Figure 7.12 New Backstage Area with the *Personal* Template Section Selected

Deleting a Custom Template

To delete a custom template that is no longer needed, use the Open dialog box to navigate to [c:]\Users*username*\Documents\Custom Office Templates. Right-click the name of the template to be deleted and then click *Delete* at the shortcut menu. Click Cancel to close the Open dialog box.

Activity 4b Using a Custom Template

Part 2 of 2

1. At a blank Excel screen, open the template created in Activity 4a by completing the following steps:
   a. Click the File tab.
   b. Click *New*.
   c. At the New backstage area, click *Personal*.
   d. In the *Personal* template section, click *NationalTemplate-StudentName*. (Your template will have your name in place of *StudentName*.)

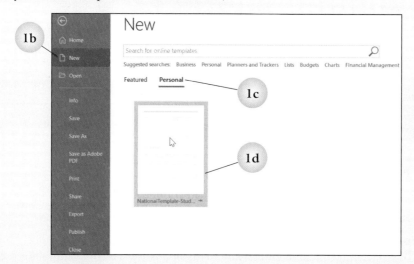

2. Look at the workbook name in the title bar. Notice that Excel has added *1* to the end of the name.
3. Enable the content.
4. Fill in the invoice as shown in Figure 7.13. **Note: Add a formula in the Line Total column for each item**.
5. Click the Print Preview button to preview the invoice and then print the invoice.
6. Save the invoice as a macro-enabled workbook by completing the following steps:
   a. Click the File tab and then click the *Save As* option.
   b. Click the Browse button.
   c. Navigate to the EL2C7 folder and then type 7-NInv2035 in the *File name* text box.
   d. Click the *Save as type* option box arrow and then click the *Excel Macro-Enabled Workbook* option.
   e. Click the Save button.
7. Close **7-NInv2035.**

Figure 7.13 Invoice for Activity 4b

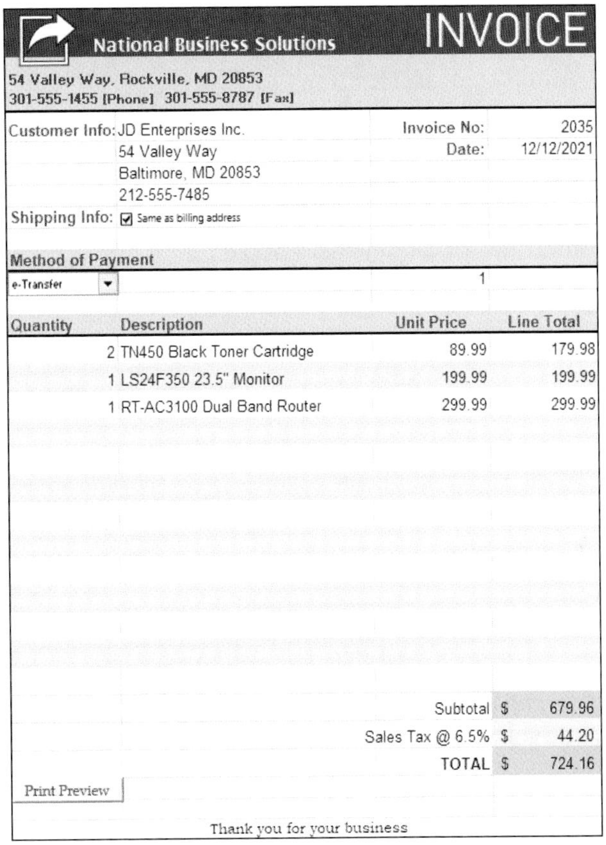
National Business Solutions INVOICE

54 Valley Way, Rockville, MD 20853
301-555-1455 [Phone] 301-555-8787 [Fax]

Customer Info: JD Enterprises Inc.
54 Valley Way
Baltimore, MD 20853
212-555-7485

Invoice No: 2035
Date: 12/12/2021

Shipping Info: ☑ Same as billing address

Method of Payment
e-Transfer 1

Quantity	Description	Unit Price	Line Total
2	TN450 Black Toner Cartridge	89.99	179.98
1	LS24F350 23.5" Monitor	199.99	199.99
1	RT-AC3100 Dual Band Router	299.99	299.99

Subtotal	$	679.96
Sales Tax @ 6.5%	$	44.20
TOTAL	$	724.16

Print Preview

Thank you for your business

Activity 5 **Manage Excel's Save Options and Trust Center Settings** **3 Parts**

You will review Excel's current save options, modify the AutoRecover options, and then recover an unsaved workbook. You will also explore the default settings in the Trust Center.

Customizing Save Options

Quick Steps

Customize Save Options

1. Click File tab.
2. Click *Options*.
3. Click *Save* in left pane.
4. Change save options.
5. Click OK.

The AutoRecover feature saves versions of your work at a specified time interval. This will be beneficial in case changes are not saved or Excel closes unexpectedly (such as during a power outage). When Excel restarts, the opening screen displays a *Recovered* section below the Recent list. Click the Recovered unsaved workbooks hyperlink and the Document Recovery task pane opens with a list of workbooks for which AutoRecover files exist.

By default, Excel's AutoRecover feature is turned on and will automatically save AutoRecover information every 10 minutes. The time interval can be adjusted to suit the user's needs. Keep in mind that data loss can still occur with AutoRecover turned on. For example, suppose the time interval is set at 20 minutes and a power outage occurs 15 minutes after an AutoRecover save. When Excel restarts, the recovered file will not contain the last 15 minutes of

Hint Do not rely on AutoRecover as you work. Saving regularly to minimize data loss and protect against unforeseen events is the best practice.

work if the workbook was not saved manually. Open the Excel Options dialog box and select *Save* in the left pane to view and/or change the AutoRecover options.

In conjunction with AutoRecover, Excel provides to Office 365 users the AutoSave feature, using OneDrive or SharePoint Online to store their files. The files are saved in real-time. To turn AutoSave on, click the AutoSave Off button located on the Quick Access Toolbar.

The save options at the Excel Options dialog box also allow changing the drive and/or folder in which to store AutoRecovered files, as well as the default file location for all new workbooks.

Activity 5a Customizing Save Options

Part 1 of 3

1. At a blank Excel screen, click the File tab and then click *Options* to open the Excel Options dialog box.
2. Click *Save* in the left pane of the Excel Options dialog box.
3. Note the current settings for *Save AutoRecover information every [ ] minutes* and *Keep the last AutoRecovered version if I close without saving*. By default, both check boxes should be checked and the time interval should be 10 minutes; however, the settings may have been changed on the computer you are using. If that is the case, write down the options so you can restore the program to its original state once you have finished this activity.
4. If necessary, insert check marks in the two check boxes to turn on the AutoRecover features.
5. Select the current value in the *Save AutoRecover information every [ ] minutes* measurement box and then type 2 to change the time interval to two minutes.

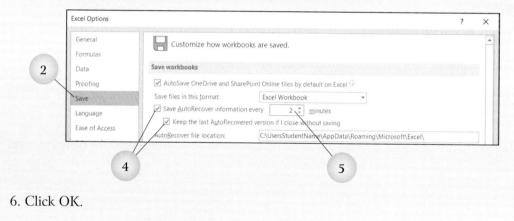

6. Click OK.

Activity 5b Recovering a Workbook

Part 2 of 3

1. Open **7-NationalJE.**
2. Save the workbook with the name **7-NationalJE-5.**
3. Note the system time in the bottom right corner of the screen. You will use this time to make sure that more than two minutes elapse before you interrupt the Excel session.

4. Make the following changes to the worksheet:
   a. Select the range A7:A17 and apply the standard dark red font color (first color in the *Standard Colors* section of the drop-down color palette).
   b. Select the range E7:E17 and apply the standard dark red font color.

4	Internal Chargeback for Computing Services Department							
5	Batch Technical Service Requests (TSRs)						GL Account	Journal Entry
6		Parts	Labor	Total	TSR	Dept Code	Number	Number
7	Accounting	$ -	$1,525.00	$ 1,525.00	CS-4042	225	011475	160101
8	Executive Administration	1,564.27	985.50	2,549.77	CS-4043	216	011482	160102
9	Finance	964.32	635.50	1,599.82	CS-4044	166	011435	160103
10	Human Resources	397.45	225.50	622.95	CS-4045	187	011485	160104
11	Graphics Design	417.45	175.50	592.95	CS-4046	210	011415	160105
12	Electronic Production	215.48	475.50	690.98	CS-4047	350	011443	160106
13	Marketing	1,048.57	725.50	1,774.07	CS-4048	452	011409	160107
14	Web Programming	975.85	854.50	1,830.35	CS-4049	284	011462	160108
15	Planning and Development	161.45	132.50	293.95	CS-4050	310	011473	160109
16	President's Office	-	425.00	425.00	CS-4051	105	011455	160110
17	Purchasing	415.87	175.50	591.37	CS-4052	243	011428	160111
18				$12,496.21				

4a   4b

5. Make sure more than two minutes has elapsed since you checked the system time in Step 3. If necessary, wait until you are sure an AutoRecover file has been saved.
6. Press Alt + Ctrl + Delete.
7. At the Windows screen, select *Task Manager*.
8. At the Task Manager dialog box, click *Microsoft Excel (32 bit)* in the task list box and then click the End task button.
9. Close the Task Manager dialog box.
10. Restart Microsoft Excel. At the opening screen, click the Recover unsaved workbooks hyperlink in the *Recent* section. Two files are available: the original version of the file used in this activity and the AutoRecovered version.

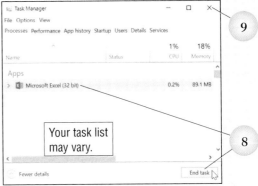

9

Your task list may vary.

8

11. Point to the first file in the Document Recovery task pane. A ScreenTip displays stating that the first file is the AutoRecover version.
12. Point to the second file in the Document Recovery task pane. A ScreenTip displays stating that the second file is the original document.
13. Click the first file in the Document Recovery task pane. Notice that the edited version of the file appears. Look at the additional information next to the file name in the Title bar. Excel includes *(version 1)* and *[AutoRecovered]* in the file name.

11

14. Click the option box arrow next to the AutoRecovered document, click the *Save As* option, and then click *Save* at the Save As dialog box to accept the default name *7-NationalJE-5 (AutoRecovered)*.

13

15. Open the Excel Options dialog box. If necessary, restore the save options to the settings you wrote down in Activity 5a. Close the Excel Options dialog box.
16. Close **7-NationalJE-5**.

Check Your Work

Viewing Trust Center Settings

In Excel, the Trust Center is responsible for blocking unsafe content when a workbook is opened. Recall the security warning that sometimes appears in the message bar when a workbook is opened. That warning is generated by the Trust Center and it can be closed by clicking the Enable Content button. The Trust Center also allows the user to view and/or modify the security options that protect the computer from malicious content.

The Trust Center maintains a Trusted Locations list of locations from which content can be considered trusted. When a location is added to the Trusted Locations list, Excel treats any files opened from that location as safe. A workbook opened from a trusted location does not cause a security warning to display in the message bar and none of its content is blocked.

If a workbook contains macros, the Trust Center checks for a valid and current digital signature from an entity in the Trusted Publishers list before enabling macros. The Trusted Publishers list is maintained by the user on the computer being used. To add a publisher to the list, enable content from that publisher and then click the option *Trust all content from this publisher*.

Depending on the active macro security setting, if the Trust Center cannot match the digital signature information with an entity in the Trusted Publishers list or the macro does not contain a digital signature, a security warning displays in the message bar. The default macro security setting is *Disable all macros with notification*. Table 7.2 describes the four macro security settings. In some cases, the user may decide to change the default macro security setting. This can be done at the Trust Center dialog box.

Quick Steps

**View Trust
Center Settings**
1. Click File tab.
2. Click *Options*.
3. Click *Trust Center* in left pane.
4. Click Trust Center Settings button.
5. Click desired trust center category in left pane.
6. View and/or modify options.
7. Click OK two times.

Hint Changing the macro security setting in Excel does not affect the macro security setting in other Microsoft programs, such as Word and Access.

Table 7.2 Macro Security Settings for Workbooks Not Opened from Trusted Locations

Macro Setting	Description
Disable all macros without notification	All macros are disabled; security alerts do not appear.
Disable all macros with notification	All macros are disabled; security alerts appear with the option to enable content if the source of the file is trusted. This is the default setting.
Disable all macros except digitally signed macros	A macro that does not contain a digital signature is disabled; security alerts do not appear. If the macro is digitally signed by a publisher in the Trusted Publishers list, the macro is allowed to run. If the macro is digitally signed by a publisher not in the Trusted Publishers list, a security alert appears.
Enable all macros (not recommended, potentially dangerous code can run)	All macros are allowed; security alerts do not appear.

1. To explore the settings in the Trust Center, complete the following steps:
    a. Click the File tab and then click *Options*.
    b. Click *Trust Center* in the left pane of the Excel Options dialog box.
    c. Click the Trust Center Settings button in the *Microsoft Excel Trust Center* section.

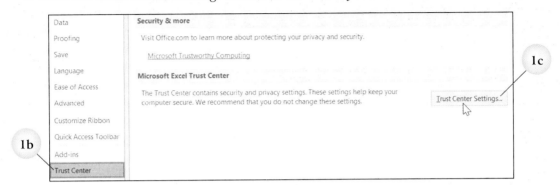

    d. At the Trust Center dialog box, click *Macro Settings* in the left pane.
    e. Review the options in the *Macro Settings* section. Note which option is active on the computer you are using. The default option is *Disable all macros with notification*.
       Note: The security setting on the computer you are using may be different from the default setting. Do not change the security setting without your instructor's permission.
    f. Click *Trusted Publishers* in the left pane. If any publishers have been added to the list on the computer you are using, their names will appear in the list box. If the list box is empty, no trusted publishers have been added.

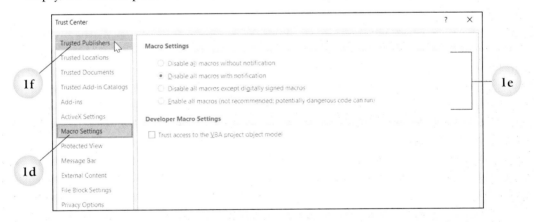

    g. Click *Trusted Locations* in the left pane. Review the paths and descriptions of the folders in the *Trusted Locations* list box. By default, Excel adds the folder created upon installation that contains the templates provided by Microsoft. Additional folders that have been added by a system administrator or network administrator may also appear.
    h. Click OK to close the Trust Center dialog box.
2. Click OK to close the Excel Options dialog box.

Chapter Summary

- Display options, found in the Excel Options dialog box in Excel are grouped as global display options, options that affect the current workbook, and options that affect only the active worksheet. Customized workbook and worksheet display options are saved with the file.

- Minimize the ribbon to provide more space in the work area when working with a large worksheet. To minimize the ribbon, click the Collapse the Ribbon button, click the Ribbon Display Options button, or Press Ctrl + F1. Clicking a tab temporarily redisplays the ribbon to allow a feature to be selected.

- To save the current ribbon and Quick Access Toolbar settings, click the File tab and then click *Options*. At the Excel Options dialog box, click *Customize Ribbon* in the left pane. Click the Import/Export button in the lower right corner of the Excel Options dialog box. Click *Export all customizations* to save the file with the custom settings. Click *Import all customizations* to import previously saved customizations.

- To customize the ribbon, open the Excel Options dialog box and then click *Customize Ribbon* in the left pane. Customize the ribbon by creating a new tab, adding buttons to a group, and/or renaming a tab, group, or command.

- Create a new tab by clicking the tab name in the *Main Tabs* list box that will precede the new tab and then clicking the New Tab button. A new group is automatically added with the new tab.

- Add buttons to a group by clicking the group name, selecting the desired command in the commands list box, and then clicking the Add button between the two list boxes.

- Rename a tab by selecting the tab name in the *Main Tabs* list box, clicking the Rename button, typing the new name, and then pressing the Enter key or clicking OK. Rename a group or command using a similar process.

- Add buttons to or delete buttons from the Quick Access Toolbar using the Customize Quick Access Toolbar button. Locate a command to add by opening the Excel Options dialog box with *Quick Access Toolbar* selected in the left pane.

- Export and import customizations to save and restore previous settings on the ribbons and Quick Access Toolbar.

- A custom view saves display and print settings so they can be applied to a worksheet when needed. Multiple custom views can be created for the same worksheet at the Custom Views dialog box. Open this dialog box by clicking the Custom Views button in the Workbook Views group on the View tab.

- Create a macro for a task that is repeated frequently and for which the steps do not vary.

- To begin recording a new macro, click the View tab, click the Macros button arrow in the Macros group, and then click *Record Macro*. At the Record Macro dialog box, assign the macro a name, an optional shortcut key, and a description. Click OK to turn on the macro recorder and close the Record Macro dialog box. All the commands and keystrokes will be recorded until the Stop Recording button is clicked.

- Workbooks that contain macros are saved in the Excel Macro-Enabled Workbook (*.xlsm) file format.

- Run a macro by opening the Macro dialog box and double-clicking the macro name. Run a macro assigned to a shortcut key by pressing Ctrl + the assigned letter. If a macro and an Excel feature are both assigned to the same shortcut key, the macro overrides the feature.

- The instructions for a macro are recorded in Visual Basic for Applications (VBA) program code. To edit a macro, open the Macro dialog box, click the macro name to be edited, and then click the Edit button. A Microsoft Visual Basic for Applications window opens, displaying a code module in which the program code for the macro can be edited. After editing the macro, save the changes, click File, and then click *Close and Return to Microsoft Excel*.

- An alternative to editing a macro in VBA is recording a new macro and then saving it with the same name to replace the existing macro.

- Delete a macro at the Macro dialog box.

- A macro is stored in the workbook in which it was created. When the Macro dialog box is open, all the macros from all the open workbooks are accessible. Therefore, to use a macro stored in another workbook, open that workbook first.

- Another option for making macros accessible to other workbooks is to create a macros workbook with a set of standard macros and then open the macros workbook when working in Excel.

- Inserting a form control allows users to enter information in a worksheet. For example, a combo box form control allows users to select an option from a list. A check box form control allows users to select an option by inserting a check mark in a check box.

- To configure and add options to a form control, right-click the control, click the *Format Control* option at the pop-up menu, and then enter information on the Control tab at the Format Control dialog box.

- Assigning a macro to a button form control allows users to quickly run the macro without having to remember the shortcut key combination or ribbon command.

- A template is a workbook that contains standard text, formatting, and formulas.

- Check the New backstage area to see if the template already exists or search online for templates using the different categories.

- Create a custom template from an existing workbook by selecting *Excel Template (*.xltx)* or *Excel Macro-Enabled Template (*.xltm)* in the *Save as type* option box at the Save As dialog box. To use a custom template, open the New backstage area, click *Personal* to display the templates, and then double-click the custom template name.

- By default, Excel's AutoRecover feature saves an open file every 10 minutes. If an Excel session is unexpectedly terminated or a file is closed without saving, the file can be recovered at the Document Recovery task pane.

- The AutoRecover feature saves the last version of a workbook in a temporary file. If a workbook is closed without saving or an earlier version is wanted, the autosaved version can be recovered using the Recover Unsaved Workbooks hyperlink.

- View and modify security options at Excel's Trust Center, which is responsible for blocking unsafe content when a workbook is opened.

Commands Review

FEATURE	RIBBON TAB, GROUP/OPTION	BUTTON	KEYBOARD SHORTCUT
customize display options	File, *Options*		
customize Quick Access Toolbar	File, *Options*		
customize ribbons	File, *Options*		
customize save options	File, *Options*		
customize view	View, Workbook Views		
delete macro	View, Macros		Alt + F8
edit macro	View, Macros		Alt + F8
insert control	Developer, Controls		
minimize ribbon			Ctrl + F1
record macro	View, Macros	OR	
ribbon display options			Ctrl + F1
save as macro-enabled workbook	File, *Save As*		F12
use custom template	File, *New*		

Microsoft®

Excel®

Protecting and Distributing a Workbook

Performance Objectives

Upon successful completion of Chapter 8, you will be able to:

1 Add information to a workbook's properties

2 Protect cells within a worksheet to prevent changes from being made

3 Protect and unprotect the structure of a workbook

4 Require a password to open a workbook

5 Check a workbook for accessibility issues

6 Scan and remove private or confidential information from a workbook

7 Mark a workbook as final

8 Use the Compatibility Checker to check a workbook for loss of functionality or fidelity with earlier versions of Excel

9 Publish an Excel workbook as a PDF or XPS file

10 Publish an Excel worksheet as a web page

11 Create an XML schema and export and import XML data

Exchanging data between programs by importing or exporting eliminates duplication of effort and reduces the likelihood of data errors or missed entries, which could occur if the data was retyped. One of the advantages of working with a suite of programs such as Microsoft Word, Excel, Access, and PowerPoint is being able to easily integrate data from one program to another. In this chapter, you will learn how to bring data into an Excel worksheet from external sources and how to export data in a worksheet to other programs. You will also learn how to use features that allow distributing Excel data using a variety of methods.

 Data Files

Before beginning chapter work, copy the EL2C8 folder to your storage medium and then make EL2C8 the active folder.

The online course includes additional training and assessment resources.

You will add the author's name and other descriptive information in a workbook's properties.

Tutorial

Adding Workbook
Properties

Quick Steps

**Add Information to
Properties**
1. Click File tab.
2. Click *Info* option.
3. Click *Add a
   [property]* next to
   property name.
4. Type text.
5. Click outside
   property box.

Adding Workbook Properties

Workbook properties include information about the workbook, such as the author's name, the title, the subject, the category to which the workbook is related (such as finance), and general comments about the workbook. This information is added to the file at the Info backstage area, shown in Figure 8.1. The document information panel found in previous versions of Excel does not exist in Excel 365.

Some information is automatically added to a workbook's properties by Excel. For example, Excel maintains statistics such as the date the workbook was created, the date the workbook was last modified, and the name of the last person to save the workbook. Workbook properties are sometimes referred to as *metadata*—a term used to identify descriptive information about data.

To add an author's name or other descriptive information about a workbook, click the File tab and then click the *Info* option. Excel displays the Info backstage area with the workbook's properties displayed at the right side of the screen. By default, when a new workbook is created, Excel inserts in the *Author* property box the name of the computer user (as defined when Microsoft Office is installed). To add another author or make a change to a workbook property (such as the title), click to open the text box next to the property's name. For example, click *Add a title* next to the Title property name. Type the appropriate title in the text box. Click outside the text box to end the entry. Properties that do not display with the message *Add a [property]* cannot be edited. Click the Show All Properties hyperlink at the bottom of the right section in the Info backstage area to add more properties.

Figure 8.1 Properties in the Info Backstage Area

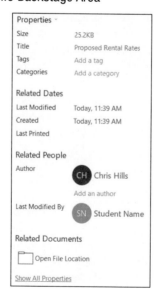

Quick Steps

Add Advanced Properties
1. Click File tab.
2. Click *Info* option.
3. Click Properties button.
4. Click *Advanced Properties*.
5. Add or edit properties as required.
6. Click OK.

To display the advanced properties shown in Figure 8.2, click the Properties button at the top of the right section in the Info backstage area and then click *Advanced Properties* at the drop-down list. Add other properties, including but not limited to information regarding the date completed, the editor, and the person who checked the document.

Having personal information available can be useful when browsing a list of files. The words *Authors*, *Size*, and *Date Modified* appear in a ScreenTip when the mouse pointer hovers over a workbook name in the Open dialog box. This information helps users to select the correct file.

Figure 8.2 Advanced Properties

Activity 1 **Adding Workbook Properties**   Part 1 of 1

1. Open **CRPricing**.
2. Save the workbook with the name **8-CRPricing**.
3. Add an additional author's name, as well as a title, subject, and comments associated with the workbook, by completing the following steps:
   a. Click the File tab and then click the *Info* option.
   b. At the Info backstage area, open an *Author* text box by clicking the *Add an author* text box below the current author's name in the *Related People* section.
   c. Type Chris Hills. If the message *We couldn't find the person you were looking for* displays, ignore it.
   d. Click outside the *Author* text box to close it.
   e. Click *Add a title* in the *Title* text box, type Proposed Rental Rates, and then click outside the text box.

f. Click the <u>Show All Properties</u> hyperlink below the *Related Documents* section to display additional properties.

g. Click *Specify the subject* in the *Subject* text box, type Rental Rates for May 2021, and then click outside the text box.

h. Click *Add comments* in the *Comments* text box, type Proposed rental rates sent for review to regional managers., and then click outside the text box.

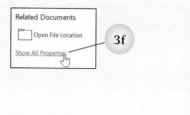

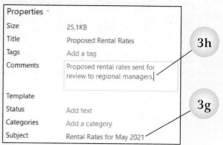

4. Right-click *Paradigm* next to the *Author* text box and then click *Remove Person* at the shortcut menu.

5. Click the <u>Show Fewer Properties</u> hyperlink at the bottom of the properties.

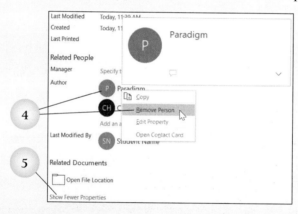

6. Compare your properties with those shown in Figure 8.1 (on page 210). The dates may vary.

7. Add advanced properties by completing the following steps:

a. Click the Properties button above the workbook properties and then click *Advanced Properties* at the drop-down list.

b. Click the Custom tab.

c. Scroll down the *Name* option box until *Forward to* appears in the list and then click this option.

d. Click in the *Value* text box, type Regional managers, and then click the Add button.

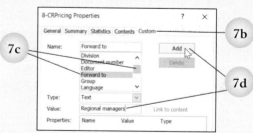

8. Compare your properties with those shown in Figure 8.2 (on page 211) and then click OK.

9. Save and then close **8-CRPricing**.

You will protect a worksheet, unlock ranges, prevent changes to the structure of a workbook, and then add a password to open a workbook.

Protecting and Unprotecting Worksheets

Unlocking Cells and Protecing a Worksheet

 Format

 Protect Sheet

Quick Steps

Protect Worksheet
1. Open workbook.
2. Activate sheet.
3. Click Review tab.
4. Click Protect Sheet button.
5. Type password.
6. Choose allowable actions.
7. Click OK.
8. Retype password if entered in Step 5.
9. Click OK.

Unlock Cell
1. Select cell(s) to be unlocked.
2. Click Home tab.
3. Click Format button.
4. Click *Lock Cell*.
5. Deselect cell(s).

Protecting and Unprotecting Worksheets

Protecting a worksheet prevents other users from accidentally deleting or modifying cells that should not be changed. By default, when a worksheet is protected, each cell in it is locked. This means that no one can insert, delete, or modify the content. In most cases, some of the cells within a worksheet contain data that other users can change. Therefore, in a collaborative environment, protecting a worksheet generally involves two steps:

1. Clear the lock attribute on those cells that are allowed to be edited.
2. Protect the worksheet.

To clear the lock attribute from the cells that are allowed to be edited, select the cells to be unlocked, click the Home tab, and then click the Format button in the Cells group. Click *Lock Cell* in the *Protection* section of the drop-down list to turn off the lock attribute. To turn on worksheet protection, click the Review tab and then click the Protect Sheet button in the Protect group. At the Protect Sheet dialog box, shown in Figure 8.3, select the actions to be allowed and then click OK. A password can be assigned to unprotect the sheet. Be cautious about adding a password, since the worksheet cannot be unprotected if the password is forgotten. If necessary, write down the password and store it in a secure location.

Figure 8.3 Protect Sheet Dialog Box

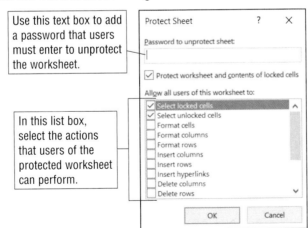

Use this text box to add a password that users must enter to unprotect the worksheet.

In this list box, select the actions that users of the protected worksheet can perform.

Unprotect
Sheet

When a worksheet has protection turned on, the Protect Sheet button in the Protect group on the Review tab turns into the Unprotect Sheet button. To remove worksheet protection, click the Unprotect Sheet button or click the Unprotect hyperlink in the Info backstage area. If a password was entered when the worksheet was protected, the Unprotect Sheet dialog box appears, as shown in Figure 8.4. Type the password and then press the Enter key or click OK.

Figure 8.4 Unprotect Sheet Dialog Box

Activity 2a **Protecting an Entire Worksheet**   Part 1 of 4

1. Open **CRFinalPrices** and save it with the name **8-CRFinalPrices**.
2. Protect the entire FinalPrices worksheet by completing the following steps:
   a. Make sure FinalPrices is the active sheet.
   b. Click the Review tab.
   c. Click the Protect Sheet button in the Protect group.
   d. At the Protect Sheet dialog box with the insertion point positioned in the *Password to unprotect sheet* text box, type eL2-C8 and then click OK.
   e. At the Confirm Password dialog box with the insertion point positioned in the *Reenter password to proceed* text box, type eL2-C8 and then click OK.

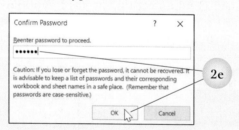

   f. Make any cell active in the FinalPrices sheet and attempt to delete the data or type new data. Since the entire worksheet is now protected, all the cells are locked. A Microsoft Excel message appears stating that the cell or chart trying to be changed is on a protected worksheet. Click OK.

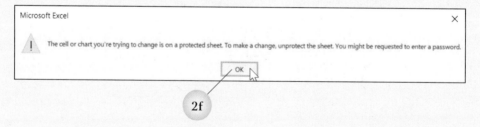

3. Notice that the Protect Sheet button changes to the Unprotect Sheet button when a worksheet has been protected.
4. Save **8-CRFinalPrices**.

1. With **8-CRFinalPrices** open, make TargetRevenue the active sheet.
2. Unlock the weekday target rental data cells for editing by completing the following steps:
   a. Select the range C5:C10.
   b. Click the Home tab.
   c. Click the Format button in the Cells group.
   d. At the Format button drop-down list, look at the icon next to *Lock Cell* in the *Protection* section. The highlighted icon indicates that the lock attribute is turned on.
   e. Click *Lock Cell* at the Format button drop-down list to turn the lock attribute off for the selected range.
   f. Click in any cell within the range C5:C10 and then click the Format button in the Cells group. Look at the icon next to *Lock Cell* in the drop-down list. The icon is no longer highlighted, which indicates that the cell is unlocked.
   g. Click within the worksheet area to close the drop-down list.
3. Unlock the remaining target rental ranges for editing by completing the following steps:
   a. Select the range F5:F10, press and hold down the Ctrl key, select the ranges I5:I10 and L5:L10, and then release the Ctrl key.
   b. Press the F4 function key to repeat the command to unlock the cells or click the Format button in the Cells group and then click *Lock Cell* at the drop-down list.
   c. Click in any cell to deselect the ranges.
4. Protect the TargetRevenue worksheet by completing the following steps:
   a. Click the Review tab.
   b. Click the Protect Sheet button in the Protect group.
   c. Type eL2-C8 in the *Password to unprotect sheet* text box.
   d. Click OK.
   e. Type eL2-C8 in the *Reenter password to proceed* text box.
   f. Click OK.
5. Save **8-CRFinalPrices**.
6. Test the worksheet protection applied to the TargetRevenue sheet by completing the following steps:
   a. Make cell B8 active and then press the Delete key.
   b. Click OK at the Microsoft Excel message box stating that the protected cell cannot be changed.
   c. Make cell C8 active and then press the Delete key. Since cell C8 is unlocked, its contents are deleted and its dependent cells are updated.
   d. Click the Undo button on the Quick Access Toolbar to restore the contents of cell C8.
7. Save **8-CRFinalPrices**.

A highlighted icon indicates that the lock attribute is active.

2d

A nonhighlighted icon indicates that the lock attribute is not active.

2f

6c

	Category	Weekday (Mo to Th)	Target Rentals	Target Revenue
4				
5	Compact	$ 45.99	675	$ 31,043
6	Mid-size	48.99	880	43,111
7	Full-size	50.99	425	21,671
8	Minivan	85.99		-
9	SUV	99.99	198	19,798
10	Luxury	109.99	86	9,459
11	TOTAL		Weekday:	$ 125,082

Protecting and Unprotecting the Structure of a Workbook

Use the Protect Workbook button in the Protect group on the Review tab to prevent changes to the structure of a workbook, such as inserting a new sheet, deleting a sheet, or unhiding a hidden worksheet. At the Protect Structure and Windows dialog box, shown in Figure 8.5, turn on protection for the workbook's structure. Click the *Windows* check box to prevent a user from resizing or changing the positions of the windows in the workbook. As with protecting a worksheet, enter an optional password that will protect the workbook.

When the structure of a workbook has been protected, the Protect Workbook button in the Protect group on the Review tab displays with a gray shaded background. To remove workbook protection, click the Protect Workbook button. If a password was entered when the workbook was protected, the Unprotect Workbook dialog box appears, as shown in Figure 8.6. Type the password and then press the Enter key.

Figure 8.5 Protect Structure and Windows Dialog Box

Figure 8.6 Unprotect Workbook Dialog Box

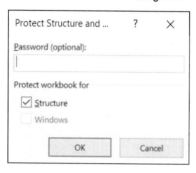

Activity 2c Protecting the Structure of a Workbook

Part 3 of 4

1. With **8-CRFinalPrices** open, protect the workbook structure by completing the following steps:
   a. If necessary, click the Review tab.
   b. Click the Protect Workbook button in the Protect group.
   c. At the Protect Structure and Windows dialog box with the insertion point positioned in the *Password (optional)* text box, type eL2-C8.
   d. Click OK.
   e. At the Confirm Password dialog box with the insertion point positioned in the *Reenter password to proceed* text box, type eL2-C8.
   f. Click OK.

1c

1d

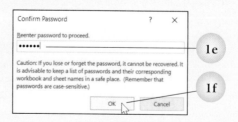

1e

1f

2. To test the workbook protection, attempt to insert a new worksheet by completing the following steps:
   a. Right-click the TargetRevenue sheet tab.
   b. Look at the shortcut menu. Notice that all the options related to managing worksheets are dimmed, which means they are unavailable.
   c. Click within the worksheet area to close the shortcut menu.
3. Save **8-CRFinalPrices**.

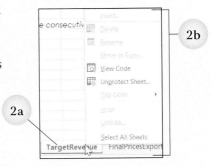

Tutorial

Adding a Password to Open a Workbook

 Protect Workbook

Adding and Removing a Password to Open a Workbook

Prevent unauthorized access to Excel data by requiring a password to open a workbook. The password to open a workbook is encrypted. In an encrypted password, the plain text that is typed is converted into a scrambled format called *ciphertext*, which prevents unauthorized users from retrieving the password. To add an encrypted password to an open workbook, click the File tab and then click the *Info* option. At the Info backstage area, shown in Figure 8.7, click the Protect Workbook button in the *Protect Workbook* section. Click *Encrypt with Password* at the drop-down list to open the Encrypt Document dialog box, shown in Figure 8.8. Save the workbook after typing and confirming the password.

Figure 8.7 Info Backstage Area with the Protect Workbook Drop-Down List

Next to the Protect Workbook button, find a description of the protection features that have been applied to the workbook and/or worksheets.

Click *Encrypt with Password* to require a password to open the workbook.

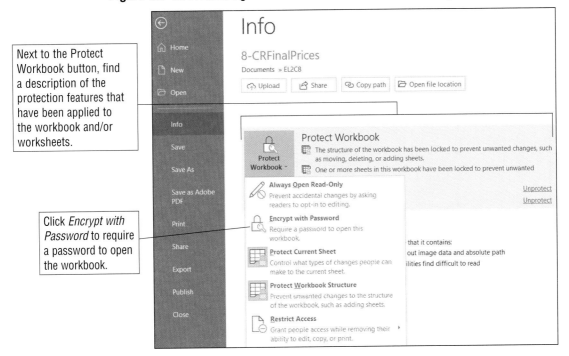

Figure 8.8 Encrypt Document Dialog Box

Quick Steps

Add Workbook Password

1. Open workbook.
2. Click File tab.
3. Click *Info* option.
4. Click Protect Workbook button.
5. Click *Encrypt with Password*.
6. Type password.
7. Click OK.
8. Retype password if entered in Step 6.
9. Click OK.
10. Save workbook.

When creating a password, it is good practice to use a combination of four types of characters: uppercase letters, lowercase letters, symbols, and numbers. A password constructed using these elements is considered secure and more difficult to crack. Note that if the password is forgotten, the workbook cannot be opened. If necessary, write down the password and store it in a secure location.

To remove a password from a workbook, open the workbook using the password. At the Info backstage area, click the Protect Workbook button. Click *Encrypt with Password* at the drop-down list to open the Encrypt Document dialog box. Delete the password, click OK, and then save the workbook.

Activity 2d Adding a Password to Open a Workbook

Part 4 of 4

1. With **8-CRFinalPrices** open, add a password to open the workbook by completing the following steps:
   a. Click the File tab. The backstage area opens with the *Info* option selected.
   b. Read the information in the *Protect Workbook* section. Since protection has already been applied to this workbook, the existing features are described and a hyperlink is provided to unprotect each protected worksheet. In a workbook with no pre-existing protection, the *Permissions* section displays the text *Control what types of changes people can make to this workbook*.
   c. Click the Protect Workbook button.

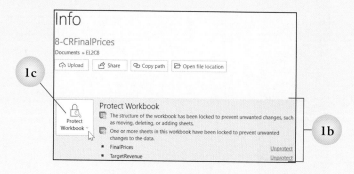

d. Click *Encrypt with Password* at the drop-down list.

e. At the Encrypt Document dialog box with the insertion point positioned in the *Password* text box, type eL2-C8.

f. Click OK.

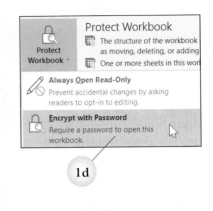

g. At the Confirm Password dialog box with the insertion point positioned in the *Reenter password* text box, type eL2-C8.

h. Click OK.

i. Notice that the description next to the Protect Workbook button now includes the text *A password is required to open this workbook.*

j. Click the Back button to return to the worksheet.

2. Save and then close **8-CRFinalPrices.**

3. Test the password security on the workbook by completing the following steps:

a. Open **8-CRFinalPrices.**

b. At the Password dialog box with the insertion point positioned in the *Password* text box, type a password that is incorrect for the file.

c. Click OK.

d. At the Microsoft Excel message box stating that the password is not correct, click OK.

e. Open **8-CRFinalPrices.**

f. Type eL2-C8 in the *Password* text box.

g. Click OK.

4. Close **8-CRFinalPrices.**

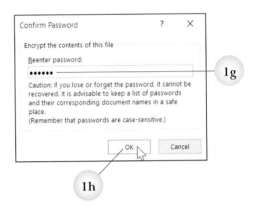

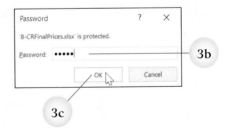

Activity 3 Prepare a First-Quarter Sales Workbook for Distribution   4 Parts

You will check for and fix any accessibility issues in a workbook, remove confidential information from a workbook, and mark the workbook as final to prepare it for distribution. In another workbook, you will check for compatibility issues with earlier versions of Excel before sending the workbook to someone who uses Excel 2003. You will also explore the default settings in the Trust Center.

Preparing a Workbook for Distribution

In today's workplace, individuals often work as part of a team both within and outside an organization. Excel workbooks are frequently exchanged between coworkers via email message attachments; saving to a shared network folder, document management server, or company website; or using other means of electronic distribution. Before making a workbook available for others to open, view, and edit, use the features provided by Excel to ensure that the workbook can be read by people with accessibility issues and that confidentiality will be protected and maintained.

Checking for Accessibility Issues

Check Accessibility

Check for Issues

Checking for Accessibility Issues

Before distributing a workbook, be sure to determine whether any of the workbook's features may make it difficult for someone who requires assistive technology to read it. After opening the file, run the Accessibility Checker by clicking the Check Accessibility button in the Accessibility group on the Review tab or click the File tab and then click the *Info* option. Click the Check for Issues button and then click *Check Accessibility* in the drop-down list. Depending on the version of Excel, a message will appear in the Status bar notifying the user of the accessibility status of the workbook. It will either notify the user that the workbook is *Good to go* or prompt the user to *Investigate*. There are three levels of errors; a description and example of each is provided in Table 8.1.

Table 8.1 Accessibility Issues

Accessibility Issue	Description	Example
Error	Workbook will be very difficult if not impossible for people with accessibility issues to understand.	Each object must have alternative text. Examples of objects are pictures, charts, tables, and shapes without text.
Warning	Workbook will be difficult in some cases for people with accessibility issues to understand.	Sheet tabs are named. Remove split or merged cells.
Tip	Workbook can be understood by people with accessibility issues but making changes might make it better organized and easier to understand.	Closed captions are included for inserted audio and video.

Inspection Results

Quick Steps

Check Accessibility
1. Click Review tab.
2. Click *Check Accessibility*.
3. Click issue.
4. Follow steps to fix issue.

After running the Accessibility Checker, refer to the Accessibility Checker task pane on the right side of the screen for a list of inspection results, as shown in Figure 8.9. The flagged object or cell, including the name of the sheet in which it is located, is listed under the relevant issue (*Errors*) and problem (*Missing alternative text*). Click a problem and Excel selects the portion of the worksheet affected by the issue, if possible. For example, objects like the table in Figure 8.9 are selected but sheet tabs are not. Once a problem is selected, an option box arrow appears. Click the arrow and choose an option to correct the problem or review the instructions in the *Why Fix?* and *Steps To Fix* sections, which appear in the *Additional Information* section at the bottom of the Accessibility Checker task pane. Once an issue has been corrected, it will no longer appear in the inspection results. Microsoft continues to update the Accessibility Checker to ensure compatibility with assistive technology, so steps may vary in the following activities.

Figure 8.9 Accessibility Checker Task Pane with Inspection Results Shown

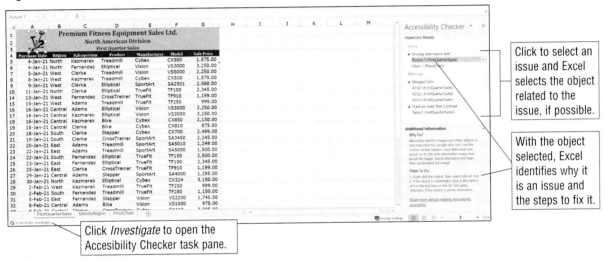

Click to select an issue and Excel selects the object related to the issue, if possible.

With the object selected, Excel identifies why it is an issue and the steps to fix it.

Click *Investigate* to open the Accessibility Checker task pane.

Activity 3a Inspecting a Workbook for Accessibility Issues

Part 1 of 4

1. Open **PFSales**.
2. Save the workbook with the name **8-PFSales**.
3. Examine the workbook for accessibility issues by completing the following steps:
   a. Click the Review tab and then click the Check Accessibility button in the Accessibility group.
   b. Expand the Errors and Warnings, if necessary, by clicking the expand button at the left of the error.
   c. Read the inspection results in the Accessibility Checker task pane.
4. Correct the errors listed in the inspection results by completing the following steps:
   a. Click *Picture 7 (FirstQuarterSales)* under *Missing alternative text*. The picture left of the title in row 1 in the FirstQuarterSales worksheet is selected.
   b. Click the option box arrow and then click the *Mark as decorative* option. The issue is removed from the *Errors* list in the *Inspection Results* section.

c. Click *Chart 1 (PivotChart)* under *Missing alternative text*. The Pivot Chart is selected.

d. Click the option box arrow and then click the *Add a description* option.

e. At the Alt Text task pane, click in the text box and type the following description: PivotChart depicting the first-quarter sales by region and by salesperson. The issue is removed from the *Errors* list.

f. Click the Alt Text task pane Close button.

5. Click *Table1 (FirstQuarterSales)* under *Hard-to-read Text Contrast*. Read the *Steps To Fix* and note that a style that has higher contrast between the text and the background is suggested.

6. Correct the issue by completing the following steps:

a. Click *Table1 (FirstQuarter Sales)* under *Hard-to-read Text Contrast*.

b. Click the option box arrow, hover the mouse pointer over *Quick Styles*, and then choose a style that has a higher contrast between the text and the background. Experiment with different styles until the issue disappears from the inspection results. Click the Light Orange, Table Style Light 16 table style (third column, third row in the *Light* section) since it meets the requirements to pass the accessibility check.

7. Close the Accessibility Checker task pane by clicking the Accessibility Checker task pane Close button.

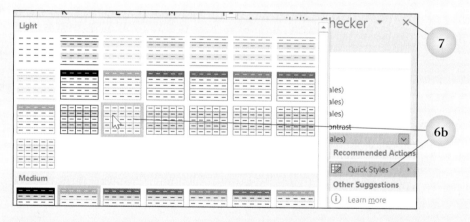

8. Save **8-PFSales**.

Inspecting a Workbook and Removing Information before Distributing It

Before distributing a workbook electronically, consider using the Document Inspector to scan the workbook for personal data and hidden information that others should not view, including information that is tracked automatically by Excel, such as the names of the individuals who have accessed and edited a workbook, or headers, footers, hidden items, and other invisible data that may not need to be viewed.

If any of this sensitive or hidden information should remain confidential, remove it before distributing the file. Before doing so, save a copy of the original file retaining all the content. To inspect the document, click the File tab and then click the *Info* option. At the Info backstage area, click the Check for Issues button in the *Inspect Workbook* section and then click *Inspect Document* at the drop-down

Use Document
Inspector to Remove
Private Information
1. Open workbook.
2. Click File tab.
3. Click the *Info* option.
4. Click Check for
   Issues button.
5. Click *Inspect
   Document.*
6. Clear check boxes
   for items not to be
   scanned.
7. Click Inspect button.
8. Click Remove All
   button in sections to
   be removed.
9. Click Close button.

list. This opens the Document Inspector dialog box, shown in Figure 8.10. By default, all the check boxes are selected. Clear the check boxes for those items that are not to be scanned or removed and then click the Inspect button.

The Document Inspector scans the workbook to look for all the checked items. When the scan is completed, a dialog box like the one in Figure 8.11 appears. Excel displays check marks in the sections for which no items were found and red exclamation marks in the sections for which items were found. Click the Remove All button in the section that contains content to be removed. Click OK when finished and then distribute the workbook as needed. If you require information such as authors and other metadata to be saved in the future, click the <u>Allow this information to be saved in our file</u> hyperlink in the *Inspect Workbook* section of the Info backstage area.

Figure 8.10 Document Inspector Dialog Box

Click to remove the check marks from the check boxes next to those items that are not to be scanned or removed from the workbook before distributing it.

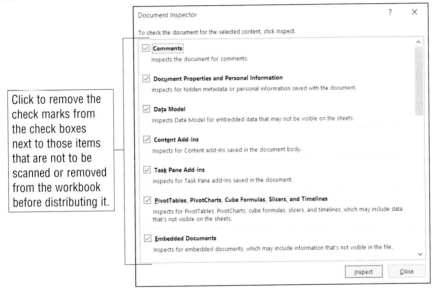

Figure 8.11 Document Inspector Dialog Box with Inspection Results Shown

Red exclamation marks indicate items that were found by scanning the workbook. Read the message about each item and then click the Remove All button next to the item to remove it.

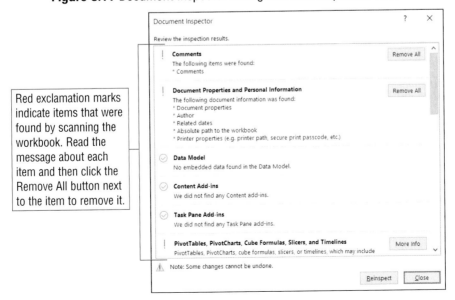

1. With **8-PFSales** open, examine the workbook for private and other confidential information by completing the following steps:

   a. Click the File tab and then click the *Info* option.

   b. Read the property information in the fields in the *Properties* section at the right side of the screen.

   c. Click the Properties button and then click *Advanced Properties* at the drop-down list.

   d. Click the Custom tab in the 8-PFSales Properties dialog box.

   e. Hover the mouse pointer over the right column boundary for the *Value* column in the *Properties* list box until the pointer changes to a left-and-right-pointing arrow with a vertical line in the middle. Drag the column width to the right until all the text in the column can be read.

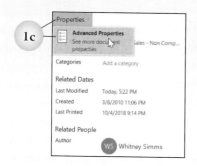
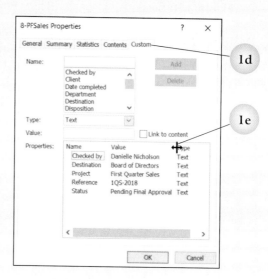

   f. Notice that the extra information added to the workbook properties contains names and other data that should perhaps remain confidential.

   g. Click OK.

   h. Press the Esc key or click the Back button.

   i. With the FirstQuarterSales worksheet active, click the Review tab, click the Notes button, and then click the *Show All Notes* option.

   j. Read the note displayed in the worksheet area.

Manufacturer	Model	Sale Price
Cybex	CX500	1,575.00
Vision	VS3000	3,250.00
Vision	VS5000	2,250.00
Cybex	CX500	1,575.00
SportArt	SA2501	2,588.00

Whitney Simms:
Price increase expected next year.

2. Use the Document Inspector to scan the workbook for other confidential information by completing the following steps:
   a. Click the File tab, click the Check for Issues button in the *Inspect Workbook* section at the Info backstage area, and then click *Inspect Document* at the drop-down list.
   b. At the message box stating that the file contains changes that have not been saved, click Yes to save the file.
   c. At the Document Inspector dialog box with all the check boxes selected, click the Inspect button to look for all the items.
   d. Read the messages in the first two sections of the Document Inspector dialog box, which display with red exclamation marks.
   e. Click the Remove All button in the *Document Properties and Personal Information* section. Excel deletes the metadata and the section displays with a check mark, indicating the information has been removed.

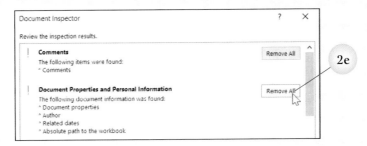

   f. Scroll down and read the message for the *PivotTables, PivotCharts, Cube Formulas, Slicers, and Timelines* section. The PivotTable and PivotChart will not be altered.
   g. Scroll down further and notice that the inspection results indicate that a header and three hidden rows were found. Review these items but do not click the Remove All buttons. Click the Close button to close the Document Inspector dialog box.
3. Display the worksheet in Page Layout view and view the header. Switch back to Normal view.
4. Look at the row numbers in the worksheet area. Notice that after row 10, the next row number is 14. Select row numbers 10 and 14, right-click the selected rows, and then click *Unhide* at the shortcut menu to display rows 11 through 13.

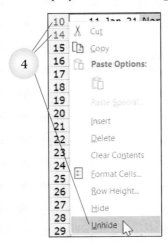

5. Click in any cell to deselect the range. Review the information in the rows that were hidden.

6. You decide that the rows that were initially hidden should remain displayed but you want to prevent reviewers of the workbook from seeing the header and comments. Use the Document Inspector to remove these items by completing the following steps:

   a. Click the File tab, click the *Info* option, click the Check for Issues button, click *Inspect Document* at the drop-down list, and then click the Yes button to save the changes to the workbook.

   b. Remove the check marks from all the check boxes except those next to the sections *Comments* and *Headers and Footers*.

   c. Click the Inspect button.

   d. Click the Remove All button in the *Comments* section.

   e. Click the Remove All button in the *Headers and Footers* section.

   f. Click the Close button.

7. Notice that the comments and/or notes and the header have been deleted from the worksheet.

8. Click the Notes button and then the *Show All Notes* option in the Notes group on the Review tab to turn off the feature.

9. Allow personal information to be saved with the workbook by completing the following steps.

   a. Click the File tab and then click the *Info* option.

   b. Click the <u>Allow this information to be saved in your file</u> hyperlink.

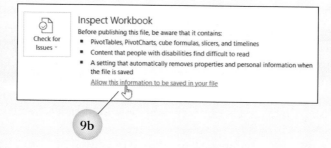

9b

10. Save **8-PFSales**.

Marking a Workbook as Final

A workbook that will be distributed to others can be marked as final, which means it is protected from additions, deletions, and modifications. When a workbook is marked as final, it is changed to a read-only file and the status property is set to *Final.* In addition to protecting the workbook, marking it as final also indicates to the recipients that the content is considered complete.

To mark a workbook as final, click the File tab and then click the *Info* option. At the Info backstage area, click the Protect Workbook button and then click *Mark as Final* at the drop-down list. (Note that marking a workbook as final is not as secure as using password-protected, locked ranges.)

A workbook marked as final displays with the ribbon minimized and a message above the Formula bar that informs the user that the author has marked the workbook as final to discourage editing. Click the Edit Anyway button in the message bar to remove the Mark as Final feature, redisplay the ribbon, and allow changes to be made to the workbook.

1. With **8-PFSales** open, save the workbook with the name **8-PFSalesFinal**.
2. Mark the workbook as final to prevent changes from being made and set the Status property to *Final* by completing the following steps:
   a. Click the File tab, click the *Info* option, click the Protect Workbook button in the Info backstage area, and then click *Mark as Final* at the drop-down list.

   b. Click OK at the message box stating that the workbook will be marked as final and then saved.
   c. Click OK at the second message box stating that the workbook has been marked as final to indicate that editing is complete and this is the final version of the file. *Note: If this message box does not appear, it has been turned off by a previous user who clicked the* **Don't show this message again** *check box.*

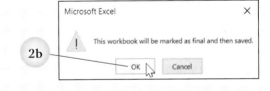

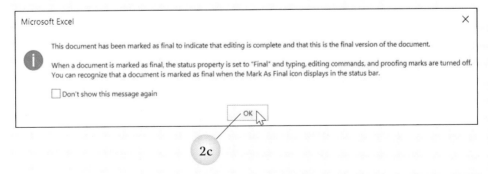

3. Click the File tab. Notice that the *Protect Workbook* section of the Info backstage area displays in yellow with a message stating that the workbook has been marked as final. Click the Back button and notice the addition of *Read-Only* next to the file name in the Title bar.
4. The ribbon is minimized and a message displays above the Formula bar indicating that the workbook has been marked as final to discourage editing. An additional message or icon may display in the Status bar.
5. Make any cell active and attempt to insert or delete text in the cell. Since the workbook is now a read-only file, the cell cannot be opened to edit or delete the contents.

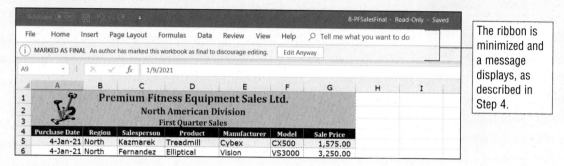

The ribbon is minimized and a message displays, as described in Step 4.

6. Close **8-PFSalesFinal**.

Using the Compatibility Checker

Quick Steps

Check Workbook for Compatibility
1. Open workbook.
2. Click File tab.
3. Click *Info* option.
4. Click Check for Issues button.
5. Click *Check Compatibility*.
6. Read information in *Summary* list box.
7. Click *Copy to New Sheet* button.
   OR
   Click Close.

A workbook can be saved in an earlier file format so it can be read by people using an earlier version of the program. For instance, a workbook can be saved as an Excel 97-2003 file format to be compatible with Excel versions prior to 2007. When a file is saved in the file format of an earlier version, Excel automatically does a compatibility check and provides prompts about any loss of functionality or fidelity. If preferred, use the Compatibility Checker feature before saving the workbook to identify the areas of the worksheet that may need changes before saving to maintain backward compatibility.

If an issue in the *Summary* list box at the Microsoft Excel - Compatibility Checker dialog box displays a <u>Fix</u> hyperlink, click the hyperlink to resolve the problem. To get more information about a loss of functionality or fidelity, click the <u>Help</u> hyperlink next to the issue. To return to the worksheet with the cells selected that are problematic for earlier Excel versions, click the <u>Find</u> hyperlink next to the issue.

Activity 3d **Checking a Workbook for Compatibility with Earlier Versions of Excel**   Part 4 of 4

1. Open **CRAnalysis**.
2. Run the Compatibility Checker to scan the workbook before saving it in an earlier Excel file format by completing the following steps:
   a. Click the File tab and then click the *Info* option.

b. Click the Check for Issues button in the Info backstage area.

c. Click *Check Compatibility* at the drop-down list.

d. At the Microsoft Excel - Compatibility Checker dialog box, read the information in the *Summary* list box in the *Significant loss of functionality* section.

e. Scroll down and read the information in the *Minor loss of fidelity* section.

f. Scroll back up to the top of the *Summary* list box.

g. Click the Copy to New Sheet button.

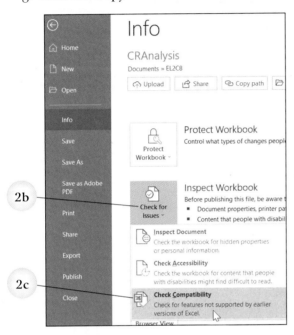

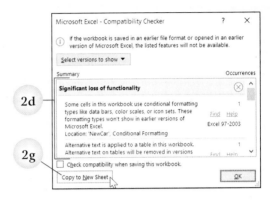

3. At the Compatibility Report sheet, read the information in the box with the hyperlink <u>NewCar'!D13:D16</u> and then click the hyperlink. The NewCar worksheet becomes active with those cells selected that have conditional formatting applied that is not supported in the earlier version of Excel (the range D13:D16).

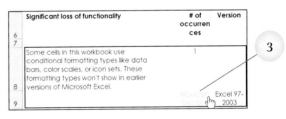

4. Make the Compatibility Report sheet active and then print the worksheet with the worksheet scaled to *Fit Sheet on One Page*.

5. Save the revised workbook with the name **8-CRAnalysisCompChk**.

6. Make NewCar the active worksheet and then deselect the range.

7. To save the workbook in an earlier version of Excel, click the File tab, click the *Export* option, click *Change File Type*, click *Excel 97-2003 Workbook* in the *Workbook File Types* section, and then click the Save As button. Click the Save button at the Save As dialog box to accept the default file name. Click the Continue button at the Compatibility Checker dialog box.

8. Close **8-CRAnalysisCompChk**.

You will publish a workbook as a PDF file and an XPS file. You will also publish a worksheet as a web page.

Tutorial

Publishing a
Workbook as a
PDF or XPS File

Distributing Workbooks

Many organizations that need to make files accessible to several users create a document management server or network share folder from which users can retrieve files. A popular method of distributing content over the internet is to publish a workbook as a PDF or XPS file. A workbook can also be published as a web page to make the content available on the internet.

Publishing a Workbook as a PDF File

Quick Steps

Publish Workbook as PDF File

1. Open workbook.
2. Click File tab.
3. Click *Export*.
4. Click Create PDF/XPS button.
5. Click Publish button.

💡 **Hint** Publish a multisheet workbook as a multipage PDF file by clicking the Options button in the Publish as PDF or XPS dialog box and then clicking *Entire workbook* in the *Publish what* section of the Options dialog box.

Publishing a workbook as a PDF file involves saving it in a fixed-layout format known as *Portable Document Format*. The PDF standard was developed by Adobe and has become a popular format for sharing files with people outside an organization. Creating a PDF file of a workbook ensures that it will look the same on most computers, with all the fonts, formatting, and images preserved. The recipient of the file does not have to have Microsoft Excel on his or her computer to read the file.

To open and view a PDF file, the recipient must have Adobe Acrobat Reader DC on his or her computer or an Internet browser such as Microsoft Edge. The reader is a free application available from Adobe and can be downloaded and installed if the computer being used does not already have it installed. (Go to http://adobe.com and click *Adobe Acrobat Reader DC* to download and install the latest version of the software.)

A PDF file can also be opened with Word 365. It converts a PDF to an editable file, converting any formulas to values and any charts to objects. The file may not look exactly like the original PDF file, however.

Activity 4a   Publishing a Workbook as a Multipage PDF File

Part 1 of 3

1. Open **8-PFSales**.
2. Publish the workbook as a PDF file by completing the following steps:
   a. Click the File tab.
   b. Click the *Export* option.
   c. With *Create PDF/XPS Document* selected in the Export backstage area, click the Create PDF/XPS button.

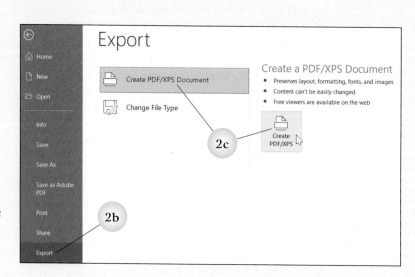

d. Click the *Open file after publishing* check box at the bottom of the Publish as PDF or XPS dialog box to insert a check mark, if necessary.

e. Click the Options button and then click the *Entire workbook* option in the *Publish what* section of the Options dialog box. This will create a PDF with three pages. Click OK.

f. With *PDF* in the *Save as type* option box and *8-PFSales* in the *File name* text box, click the Publish button.

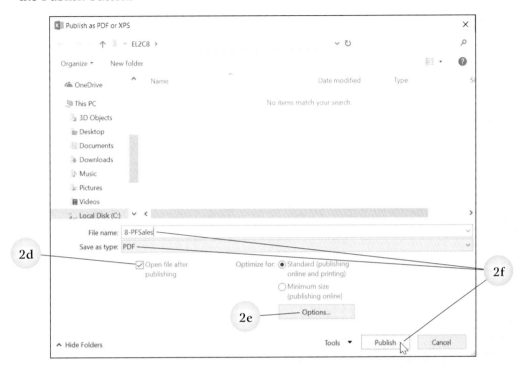

3. An internet browser such as Microsoft Edge or an Adobe Acrobat Reader DC application window opens with the published workbook displayed. Notice that the workbook has retained all the Excel formatting and other visual features and contains three pages.

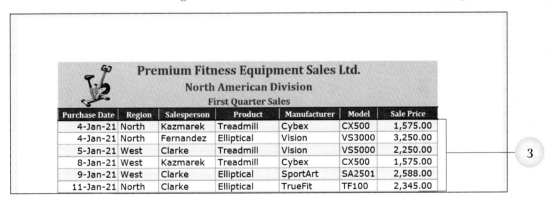

4. Close the application window.
5. Return to Excel and leave **8-PFSales** open for the next activity.

Publishing a Workbook as an XPS File

Quick Steps

Publish Workbook as XPS File
1. Open workbook.
2. Click File tab.
3. Click *Export.*
4. Click Create PDF/XPS button.
5. Click *Save as type* option box.
6. Click *XPS Document.*
7. Click Publish button.

XPS stands for *XML paper specification*, which is another fixed-layout format that has all the same advantages as PDF. XPS was developed by Microsoft with the Office 2007 suite. Similar to PDF files, which require Adobe Acrobat Reader DC for viewing, XPS files require the XPS viewer. The viewer is provided by Microsoft and is packaged with Windows 10, Windows 8, Windows 7, and Windows Vista.

Activity 4b Publishing a Worksheet as an XPS File

Part 2 of 3

1. With **8-PFSales** open, publish the FirstQuarterSales worksheet as an XPS file by completing the following steps:
   a. Click the File tab.
   b. Click the *Export* option.
   c. With the *Create PDF/XPS Document* option selected in the Export backstage area, click the Create PDF/XPS button.
   d. At the Publish as PDF or XPS dialog box, click the *Save as type* option box below the *File name* text box and then click *XPS Document* at the drop-down list.

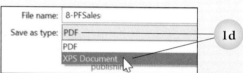

   e. With a check mark in the *Open file after publishing* check box and *8-PFSales* in the *File name* text box, click the Publish button.

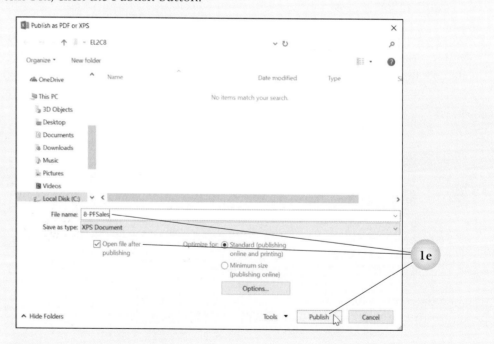

2. The XPS Viewer application window opens with the published worksheet displayed. *Note: Choose the XPS Viewer application if a dialog box opens asking which application should be used to view the file.*
3. Close the XPS Viewer application window.

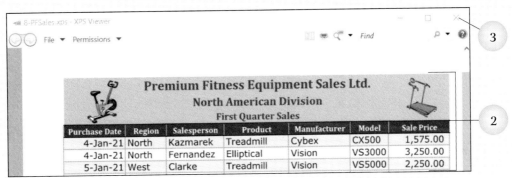

4. Leave **8-PFSales** open for the next activity.

Check Your Work

Publishing a Worksheet as a Web Page

Quick Steps

Publish Worksheet as Web Page
1. Open workbook.
2. Click File tab.
3. Click *Export.*
4. Click *Change File Type.*
5. Click *Save as Another File Type* option.
6. Click Save As button.
7. Click *Save as type* option box.
8. Click *Web Page.*
9. If necessary, change drive, folder, and/or file name.
10. Click Change Title button, type title, and then click OK.
11. Click Publish button.
12. Set options.
13. Click Publish.

Publish the worksheet in the traditional Hypertext Markup Language (HTML) file format for web pages by changing the *Save as type* option to *Web Page.* In the *html* option, Excel creates additional files for supplemental data and saves them in a subfolder. Alternatively, publish a worksheet as a web page by changing the *Save as type* option to *Web Page.* In this format, all the data in the worksheet, including graphics and other supplemental data, is saved in a single file that can be uploaded to a web server.

When a web page option is chosen at the *Save as type* list, the Save As dialog box changes, as shown in Figure 8.12. At this dialog box, specify whether to

Figure 8.12 Save As Dialog Box with File Type Changed to *Web Page*

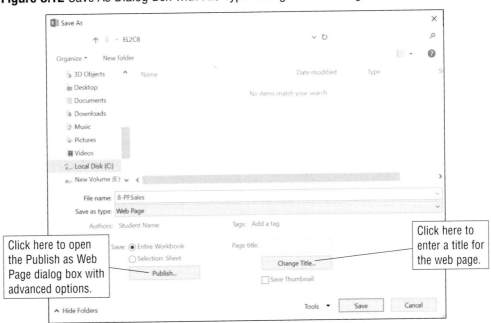

publish the entire workbook or only the active sheet. Click the Change Title button to add a title to the web page. The page title displays in the Title bar of the browser window and on the Microsoft Edge tab when the page is viewed online. Click the Publish button and the Publish as Web Page dialog box appears, as shown in Figure 8.13, providing additional options.

Figure 8.13 Publish as Web Page Dialog Box

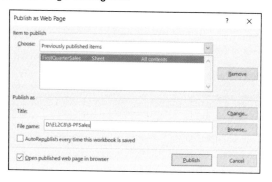

Activity 4c Publishing a Worksheet as a Web Page

Part 3 of 3

1. With **8-PFSales** open, prepare the worksheet to be published as a web page by completing the following steps:
   a. Select the range G5:G47; click the Home tab, if necessary; and then click the Alignment dialog box launcher.
   b. Click the Horizontal option box arrow and then click the *Right (Indent)* option.
   c. Click the *Indent* measurement up arrow once so that *1* displays in the *Indent* measurement box.
   d. Click OK and then click in any cell to deselect the range.
2. Publish the worksheet as a web page by completing the following steps:
   a. Click the File tab.
   b. Click the *Export* option.
   c. Click the *Change File Type* option and then click the *Save as Another File Type* option in the *Other File Types* section.
   d. Click the Save As button.
   e. Click the *Save as type* option box and then click *Web Page* at the drop-down list.
   f. Click the Change Title button.
   g. At the Enter Text dialog box, type Premium Fitness Equipment Sales Ltd. 1st Q Sales in the *Page title* text box and then click OK.
   h. Click the Publish button.

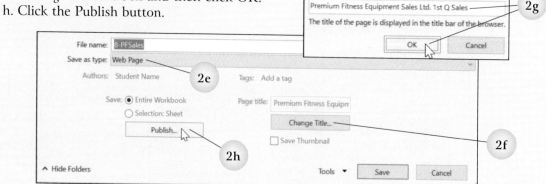

i. At the Publish as Web Page
    dialog box, click the *Open
    published web page in browser* check
    box to insert a check mark and
    then click the Publish button.
    Choose how you want to view
    the web page.
3. After viewing the web page, close
    the browser window.
4. Save and close **8-PFSales**.

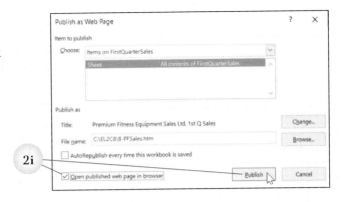

Activity 5 **Export a Final Prices Worksheet in XML Format**   **2 Parts**
and Import an XML File Containing Customer Data

You will create a schema and convert final prices data to an XML file and then
import customer information from an XML file.

Exporting and Importing XML Data

Extensible Markup Language (XML) defines a set of rules that allows users to
customize the markup language used to encode the data in a worksheet. XML
code is easily understood and can be used to present workbook data in a browser.
The standards of XML coding are developed and maintained by the World Wide
Web Consortium (W3C), an international organization.

Creating an XML Schema

To export an Excel worksheet as an XML file, you first need to create an XML
schema for the worksheet, as shown in Figure 8.14. It is created in a text editor,
such as Notepad. The first two lines of code for an XML schema contain the XML
declaration, which provides information on the XML version, the encoding being
used to denote the characters, whether the document needs information from
external sources, the file name, and where information about the standards can be
found.

XML code is written using tags. Each tag is enclosed in angle brackets (< and
>), and tags must be used in pairs, with an opening tag and a closing tag. The
closing tag includes a forward slash (/). Use the basic code shown in Figure 8.14
as a template for writing an XML schema. Provide code for at least two records,
with the opening tag <record> indicating the start of a record and the closing tag
</record> indicating the end of a record. Excel will complete the schema based on
the pattern established for those records.

Figure 8.14 Basic Schema Code

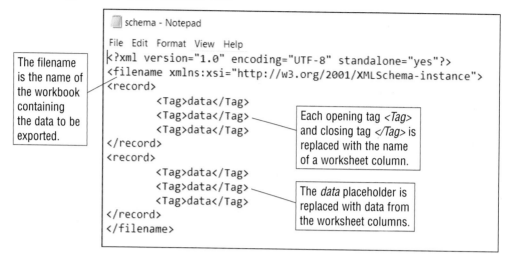

The filename is the name of the workbook containing the data to be exported.

```
schema - Notepad
File  Edit  Format  View  Help
<?xml version="1.0" encoding="UTF-8" standalone="yes"?>
<filename xmlns:xsi="http://w3.org/2001/XMLSchema-instance">
<record>
        <Tag>data</Tag>
        <Tag>data</Tag>
        <Tag>data</Tag>
</record>
<record>
        <Tag>data</Tag>
        <Tag>data</Tag>
        <Tag>data</Tag>
</record>
</filename>
```

Each opening tag *<Tag>* and closing tag *</Tag>* is replaced with the name of a worksheet column.

The *data* placeholder is replaced with data from the worksheet columns.

Figure 8.15 Schema Code for Activity 5a

```
crschema - Notepad
File  Edit  Format  View  Help
<?xml version="1.0" encoding="UTF-8" standalone="yes"?>
<crfp xmlns:xsi="http://www.w3.org/2001/XMLSchema-instance">
<record>
        <Category>Compact</Category>
        <Weekday>35.99</Weekday>
        <Weekend>55.99</Weekend>
        <Weekly>175.99</Weekly>
        <Monthly>675.99</Monthly>
        <Corporate>12%</Corporate>
</record>
<record>
        <Category>Mid-size</Category>
        <Weekday>38.99</Weekday>
        <Weekend>62.99</Weekend>
        <Weekly>185.99</Weekly>
        <Monthly>692.99</Monthly>
        <Corporate>15%</Corporate>
</record>
</crfp>
```

The columns must be listed in the same order in the schema as they are in the worksheet, but the column names do not have to be exactly the same.

Provide at least two examples of records in the schema. When the data is imported, Excel will fill in the rest.

 Tutorial

Exporting a Worksheet as an XML file

 Source

Exporting a Worksheet as an XML File

To export data in an Excel worksheet as an XML file, complete the following steps:

1. Click the Source button in the XML group on the Developer tab.
2. Click the XML Maps button at the XML Source task pane, shown in Figure 8.16.
3. Click the Add button at the SML Maps dialog box, navigate to the XML schema file at the Select XML Source dialog box, click the XML schema file in the file list pane, and then click the Open button.
4. Click the OK button at the message box that displays, stating that the specific XML source does not refer to a schema and that Excel will create a schema based on the XML source data.

5. Click the OK button at the XML Maps dialog box.
6. Drag each element in the *XML maps in this workbook* list box at the XML Source task pane to its corresponding column header in the worksheet.
7. Click the Developer tab and then click the Export button in the XML group.
8. Type the file name in the *File name* text box and then click the Export button.

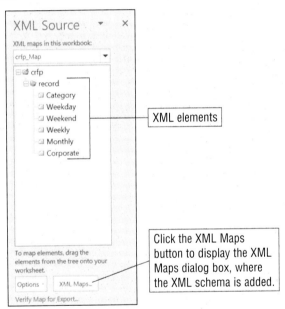

Export

When the schema file is added to the workbook, each *<Tag>* in the XML code appears as an XML element in the *XML maps in the workbook* list box at the XML Source task pane. An XML data map connects the schema file to the worksheet. Create an XML data map by dragging each element from the list box at the XML Source task pane to its respective column header in the worksheet. When a worksheet column has been mapped to an XML element, it becomes an XML element and changes to a table format.

If an Error in XML message box displays, stating that Excel cannot load the specified XML or schema source, click the Details button, read the information about the error at the XML Error dialog box, and then click the OK button to close the dialog box. Correct the error and then add the schema file again.

Figure 8.16 XML Source Task Pane

Activity 5a **Exporting an XML File**   Part 1 of 2

1. Open the data file **crschema** in Notepad.
2. Move the insertion point to the beginning of the first blank line and then type the following code, using the Tab key to indent the lines as shown:

```
<record>
      <Category>Compact</Category>
      <Weekday>35.99</Weekday>
      <Weekend>55.99</Weekend>
      <Weekly>175.99</Weekly>
```

```
        <Monthly>675.99</Monthly>
        <Corporate>12%</Corporate>
    </record>
    <record>
        <Category>Mid-size</Category>
        <Weekday>38.99</Weekday>
        <Weekend>62.99</Weekend>
        <Weekly>185.99</Weekly>
        <Monthly>692.99</Monthly>
        <Corporate>15%</Corporate>
    </record>
</crfp>
```

3. Compare your schema with Figure 8.15 (on page 236). Save and then close **crschema** and Notepad.

4. Open **8-CRFinalPrices** using the password *eL2-C8* and then save the file with the name **CRFP**. Make the FinalPricesExport worksheet active.

5. Add the Developer tab to the ribbon, if necessary, by completing the following steps:
   a. Right-click on any part of the ribbon and then click the *Customize the Ribbon* option.
   b. Click the *Developer* check box in the *Main Tabs* list box and then click OK.

6. Click the Developer tab and then click the Source button in the XML group.

7. Click the XML Maps button in the XML Source task pane.
8. At the XML Maps dialog box, click the Add button.
9. Navigate to your EL2C8 folder at the Select XML Source dialog box, click the *All XML Data Sources* option box arrow, click the *All Files* option at the drop-down list, click **crschema** in the file list pane, and then click the Open button.
10. Click the OK button at the message box stating that the XML source does not refer to a schema and that Excel will create a schema based on the XML source data.
11. Click the OK button at the XML Maps dialog box.

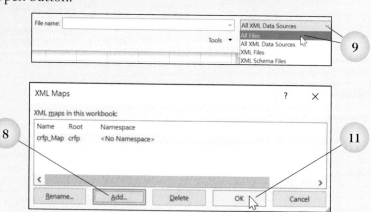

12. Drag the *Category* element in the list box at the XML Source task pane to cell A4.

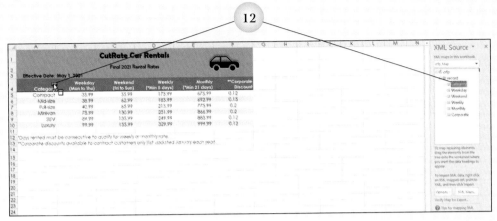

13. Drag the *Weekday* element in the list box to cell B4.
14. Repeat Step 11 to map the *Weekend*, *Weekly*, *Monthly*, and *Corporate* elements in the list box at the XML Source task pane to the corresponding column headers in the worksheet.
15. Click the Developer tab, click the Export button in the XML group, navigate to your EL2C8 folder, click in the *File name* text box, type FinalPrices, and then click the Export button.
16. Open File Explorer, navigate to your EL2C8 folder, and then double-click the data file **FinalPrices** in the file list pane. Choose an application to open the file, if necessary.
17. Scroll through the file and notice that Excel added the rest of the categories and prices.
18. Click the Close button on the **FinalPrices** file and then click the Close button on the File Explorer window.
19. Save **CRFP**.

Check Your Work

Importing an XML File

 Tutorial

Importing an XML File

 GetData

To import an XML file, click the Data tab, click the Get Data button, point to the *From File* option at the drop-down list, and then click the *From XML* option at the second drop-down list. At the Import Data dialog box, navigate to the drive and/or folder in which the source file resides and then double-click the XML file name in the file list. At the Navigator dialog box, click the record that contains the data to be imported (it is named *record*). Click the Load button to import the data into a new worksheet, or click the Load button arrow and then click the *Load To* option to open the Import Data dialog box, which contains more options for viewing and placing the data. Another option is to click the Edit button to edit and then import the data. This process is similar to importing an Access table into Excel, where a query is created.

1. With **CRFP** open, click the Review tab and then click the Protect Workbook button in the Protect group.
2. At the *Password* text box in the Unprotect Workbook dialog box, type eL2-C8 and then click OK.
3. Import the Customers XML file into a new worksheet by completing the following steps:
   a. Click the Data tab.
   b. Click the Get Data button in the Get & Transform group. Point to the *From File* option and then click the *From XML* option at the second drop-down list.
   c. Navigate to your EL2C8 folder and then double-click **CRCustomers**.
   d. Click *record* in the left panel. A preview of the data displays in the right panel.
   e. Click the Load button.
   f. Rename the worksheet **Customers**.
   g. Print the worksheet.
   h. Save and then close **CRFP**.

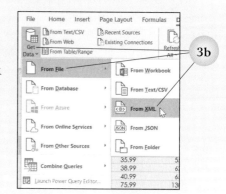

Check Your Work

Chapter Summary

■ Workbook properties include descriptive information about the workbook, such as the author's name and the workbook title, subject, category, and comments. Display the Info backstage area to add information to a workbook's properties. Workbook properties are sometimes referred to as *metadata*.

■ When Microsoft Office is installed, a user name is defined for the computer. Excel automatically inserts this name in the *Author* property box when a new workbook is created.

■ Protect an entire worksheet to prevent other users from accidentally inserting or deleting data. Protect a worksheet using the Protect Sheet button in the Protect group on the Review tab.

■ By default, each cell in a worksheet has a lock attribute that activates when the worksheet is protected. To allow editing of individual cells in a protected worksheet, select the cells and turn off the lock attribute before protecting the worksheet. Add a password to unprotect a worksheet.

■ Use the Protect Workbook button in the Protect group on the Review tab to prevent changes to the structure of a workbook, such as inserting, deleting, renaming, or otherwise managing worksheets within it. To remove workbook protection, click the Protect Workbook button. If a password was entered when the workbook was protected, the Unprotect Workbook dialog box appears. Type the password and then press the Enter key.

■ Prevent unauthorized access to an Excel workbook by requiring a password to open it. The plain text of the password is encrypted, which prevents unauthorized users from retrieving it.

■ Add a password at the Info backstage area by clicking the Protect Workbook button and then clicking *Encrypt with Password*. Save the workbook after typing and confirming the password.

- Before distributing a workbook for others to open, view, and edit, use Excel features to ensure that the file can be read by individuals who require assistive technology to read the workbook. Run the Accessibility Checker by clicking the Check Accessibility button in the Accessibility group on the Review tab or click the File tab and then click the *Info* option.

- Before distributing a workbook, also check it to ensure that confidentiality will be protected and maintained. The Document Inspector scans a workbook for personal or hidden information. Identify and then remove any information that should remain confidential at the Document Inspector dialog box.

- After a workbook has been inspected, Excel displays a red exclamation mark in each section in which Excel detected a requested item. Click the Remove All button to delete all such items from the workbook.

- Marking a workbook as final changes it to a read-only file and sets the status property as *Final*. To mark a workbook as final, click the File tab and the click the *Info* option. At the Info backstage area, click the Protect Workbook button and then click *Mark as Final* at the drop-down list.

- Run the Compatibility Checker before saving a workbook in an earlier version of Excel to identify areas of the worksheet that may need changes to maintain backward compatibility. The results of the compatibility check can be copied to a new worksheet for easy referencing and documentation purposes.

- Saving a workbook in a fixed-layout format such as PDF or XPS preserves all the Excel formatting and layout features. Adobe Acrobat Reader or Word 365 is required to open and view a workbook saved as a PDF file. The XPS Viewer is provided with Windows. Adobe Acrobat Reader can be downloaded for free from the Adobe website.

- To publish the current worksheet as a web page, open the Save As dialog box and change the *Save as type* option to *Web Page* or *Web Page*.

- Extensible Markup Language (XML) defines a set of rules that allows users to customize the markup language used to encode the data in a worksheet. To export an Excel worksheet as an XML file, the user first needs to create an XML schema for the worksheet. An XML schema is a document created in Notepad that defines the XML file structure. XML code is written using tags. Each tag is enclosed in angle brackets (< and >), and tags must be used in pairs, with an opening and a closing tag. An XML data map connects the schema file to the worksheet.

- To import an XML file, click the Data tab, click the Get Data button, point to the *From File* option at the drop-down list, and then click the *From XML* option at the second drop-down list. At the Import Data dialog box, navigate to the drive and/or folder in which the source file resides and then double-click the XML file name in the file list. At the Navigator dialog box, click the record containing the data to be imported. Click the Load button to import the data in a new worksheet, click the *Load to* button arrow and then click the *Load To* option at the drop-down list to open the Import Data dialog box, or click the Edit button to Edit and then import the data.

Commands Review

FEATURE	RIBBON TAB, GROUP/OPTION	BUTTON, OPTION	KEYBOARD SHORTCUT
Accessibility Checker	Review, Accessibility OR File, *Info*	, *Check for Issues* , *Check for Issues*	
Compatibility Checker	File, *Info*		
Document Inspector	File, *Info*	, *Check for Issues*	
export data as XML file	Developer, XML		
import XML file into Excel	Data, Get & Transform Data		
mark workbook as final	File, *Info*	, *Protect Workbook*	
protect workbook	Review, Protect		
protect worksheet	Review, Protect		
save as	File, *Save As*		F12
save as PDF/XPS	File, *Export* OR File, *Save As*		F12
save as web page	File, *Export* OR File, *Save As*		F12
unlock cells	Home, Cells		

Index

A

absolute reference, range name and, 32

Access
- copying and pasting worksheet data to, 150–151
- importing data from, 154–156

Accessibility Checker task pane, 221

accessibility issues, checking, 220–222

adding buttons to ribbon, 178

Adobe Reader, 230

Advanced Filter button, 26

Advanced Filter dialog box, 27

AND logical function, 50–53

argument, in function formula, 31

array formula, 13

* (asterisk), in custom filter, 22

auditing tools, 132–139
- circling invalid data, 137–139
- tracing precedent and dependent cells, 133
- troubleshooting formulas, 134–137
- viewing relationships between cells and formulas, 133–134
- watching formula cells, 137–139

Author property name, 210

AutoCorrect Option button, 61

AutoFilter, filtering worksheet using custom, 21–23

automating tasks using macros, 186–194

AutoRecover feature, 201–203

AutoSave feature, 202

AVERAGE function, 33

AVERAGEIF function, 38–39

AVERAGEIFS function, 38, 40

B

banding rows, 63

Break Link button, 90, 147

button form control, 195

C

calculated column, adding to table, 61–63

cells
- dependent cells, 133
- filtering and sorting by attributes of, 23–26
- formatting
  - based on Top/Bottom Rules list, 4, 6
  - based on value comparison, 4, 15
  - new formatting rule, 6–8
- precedent cells, 133
- unlocking, 215
- viewing relationships between cells and formulas, 133–134
- watching formula cells, 137–139

Change Source button, 90

Change Source dialog box, 90

Chart Elements button, 107

Chart Styles button, 107

Check Accessibility button, 220

check box form control, 195, 197

Check Compatibility button, 228

Check for Issues button, 220

ciphertext, 217

Clear button, 24

Clear Format button, 9

Clipboard task pane, 150

col_index_num, 43

Collapse the Ribbon button, 175

color
- filtering by font color, 23–26
- sorting by cell color, 23–26

[color] in custom number format code, 20

color scales, conditional formatting using, 12–13

Column button, 110

columns
- adding calculated column to table, 61–63
- banding, 63

converting data from rows to columns, 119–121

converting text to, 68–69

Flash Fill feature, 164–165

removing duplicate records, 69–71

combo box form control, 195–197

commands
- adding to quick Access toolbar, 183
- renaming, 178–179

comma separated file format, 158–159

compatibility checker feature, 228–230

CONCATENATE function, 165

CONCAT function, 165, 167, 170

conditional formatting, 4–15
- cell formatting
  - based on Top/Bottom Rules list, 4, 6
  - based on value comparison, 4, 15
  - using Highlight Cells Rules option, 4, 5
- color scales in, 12–13
- create and apply new formatting rule, 6–8
- data bars in, 12–13
- defined, 3, 4
- drop-down list, 4
- editing and deleting rules, 8–10
- filtering and sorting using, 23–26
- formatting using Quick Analysis, 15
- formulas in, 13–14
- icon set for applying, 11–12
- Quick Analysis button, 15

Conditional Formatting button, 4, 8

Conditional Formatting Rules Manager dialog box, 8–10

conditional test, 34, 38, 49

Consolidate button, 93

Consolidate dialog box, 93–94

Consolidate feature,
summarizing data
using, 85, 93–95
Convert Text to Columns
Wizard, 68–69
Convert to Range button, 76
copying and pasting Excel data
to Access, 150–151
to PowerPoint, 147–149
to Word, 144–145
COUNTA function, 33
COUNTBLANK function, 33,
35–36
COUNT function, 33, 170
COUNTIF function, 34–36
COUNTIFS function, 34–37
Create Sparklines dialog box,
110, 111
CSV file format, 151
Custom AutoFilter dialog box,
21–23
Custom AutoFilter feature,
filtering worksheet
using, 21–23
Customize Quick Access Toolbar
button, 181
customizing
creating and applying custom
views, 184–185
display options, 174–175
exporting and importing, 177
macros, 186–194
Quick Access toolbar, 181–
184
ribbon, 175–176, 176–181
save options, 201–204
Sparklines, 111–112
custom number format, creating,
19–21
Custom Sort, 24
custom view, creating and
applying, 184–185
Custom View button, 184
Custom View dialog box, 184,
185

D

data
circling invalid data, 137–139
converting, from rows to
columns, 119–121
Data Tools group, 68–75

exporting, 144–153
to Access, 150–151
breaking link to Excel
object in Word, 147
by copying and pasting to
Access, 150–151
PowerPoint, 147–149
Word, 144–145
to PowerPoint, 147–149
as text file, 151–153
to Word, 144–146
filtering and sorting,
using conditional
formatting or cell
attributes, 23–26
formatting as table, 60–65
grouping and ungrouping,
81–82
importing, 154–159
from Access, 154–157
editing or removing source
of query, 163–164
refreshing, modifying and
deleting queries,
160–163
from text file, 158–159
maintaining external
references for, 90–93
modifying, with Power Query
Editor, 156–157
pasting, using Paste Special
options, 118–122
PivotCharts, 106–109
PivotTables, 95–109
populating, using Flash Fill,
164–165
restricting data entry, 72–73
separating, using Text to
Columns, 68–69
subtotaling related data,
76–81
summarizing
with consolidate feature,
93–95
linking to ranges in
other worksheets/
workbooks, 89–90
in multiple worksheets
using range names
and 3-D references,
86–88
with Sparklines, 110–112
transposing, 119–121
validating data entry, 71–75

What-If analysis
with data tables, 129–132
with Scenario Manager,
124–128
data bars, conditional formatting
using, 12–13
Data source settings dialog box,
163–164
Data tab, 68, 70, 154
data table
defined, 129
one-variable data table,
129–130
two-variable data table,
131–132
Data Tools group, 68–75
convert text to columns,
68–69
overview, 68
populating data using Flash
Fill, 164–165
removing duplicate records,
69–71
validating and restricting data
entry, 71–75
data validation
circling invalid data, 137–139
ensuring data entered in
specified text length,
75
error alert message, 71–72
input message, 71
restricting data entry to dates
within range, 72–73
restricting data entry to values
within list, 74
Data Validation button, 71, 137
Data Validation dialog box,
71–72
Defined Names group, 32
deleting
conditional formatting rules,
8–10
custom number format, 20
custom template, 200
macro, 194
queries, 160, 163
range name, 32–33
Scenario Manager, 127
delimited file format, 158
dependent cell, tracing, 133
destination file, 144
destination workbook, 89
Directional icon set, 11–12

display options
    customizing, 174–175
    restoring default, 176
distribution of workbooks/
        worksheets
    checking accessibility issues,
        220–222
    compatibility checker, 228–
        230
    marking as final, 226–228
    preparation for, 220–229
    publishing
        as PDF document, 230–
            231
        as web page, 233–235
        as XPS document, 232–233
    removing information before,
        222–226
document information panel,
    210
Document Inspector dialog box,
    223
Document Inspector feature,
    222–226

E

Edit Anyway button, 226
editing
    conditional formatting rules,
        8–10
    macro, 192–194
    range name, 32–33
    scenarios using Scenario
        Manager, 126–127
    source data, 91–92
    source for query, 163–164
Edit Links button, 90
Edit Links dialog box, 90–91
email addresses
    using CONCAT, LOWER, and
        LEN functions, 170
embedding Excel data
    in PowerPoint presentation,
        148–149
    in Word document, 144–145
Encrypt Document dialog box,
    217, 218
encrypted password, 217
Error (accessibility issue), 220
error alert message, 71–72
Error Checking button, 135
errors

error codes, 135–137
logic errors, 134
troubleshooting formulas,
    134–137
Evaluate Formula button, 135
Excel Options dialog box,
    177–178
exponential notation, 16–17
Export button, 237
exporting customizations, 177
exporting data, 144–153
    breaking link to Excel object,
        147
    copying and pasting
            worksheet data to
        Access, 150–151
        PowerPoint, 147–149
        Word, 144–146
    text file, 151–153
    XML file, 235–239
Extensible Markup Language
        (XML)
    exporting, 235–239
    importing, 235, 239–240
External Data tab, 150
external reference
    editing source data and
            updating external
            link, 91–92
    point-and-click approach to
            creating, 89
    removing, 92–93

F

FALSE, 43
field names row, 60
fields, defined, 60
Field Settings button, 101
files
    comma separated file format,
        158–159
    delimited file format, 158
    importing data from text file,
        158–159
File tab, 210
filtering
    by font color, 25–26
    by icon set, 24–25
    PivotTables
        overview, 100–101
        using Slicers, 102–104
        using Timelines, 104–105

removing filter, 24
tables, 65–67
using advanced filter, 26–29
    in another location, 28
    in place, 29
using conditional formatting
        or cell attributes,
        23–26
worksheet using Custom
        AutoFilter, 21–23
Financial button, 46, 47
financial functions
    IPMT function, 46
    PMT function, 46
    PPMT function, 46–48
Find & Select button, 80–81
Flash Fill, populating data using,
    164–165
Flash Fill button, 165
Format as Table button, 60
Format button, 213
Format Cells dialog box
    applying fraction and
            scientific formatting,
            16–17
    applying special number
            formatting, 18–19
    formatted text (space delimited)
            file format, 151
formatting
    conditional, 4–15
    custom number format, 19–21
    filtering and sorting
            using conditional
            formatting, 23–26
    fraction, 16–17
    PivotTables, 100–101
    scientific, 16–17
    special number, 18–19
    subtotals, 80–81
    table, 60–65
    with text functions, 165–170
form controls
    check box form control, 195,
        197
    combo box form control,
        195–197
    configuring, 195–196
    inserting, 194–197
    list box form control, 195
    macro button form control,
        197–198
    types of, 195

Formula Auditing group, 132–139
  circling invalid data, 137–139
  tracing precedent and dependent cells, 133
  troubleshooting formulas, 134–137
  viewing relationships between cells and formulas, 133–134
  watching formula cell, 137–139
Formula bar, viewing long formulas in, 54
formulas
  array formula, 13
  auditing tools for, 132–139
  conditional formatting using, 13–14
  named ranges for, 32–33
  one-variable data table, 129–130
  proof formula, 134
  referencing cell in separate worksheet, 86–88
  3-D formulas, 86
  two-variable data table, 131–132
  viewing long, in Formula bar, 54
  viewing relationships between cells and formulas, 133–134
Formulas tab, 32, 132, 165
fraction formatting, 16–17
From Text/CVS button, 158
function formula
  argument in, 31
  creating named range, 32–33
  editing and deleting range names in, 32–33
  structure of, 31
functions
  changing in PivotTable, 101–102
  defined, 31
  Lookup & Reference functions, 43–46
  math and trigonometry functions, 41–42
  nested functions, 49–56
  search for, 56
  Sum function, 63, 94
  text functions, 165–170

G

Get Data button, 154, 239
Goal Seek, 122–123
Gradient Fill section, 12–13
Green Up Arrow icon, 11
group
  adding button to, 178
  renaming, 178–179
Group button, 81–82

H

header row, 60
  formatting, 63
health and dental costs
  calculating using nested IF and OR functions, 52–53
Hide Detail button, 81
Highlight Cells Rules option, 4, 5
HLOOKUP function, 43, 46

I

icon set
  conditional formatting using, 11–12
  filtering by, 24–25
IF function, nested, 49–54
IFS function, 54–56
IF statement
  conditional formatting using, 13–14
  structure of, 49
Import Data dialog box, 154
importing customizations, 177
importing data, 154–159
  from Access, 154–157
  from text file, 158–159
  XML file, 235, 239–240
Import Text File dialog box, 158
Indicators icon set, 11–12
Info backstage area, 210
Information error alert message, 72
Insert Form Control button, 195
Insert Function button, 34
Insert Function dialog box, 34, 35
Insert Slicer button, 65–66, 102
Insert tab, 95, 110
Insert Timeline button, 104

Inspect Document button, 222
IPMT function, 46

K

keyboard shortcut, creating and running macro to, 190–192

L

LEFT text function, 165–166, 167–169
legacy wizards, 154
LEN function, 170
Line button, 110
linking Excel data to Word document, 144, 146
  breaking link, 147
Links dialog box, 147
list box form control, 195
loan payments, calculating principal portion of, 47–48
Logical button, 49
logical functions
  AND functions, 50–52
  IF function, 49–54
  IFS function, 54–56
  nested functions, 49–56
  OR functions, 50–53
  ROUND function, 51–52
logic errors, 134
Lookup & Reference button, 43
  HLOOKUP function, 43, 46
  VLOOKUP function, 43–45
Lookup & Reference functions, 43–46
lookup table, 43
lookup_value, 43
LOWER text function, 165–166, 170

M

Macro dialog box, 189
macros, 186–194
  assigning to shortcut key, 190–192
  creating, 186–188
  defined, 186
  deleting, 194
  editing, 192–194

Protect Sheet button, 213, 214
Protect Sheet dialog box, 213–214
Protect Structure and Windows dialog box, 216
Protect Workbook button, 216, 217
Publish as Web Page dialog box, 234

Q

queries
  deleting, 160, 163
  editing or removing source for, 163–164
  modifying, 160–162
  refreshing, 160–162
Queries & Connections button, 161
Queries & Connections Group, 160
Query dialog box, 161
Query Properties dialog box, 160
? (question mark)
  in custom filter, 22
  in custom number format code, 20
Quick Access toolbar
  adding commands to, 183
  customizing, 181–183
  importing customizations to, 184
  removing buttons from, 183
  resetting to original setting, 183–184
Quick Analysis button, 9, 15

R

range
  converting table to normal range, 76–78
  converting table to range and creating subtotals, 76–81
  converting to table, 60–61
  restricting data entry to dates within range, 72–73
range_lookup, 43
range name
  creating, 32–33
  deleting, 32–33

editing, 32–33
  summarize data in multiple worksheets using, 86–87
Ratings icon set, 11–12
Recommended PivotTables, 96–98
Recommended PivotTables button, 96
Record Macro dialog box, 186
  with shortcut key assigned, 190
records
  defined, 60
  removing duplicate, 69–71
recovering workbook, 203–204
Red Down Arrow icon, 11
references
  3-D reference, 86
  worksheet reference, 86
Refresh All button, 160
Remove Arrow button, 133
Remove Duplicate dialog box, 69–71
Remove Duplicates button, 70
removing
  buttons from ribbon, 178
  password from workbook, 217–219
Rename button, 178
Reset button, 183–184
ribbon
  adding buttons to a group, 178, 180
  creating a new tab, 178–179
  customizing, 176–181
  importing customizations, 184
  minimizing, 175–176
  renaming tab, group, or command, 178–180
  resetting, 183–184
Ribbon Display Options button, 175
RIGHT text function, 165–166, 167–169
ROUND function, 51–52
rows
  adding to table, 61–63
  banding, 63
  converting data from rows to columns, 119–121
  header row formatting, 63
  removing duplicate, 69–71
  Total row, adding, 64–65
Run button, 189

S

Save As dialog box, 151, 233
Save As option, 144, 187
Save button, 187
saving
  AutoRecover and AutoSave, 201
  customizing save options, 201–204
  workbook as template, 198–201
  workbooks containing macros, 187–188
Scenario Manager
  adding scenario to worksheet using, 125–126
  applying scenarios with, 126–127
  creating assumptions for What-If analysis, 124–128
  deleting scenarios with, 127
  editing scenarios with, 126–127
  generating scenario summary report, 128
Scenario Manager dialog box, 125
Scenario Summary dialog box, 128
Scenario Values dialog box, 125
scientific formatting, 16–17
security setting, Trust Center settings, 204–205
; (semi colon), in custom number format code, 20
Shapes icon set, 11–12
shortcut key, creating and running macro to, 190–192
Show Detail button, 81
Show Formulas button, 133
Slicer feature, filtering table with, 65–67
Slicer pane, 65–67, 102
Slicers, filtering PivotTable using, 102–104
Slicer Tools Options tab, 104
Sort Dialog Box, 24
Sort & Filter button, 22
sorting
  by cell color, 24–26
  custom sort, 24

tables, 65–67
   using conditional formatting
      or cell attributes,
      23–26
Source button, 236
source data, editing and
   updating external
   link, 91–92
source file, 144
source workbook, 89
Sparklines
   creating, 110–111
   customizing, 111–112
   defined, 110
Sparkline Tools Design tab, 111
special number format, 18–19
statistical functions
   AVERAGE function, 33
   AVERAGEIF function, 38–39
   AVERAGEIFS function,
      38–39, 40
   COUNTA function, 33
   COUNTBLANK function, 33,
      35–36
   COUNT function, 33
   COUNTIF function, 34–36
   COUNTIFS function, 34–37
   MAX function, 33
   MIN function, 33
Stop error alert message, 72
Stop Recording button, 187
structured reference formula,
   adding to table, 64–65
SUBSTITUTE text function,
   165–166
Subtotal button, 76
subtotals
   converting table to range and
      creating subtotals,
      76–81
   modifying, 79–81
   overview, 76
Sum function, 63, 94
   changing in PivotTable,
      101–102
SUMIF function, 41–42
SUMIFS function, 41
summarizing data
   with consolidate feature,
      93–95
   by linking to ranges in
      other worksheets/
      workbooks, 89–90

in multiple worksheets using
   range names and 3-D
   references, 86–88
with Sparklines, 110–112

T

tab
   creating new, 178
   renaming, 178–179
table_array, 43
Table button, 60
tables
   adding row and calculated
      column to, 61–63
   automatic expansion of, 61
   banding rows and columns, 63
   converting
      to normal range, 76–78
      range to table, 60–61
      table to range and creating
         subtotals, 76–81
   copying and pasting data from
      Access to, 150–151
   creating, 60–61
   defined, 59
   field names row in, 60
   fields in, 60
   filtering, 65–67
   formatting, 64–65
   header row in, 60
   importing from Access,
      154–156
   modifying, 61–62
   PivotTables, 95–109
   records in, 60
   sorting, 65–67
   structured reference formula,
      adding, 64–65
   style options for, 63
   subtotaling related data,
      76–81
   Total row, adding, 64–65
Table Styles gallery, 63
Table Tools Design tab, 63, 70,
   76
target value, Goal Seek to find,
   123
template
   deleting custom template, 200
   saving workbook as, 198–201
   using custom template,
      199–201

text
   converting to columns, 68–69
   converting using text
      functions, 169
   extracting and combining
      using text functions,
      167–169
Text button, 165
text file
   exporting worksheets as,
      151–153
   importing data from, 158–159
text (tab delimited) file format,
   151
text functions, 165–170
   converting text using, 169
   extracting and combining text
      using, 167–169
"text" in custom number format
   code, 20
TEXTJOIN function, 166–169
text #NAME? error message, 32
Text to Columns button, 68
3 Arrows (Colored) icon set,
   11–12
3-D formulas, 86
3-D references
   defined, 86
   summarize data in multiple
      worksheet using, 88
Time Level indicator, 104
timelines, filtering PivotTables
   using, 104–105
Timeline Tools Options tab, 104
Tip (accessibility issue), 220
Title property name, 210
Top/Bottom Rules list,
   formatting cell based
   on, 4, 6
Total row, 64–65
Trace Dependents button, 133
Trace Precedents button, 133
Transpose button, 119
transposing data, 119–121
trigonometry functions, 41–42
TRIM text function, 165
troubleshooting formulas,
   134–137
TRUE, 43
Trust Center settings, 204–205
Trusted Locations list, 204
Trusted Publishers list, 204
two-variable data table, 131–132

U

Undo feature, 90
Ungroup button, 81–82
Ungroup dialog box, 81–82
unicode text, 151
Unprotect Sheet dialog box, 214
unprotecting
    workbook, 216
    worksheet, 213–217
Unprotect Sheet button, 214
Unprotect Workbook dialog box,
    216
UPPER text function, 165–166,
    169

V

value comparison, formatting
    cells based on, 4, 15
#VALUE! error, 134, 135
Value Field Setting dialog box,
    101–102
Visual Basic for Applications
    (VBA), 187, 192
VLOOKUP function, 43–45

W

Warning (accessibility issue), 220
Warning error alert message, 72
Watch Window button, 137
website, publishing worksheet as
    web page, 233–235
What-If analysis
    creating assumptions with
        Scenario Manager,
        124–128
    with data tables, 129–132
    Goal Seek to find target value,
        122–123
What-If Analysis button, 122
wildcard characters, in custom
    filter, 22
Win/Loss button, 110
Word document
    breaking link to Excel object
        in, 147

copying and pasting
        worksheet data to,
        144–145
embedding Excel data into,
        144–145
linking Excel data to, 144,
        146
workbooks
    creating macros workbook,
        194
    destination, 89
    distributing, 230–240
        checking accessibility
            issues, 220–222
        compatibility checker,
            228–230
        marking as final, 226–228
        preparing for, 220–229
        publishing as PDF
            document, 230–231
        publishing as XPS
            document, 232–233
        removing information
            before, 222–226
    passwords, adding and
        removing, 217–219
    properties, adding, 210–212
    protecting and unprotecting
        structure of, 216–217
    recovering, 203–204
    saving as template, 198–201
    saving containing macros,
        187–188
    source, 89
    summarizing data by linking
        ranges in another
        workbook or
        worksheet, 89–90
worksheets
    converting range to table,
        60–61
    custom view for, 184–185
    distributing, as web page,
        233–235
    exporting, 144–153
        breaking link to Excel
            object, 147

copying and pasting
        worksheet data to
        Access, 150–151
        PowerPoint, 147–149
        Word, 144–145
    as text file, 151–153
filtering, using Custom
    AutoFilter, 21–23
importing data, 154–159
    from Access, 154–157
    from text file, 158–159
protecting and unprotecting,
    213–217
range name and worksheet
    references, 32
summarizing data
    Consolidate feature, 93–95
    by linking ranges in
        another workbook,
        89–90
    in multiple worksheets
        using range names
        and 3-D references,
        86–88
worksheet references, 86

X

XML file
    creating XML schema, 235–
        236
    exporting, 235–239
    importing, 235, 239–240
XML paper specification, 232
XML Source task pane, 237
XPS document, publishing
    workbook as, 232–
    233

Y

Yellow Sideways Arrow icon, 11

Z

0 (zero), in custom number
    format code, 20

Interior Photo Credits